Airbnb®

2nd Edition

by Symon He, MBA
Co-founder of LearnBNB.com

James Svetec
Founder of BNB Mastery

A Wiley Brand

Airbnb® For Dummies®, 2nd Edition

Published by: **John Wiley & Sons, Inc.,** 111 River Street, Hoboken, NJ 07030-5774, www.wiley.com

Copyright © 2023 by John Wiley & Sons, Inc., Hoboken, New Jersey

Published simultaneously in Canada

For general information on our other products and services, please contact our Customer Care Department within the U.S. at 877-762-2974, outside the U.S. at 317-572-3993, or fax 317-572-4002. For technical support, please visit https://hub.wiley.com/community/support/dummies.

Wiley publishes in a variety of print and electronic formats and by print-on-demand. Some material included with standard print versions of this book may not be included in e-books or in print-on-demand. If this book refers to media such as a CD or DVD that is not included in the version you purchased, you may download this material at http://booksupport.wiley.com. For more information about Wiley products, visit www.wiley.com.

Library of Congress Control Number: 2023933109

ISBN 978-1-394-15463-0 (pbk); ISBN 978-1-394-15464-7 (ebk); ISBN 978-1-394-15465-4 (ebk)

SKY10044010_030323

Contents at a Glance

Table of Contents

Introduction

Welcome to the incredible world of Airbnb hosting. Airbnb is one of the fastest growing companies in the world and an incredible opportunity for people all around the world to earn extra income from their unused space. In addition to the extra income, meeting new people from all around the world is one of the many great perks of hosting on Airbnb.

When the 2020 pandemic all but shut down travel around the world, many began to question the viability of short-term rentals — would it ever be profitable again? Not only is the answer a resounding "Yes!", the new normal for travel has created both new opportunities and challenges. Hosts in previously obscure, little known travel destinations are fully booked and turning tidy profits.

Or you may have heard horror stories about hosting on Airbnb, be it unwanted parties or guests trashing a host's house. Circumstances aren't always perfect. When a platform such as Airbnb facilitates more than a half billion guest stays, they're bound to have a few rare instances that are less than ideal.

The vast majority of all Airbnb hosts never encounter a single major issue with their guests. The odd coffee cup may break, but if you follow proven strageies, hosting can be rewarding and profitable.

About This Book

Airbnb For Dummies serves as the perfect roadmap for current and aspiring Airbnb hosts who want to host the right way and optimize their earnings on Airbnb. This book includes everything you need to know in order to get the most out of your hosting and truly enjoy the experience.

Becoming a top performing host on Airbnb isn't easy; however, with the strategies we cover in this book you have everything you need to make it happen. You can read about everything you need to know about the following:

>> **The Airbnb basics:** From how Airbnb works as a platform to what it really means to host your space on Airbnb to setting goals for your specific listing.

We walk you through so that you understand the game you're playing and how to win at it, whatever that means for you.

» **Setting up the perfect listing:** We cover everything you need to know to get your property and your listing set up for success. We tell you what you need to do to ensure your property is guest ready and hassle-free. We show you how to set up your listing so that guests are excited to book your place. Whether you're brand new to hosting or have been at it for several years, we show you how to optimize your listing from every angle.

» **Maximizing hosting returns:** You can discover what you need to keep your place booked as much as you want it to be and at the best possible rates.

» **Minimizing hosting hassle:** You get plenty of helpful tips and resources that help you to make your hosting as enjoyable as possible. Hosting is meant to be fun and exciting, and we show you how to keep it that way for as long as you host.

» **Using the right tools and systems:** With the right tools and the right systems in place, you can all but guarantee any hosting nightmare doesn't take place at your listing, while maximizing your profit and minimizing your stress levels.

» **So much more:** You can discover how to get involved with new opportunities for fun and for income such as Airbnb Experiences.

This book is meant to give you everything you need to make your hosting both profitable and enjoyable.

Foolish Assumptions

If you fall into one of the following categories, then this book is for you:

» You're an absolute beginner to Airbnb. You've never hosted or even stayed at an Airbnb before, and you don't know where to begin.

» You started hosting, but you're not really sure if you're making the right hosting decisions or if you're performing as well as you could be.

» You've been hosting for a while and everything is going well, but you're starting to get tired and you need to find a better way to operate. You want hosting to be as fun and enjoyable as it was in the beginning again.

» You're an experienced host with years of guest stays under your belt and you have a Superhost badge to show for it. You're doing a fantastic job of hosting, and you want to continue to improve and find out how to take your hosting to the next level.

>> You don't have a property that you can list on Airbnb, but you want to host other people's properties, and you're not quite sure where to get started.

>> You're curious about what some of the most successful Airbnb hosts in the world are doing or about some of the new and exciting features that Airbnb has to offer. You realize that Airbnb currently presents a huge opportunity and you want to get in on it.

Icons Used in This Book

Throughout this book, you notice a number of helpful little icons over in the margins. Here's what they mean:

TIP

This icon indicates a pro tip that can likely save you a lot of time or make your hosting more successful. We learned these little tips through trial and error so that you don't have to.

WARNING

We use this icon to highlight anything that, if done improperly, could lead to some headaches down the road. Be sure not to overlook these points because they can save you from potential mistakes.

REMEMBER

This icon indicates an important tidbit that you're going to want to remember so that you make the best decisions and understand the reasoning behind our advice.

ON THE
WEB

As an additional value to our readers, we gathered a collection of useful resources and made them available for download or access online. Where noted, we provide a web URL address to direct you to them.

Where to Go from Here

This book doesn't need to be and isn't meant to be read from cover to cover. If you want to read it that way, then of course you may; however, if you only need specific pieces or solutions, then feel free to jump around and gather what you need to accomplish your goals. Just use the table of contents or index to find the topics that interest you and go from there. You can also refer to the Cheat Sheet at www.dummies.com for more helpful advice that you can refer whenever you need to. Start with your needs and interests.

That being said, oftentimes as a host you may not properly identify the source of a specific problem, which makes coming up with the right solution more difficult. If, for example, your property isn't generating the returns that you want it to, you may decide to first look at Part 3 for optimizing your pricing strategy. You may find however that improving your listing photos or adding some much-needed amenities is what you actually needed to do in order to increase your performance. If so, check out Part 2.

If at first you don't succeed, reassess, revisit, and rework your approach. Having your Airbnb operation go exactly as you want them to go may not necessarily be easy, however we can assure you that doing what it takes to get there will be very much worthwhile.

1

Getting Started with Airbnb

Understand the big picture view of Airbnb, its place in the sharing economy, and why it's a great opportunity to earn extra income from your unused space.

Discover what you need to have and do before hosting so that you can get the best possible start.

Ask yourself key questions before becoming a host to understand clearly whether hosting is right for you.

Determine if buying or building a property for Airbnb is worth the extra cost and effort involved.

Know how to figure your profit potential on Airbnb and determine how much money you can make as a host.

Chapter **1**

The Lowdown on Airbnb, Just the Basics

A irbnb is a home-sharing platform founded in 2008 that now offers more listings than all the top five hotel brands in the world combined. It started out as two guys hosting friends and guests on an air mattress in a San Francisco living room. They didn't know at the time that they were starting a wave that would spread across the world, where people could open their homes and properties to travelers seeking a more personal stay. If you're reading this book (and clearly you are), more than likely you're interested in listing your property on Airbnb to meet interesting new people and make money at the same time.

If so, you've come to the right place. Consider this chapter your jumping-off point into the world of Airbnb hosting. Here we dive into the lowdown on Airbnb and share just what you need in order to understand how Airbnb works so you can start hosting.

Looking at the Big Picture

Airbnb is a marketplace to connect people who are looking to stay at someone's property with someone who has said property and is looking to have people stay there. It's a community for both guests and host to connect with one another.

Airbnb provides the front-end and back-end tools to easily and effectively connect the dots.

These sections clarify a few ideas behind Airbnb a bit more, including what a sharing economy is, what short-term rentals are, and what you need to start hosting.

The sharing economy — putting underutilized resources to use

A *sharing economy* is defined as an economic system in which assets or services are shared between private individuals. This system can be free or require a fee and typically occurs over the Internet. These transactions are effectively consumer-to-consumer rather than the more traditional business-to-consumer. It's a whole economy run by consumers rather than big corporations.

In other words, individuals connect with one another to share (either for free or for a fee) different assets or services. Individuals typically already have these assets and services at their disposal.

Examples of this sharing economy have become widespread today. Uber and its main competitor Lyft are prime examples. People take advantage of an asset they possess (their car) and a service they can offer (the driving of that car). One individual is providing that asset and service and another individual is benefitting. It exists entirely between two private individuals. Uber or Lyft provide the marketplace for those interactions and transactions.

Airbnb acts the same in bringing together homeowning individuals (or anyone with a spare space) with other individuals who are looking for that asset (an accommodation) and service (a night to stay and someone to host them).

Consider two strangers trying to find one another in the world and all the circumstances that would need to line up for them to successfully do that. Instead, Airbnb acts as the marketplace that enables these individuals to find and connect with one another. It makes facilitating that transaction quite easy.

Understanding what short-term rentals are

Airbnb is an online platform that enables hosts to make their space available to guests who are seeking short-term rental accommodations. *Short-term rentals* are accommodations that meet the following:

PAVING THE WAY: THE ORIGINAL SHARING ECONOMY

Although Uber and Airbnb were arguably the first companies to popularize the sharing economy, several other companies came before them in the sharing economy space.

In 2008, there was Taxi Magic. Taxi Magic was Uber before Uber was Uber. However where Uber gained widespread success and was adopted nearly worldwide, Taxi Magic was a failure.

Many other companies tried to make the sharing economy happen and operated in that space. Back before Uber and Airbnb became successful, the idea of getting into a stranger's car so he could drive you somewhere or staying in a stranger's house was crazy. It was a scary and ridiculous idea.

Today, you likely don't think twice about requesting an Uber and getting into a stranger's car. Most people are completely open to booking an Airbnb and staying with a stranger. Uber and Airbnb paved the way and normalized the idea of the sharing economy among the masses.

» **Furnished:** The space must be furnished with the basics that guests would need and expect when staying overnight somewhere. Guests will need a place to sleep, not just a barren room. Refer to Chapter 5 where we discuss what necessities to include.

» **Transient occupancy:** Under most regulations a short-term rental is defined as a stay that lasts for less than 28 or 30 days. This definition may change slightly depending on the location, but essentially it's any stay that lasts for less than one month.

In other words, a short-term rental is when guests are staying for a short, fixed time period and for a specific purpose. They're visiting your city and want to stay at a property for a couple days or weeks to see the city, attend a conference or event, conduct business, or visit family and friends.

Knowing what you need to host

In order to host on Airbnb, you need the following:

» **A space:** The first and most important aspect to hosting is having a space. This space can range from an air mattress in your living room to a tree house or an entire property. Essentially, it's anywhere someone can sleep that you can post on Airbnb. You need to be able to define your space so people don't come to your mattress expecting a castle. However, you can truly list any spare space on Airbnb. Chapter 5 covers everything you need to know about getting your space setup for Airbnb. Chapter 6 discusses how to word your Airbnb listing so that guests arrive with the right expectations.

» **A listing:** Before you can host, you need to create a listing for that space on Airbnb. This listing tells guest what to expect and highlights the space. Chapter 6 gives you tips for making your listing stand out. In addition, your listing sets the rates so people can book the space for the time period they want and for a specific price. Just as important, your listing includes photos of your space. Including photos that capture the essence of your space is important. Check out Chapter 7 for in-depth advice about what you need to do to ensure your photos stand out and get prospective guests' attention.

» **The right tools:** Having the right tools make hosting on Airbnb much easier. In Chapter 10 we discuss several different tools, both hardware and software, that make tasks such as messaging guests, pricing your listing, and checking guests into your space much less time consuming.

» **The right methods and strategies:** You need an actual system that contains different methods and strategies to best perform as a host. With this base knowledge you continue discovering what hosting entails. Consider learning how to drive. In order to drive, you first need to have a car, but you also need to know how to drive that car. Similarly with Airbnb, if you have a space and a listing, you also need to know how to combine the two and make them work together. In other words, you need to know how to continually operate your listing to the best of your abilities with no issues. Throughout the rest of this book, our goal is to show you those strategies so that you can host successfully without needing to learn through trial and error.

Understanding How the Pandemic Changed Airbnb Hosting

The global pandemic of 2020 changed Airbnb hosting in a few notable ways:

» **It changed the way people travel.** During the pandemic, the most notable shift was a near total elimination of interational travel. With national borders closed in many parts of the world and reluctancy to board crowded airplanes, we saw more people traveling locally than ever before. This lead to many markets just outside of major urban centers to experience substantial demand growth, and many markets that relied on international tourism to see the exact opposite. Post-pandemic, we're seeing a new era of remote work, where many travelers are looking to stay for months instead of weeks given their new-found freedom to work from anywhere.

» **It changed the way people host.** Hosts have become much more focused on cleanliness and sanitation, and many hosts who offered up a shared space within their home turned off their listings. This change meant that Airbnb was dominated by whole-home listings even more than before.

» **It changed the way Airbnb structured it's platform.** In light of the changes that Airbnb recognized were taking place in the travel industry, Airbnb restructured their entire platform in some big ways. The platform is more focused than ever on catering to longer-term stays and cool getaways. If you've got a cool or unique space to list, your odds of success are higher now than ever before.

AIRBNB — THEN VERSUS NOW

In the early days of Airbnb the company hosted guests with air mattresses in apartment living rooms. Today, Airbnb has more than six million listings worldwide, ranging from luxury mansions to tree houses and apartment living rooms. The platform gained traction during the recession in 2009 with the company name coming from the idea of an "air bed and breakfast" — a play on the traditional bed and breakfast by including an air mattress.

Founders Brian Chesky, Joe Gebbia, and Nathan Blecharczyk rented out an air mattress set up in their living room for $80 per night. They realized there was a need for affordable accommodations apart from hotels or budget motels. They also found that most people have extra space in their homes that could easily house a guest.

It was a need with a clear solution, and both groups stood to gain. The traveling guest would pay an affordable rate for a place that wasn't being utilized and the host could utilize and capitalize on that spare space while deriving an income from it.

Answering Common Questions That You as a Potential Host May Have

Whether you're curious about the types of guests and how to properly screen or have a fear of letting a stranger into your home, this section provides answers to your most pressing questions. Many now-passionate hosts at one point would have never considered renting out their personal apartments or vacation homes. Oftentimes after they realized how the Airbnb systems create a safe, enjoyable, and successful experience, they were eager to commit to and later enjoy hosting. As an aspiring host, you may have been wondering about a lot of the answers to these questions. Keep reading to see.

Why would I allow strangers into my house?

The best reasons to let strangers into your house is that they're willing to pay to stay in your unused space and you can meet cool people:

>> **Generate additional income.** Making more money is the main reason most people start hosting. By taking a spare space in your home and offering it to your guests, you can bring in more money. Even better, the additional income you can make is disproportionate to the time you'll spend on hosting responsibilities. You're leveraging a little of your time for tasks such as cleaning or guest communication, but mainly you're leveraging an asset that otherwise is unutilized. In Chapter 4 we show you how to determine your listing's profit potential.

>> **Meet interesting people from all around the world.** By hosting strangers you can meet interesting people, many who are from a different background or walk of life. They're coming from a different part of the world and have their own set of experiences. You can share part of your neighborhood and world, offering them tips of what to see and do. You can even build long-lasting relationships. In Chapter 12 we discuss what it means to be a great host, not the least of which is caring about the relationships you establish with each guest.

Is it safe to host on Airbnb?

There are some common misconceptions about Airbnb, most prominently of which is the nightmare guest. Stories of nightmare guest experiences can be a huge deterrent to hosting guests in your space. However, these stories serve as the exception rather than the rule.

HOW AIRBNB ALMOST NEVER GOT OFF THE GROUND

When Airbnb began, it didn't immediately experience widespread acceptance because the idea seemed so crazy that nobody thought it would work. The concept of strangers staying in other strangers' homes was weird and scary. The founders didn't have a seamless launch; they were maxing out credit cards by the dozen to keep the idea afloat.

At one point, they had completely run out of cash and were desperate to sustain their company. They brainstormed some ideas to use at the 2008 Democratic National Convention to raise some funds for their scrappy start-up. They started packaging and selling "Obama O's" and "Cap'n McCain" cereal at the convention.

They'd run around to stores buying cereal, repackaging it in their own Obama O and Cap'n McCain containers and quickly selling it. The campaign went viral and gained more success than Airbnb at the time. The $30,000 profit sustained them so that they didn't run out of money again before finding success.

While pitching Airbnb, the founders were laughed out of the room more than once. Today it's hard to believe that Airbnb was initially widely criticized and misunderstood.

Many people have the idea that if they host on Airbnb their property will get absolutely trashed. They believe the guests will be awful and there's a huge risk of parties where people will burn your house to the ground.

However, that's the exception and an anomaly. Recently, Airbnb welcomed its 500 millionth guest. It's understandable that among half of one billion guests there would be some stays that didn't go as planned. Yet when you look at the percentage of terrible stays, they make up the tiniest of amounts. Barely a fraction of 1 percent of all stays result in any kind of major issue or damage — far from the norm. And, you can prevent these rare incidents from happening.

Airbnb has developed several safety features to ensure that hosting is safe and secure. Here are some of these features you can take:

>> **Hosts and guests never exchange money.** All money is exchanged directly through the platform. Because Airbnb acts as an intermediary, there's no way to get scammed as either a guest or a host.

>> **Hosts can see prospective guests' profiles and require that guests show a government-issued photo ID.** A government-issued photo ID can include

a passport or a driver's license. Guests also can offer other verifications, such as a personal email address, a work email address, a phone number, a Facebook account, and a photo. You can reach out to guests who make reservations and ask questions such as who they are and why they're staying in your area. If guests haven't provided these verifications, you can ask them to do so, making it safer depending on your level of comfort.

» **Hosts can set their own booking preferences.** As a host, you can set your own pricing and minimum stay requirements so that you attract the right types of guests into your space. We discuss this more in Chapter 8.

» **Hosts can make their own rules.** As a host, you can create House Rules that make it clear to guests what is and isn't allowed. In addition, you can set your own security deposit so that guests have a financial stake in following the rules. We cover House Rules and security deposit specifics in Chapter 6.

Is my property suited for Airbnb?

In general, the answer is overwhelmingly yes. You can list almost any property on Airbnb. Here are two considerations for listing your property on Airbnb:

» **An accurate listing:** You need to make sure you're listing your space accurately on Airbnb. You don't want guests showing up to your air mattress when they were expecting a castle. You must start by setting up the expectation with an accurate description for your property.

» **The bed and the space:** You must have something considered to be a bed and it must be in a private or common space. A private space can range from a private bedroom to an entire house or apartment. On the other hand, a common space can be any room in a space that is shared with other people. For example, the minimum listing is an air mattress in a common space, such as a living room. However, consider that how well the listing performs is up to you and up for question. Success varies wildly from place to place and depends on the guest you're trying to attract. You may want to add amenities to your property to make it better suited for success on Airbnb.

Is it legal to host?

Legally hosting on Airbnb depends entirely on where you're hosting. Each municipality has its own set of regulations, so check with your jurisdiction to ensure you're compliant with the law. If it's legal to host, then an area typically has no regulations so you can do whatever you want. However, certain areas may make hosting on Airbnb outright illegal. Other jurisdictions have different criteria that make hosting legal as long as you follow certain requirements, such as the number of days per year you can host.

TIP

Do your research for your specific municipality. The best place to start is to search online for "regulations on short-term rentals and Airbnb hosting" in your area.

Am I suited to host on Airbnb?

If you're ready to take on the commitment and responsibility of hosting and you have the space for it, you're suited to host on Airbnb.

Go into this experience with your eyes wide open to the reality of hosting and welcoming guests into your home. Here are some important factors to consider:

» **Your property cleaning and upkeep:** When your guests make a reservation to stay in your listing, they expect a clean and well-maintained property. Chapter 15 discusses the importance of maintaining and cleaning your property.

» **Your personal bandwidth:** Decide how much you're willing to communicate with guests and answer their questions. Guests expect you to answer their questions and be relatively quick to respond, so you need to be ready for that. Depending on your property, expectations may also be quite different. For instance, guests booking an air mattress for $10 per night more than likely have much lower expectations than guests booking a private villa for $800 per night. Chapter 10 discusses a few ways to ease the burden of communicating with guests.

» **Your lifestyle, including noise levels:** If you're hosting guests in the space where you live, consider how often you'll be around and available for guests. Also consider how much noise you typically make in your home. Guests expect at a minimum that you won't disturb their sleep, so if you plan on having friends over every weekend, you may need to reconsider. We discuss all the key elements to a perfect guest stay in Chapters 12–14.

What if a guest gets hurt?

If you provide a well-maintained property, the likelihood of your guests getting hurt is low. Nevertheless, you want to make sure you have the proper insurance to protect you whether a guest suffers an injury or your property is damaged. Airbnb's $1 million liability insurance policy protects you as the host in the event of any damages or any issues.

TIP

Don't depend solely on Airbnb's policy. Research Airbnb's liability insurance policy and find out what it does and doesn't cover. Speak with your local insurance agent and make sure you have all the protection you need for your specific situation. We walk through the specifics on getting proper insurance in Chapter 5.

What is the difference between Couch Surfing and Airbnb?

The main difference between Airbnb and couch surfing is money. On Airbnb you're charging money for your space while on the Couch Surfing platform, you aren't charging money. The adage "you get what you pay for" accurately explains the difference between the two.

Because the guest isn't paying for anything when couch surfing, the guest can't have any real expectations for the space the host has provided. The guest can't expect the space will be clean. The guest can't expect washed sheets or soap. Oftentimes the host has those items, but nothing is guaranteed. There's also no guarantee that the host will message the guest back on Couch Surfing because the platform runs that way. Airbnb is completely the opposite. A guest on Airbnb is looking for more stability, more guarantees, and an overall more organized experience. This guest is open to paying money to get those additional benefits.

Couch Surfing is for a specific type of host and guest. If you're a host who doesn't care about making money and wants the least amount of commitment while still meeting cool people, then Couch Surfing may work for you. If you're a host who wants additional income and desires more organization with your planning, then Airbnb is a better option.

Chapter 2

Hosting on Airbnb: What It Really Means

Becoming an Airbnb host isn't for everyone, and even though you may want to start immediately, holding off for a bit may be in your best interest. Having the right type of hosting mind-set is important if you want to host successfully on Airbnb. In this chapter we walk you through some important points to consider prior to hosting and help you to determine whether or not you're currently ready to start hosting on Airbnb.

Having a Hospitality Mind-Set — What It Takes to Be a Host

An Airbnb host and a landlord are two different positions. Many people think nothing will change when switching from acting as the landlord of a long-term rental property to the host of a short-term Airbnb rental. You may think that the only changes concern money and overall operations. However, when you decide to host on Airbnb, you're signing up for a much different experience.

As an Airbnb host, you're inviting someone into your home and space. You're actually in the hospitality industry rather than the real estate industry. With this change comes a new way of thinking. After all, you're opening your home and welcoming guests into it. Hosting family or friends is a more similar experience to what hosting on Airbnb entails rather than renting a space to someone for 6 or 12 months at a time.

As an Airbnb host, you need to set your expectations clearly on your listing and then reliably deliver on those expectations. Most importantly, you need to maintain a guest-focused mind-set. Your main focus should be on making your guests' stay as great as possible. Ensure you have the following in place to effectively deliver on all those expectations.

THE HOSPITALITY MIND-SET: HOW HOSTING ON AIRBNB DIFFERS FROM BEING A LANDLORD

Being an Airbnb host versus being a landlord differs more than you may think. The alternative to hosting on Airbnb is renting your space long term to a tenant. When you make that choice, you leave the hospitality industry and enter the real estate industry. Essentially, within the real estate space you're providing someone a space — anything from a room to an apartment or house — and it's that tenant's choice where to go from there.

The tenant must deal with everything from the furniture to decorations and any other amenities. Responsibilities such as cleaning and maintenance of the property is the tenant's responsibility, although there's a small degree of the service element in real estate. If there's an electrical issue or structural damage, you tend to that. However, to a certain extent, you're just offering a space.

With Airbnb you go further: You're providing an overall experience. You're making sure your guest's stay is perfect. You aren't just giving them a room with four walls. Rather, you're offering all the amenities and services. You're not only tending to the property maintenance and service, but you're also communicating with guests and offering recommendations of where to go, where to eat, and what to do in the area. You're part of a different industry, and realizing that difference is important.

Opening your heart and your home to guests

If you're offering your personal space to guests, you're letting people right into your life. You must be ready to welcome them into your home and not just on the good days. Some days you may be stressed and not want to talk to people. Even though other matters are going on in your life, as an Airbnb host you're still welcoming people into your home whenever your calendar is open. You really have to be ready for that reality. You can't let any of your day-to-day life impact your guests' stay.

On the flip side, being a great host doesn't mean you have to spend all your time with your guests. Be mindful of what sharing your space looks like and the extent to which you're letting guests into your life. The most involved way to host is by offering your spare bedroom or living room in the place where you're living. Doing so can be challenging at times but also rewarding because you can meet and get to know your guests and build relationships.

However, pursuing that arrangement means going in with your eyes wide open because more than likely you won't want to interact and help guests every day (or however many days you set your listing available). Essentially, be prepared to be there for your guests whether you want to or not.

If you have a vacation home that you're welcoming people into and you're not living there with them, you still need to remember the "mi casa es su casa" mentality. You want to avoid thinking "Hey, you're in my home for this set amount of time." Instead, you're setting an expectation that "While you're here, make yourself at home." Be prepared for that type of hospitality. You want your guests to feel comfortable and be able to enjoy themselves. They shouldn't be walking on eggshells worried about upsetting you or messing up your space.

TIP

To avoid having your guests feel that way, consider putting away anything that carries extreme sentimental value to you that may risk being damaged by guests. Doing so can put you at ease with having guests in your space.

Also be sure to clearly communicate anything that you're particular about, such as how certain items get organized or put away. If you don't communicate clearly, then you risk becoming frustrated with your guests, which is the opposite of what you want.

You have to be comfortable with your guests during their stay. Physically and mentally prepare yourself. Doing so can be tough. If you're not ready to welcome people and have your home be their home, then being an Airbnb host may not be the best fit. Ultimately, as soon as you can fully welcome guests into your space, you'll be able to offer the best experience.

REMEMBER

Make known any concerns about your space so your guests can meet those expectations and enjoy a stress-free stay.

Establishing trust through transparency and dependability

Because you're essentially operating in the hospitality industry as an Airbnb host, a high degree of customer service comes into play. Unmet expectations can frustrate your guests. As a result, you want to establish your guests' trust by being transparent and dependable.

Keeping an eye on the big picture and remembering that each individual guest stay adds up to create an overall level of guest satisfaction is important. No single guest can be looked at as being insignificant or unimportant. If you don't consistently offer transparency and dependability, you're going to lose trust and credibility in your reviews. When you aren't meeting the expectations you set, your guests are going to let you know.

REMEMBER

Clear and fast communication is a good example of what shows up in the reviews. People won't trust you to get back to them when they have questions in the future if they see a high number of past guests complaining about the time it took you to respond to their messages. This applies to any expectation you're setting for your listing as well as the baseline expectations for staying in any Airbnb accommodation. Essentially, ensure that you're thinking in the long term and that you maintain trust by always meeting and exceeding guests' expectations.

Keeping your place clean and well equipped

From your own standpoint as the owner of your listing you may be perfectly content with some weeds in the front lawn or some dust on the baseboards. However, when you become a host, you need to consider these different elements from a different mind-set. Keeping your place clean and well maintained is an important part of being a great host.

Similarly, you may not often cook for yourself and you may therefore have a relatively limited supply of cooking utensils. Though that amount may be entirely acceptable for you, as a host you have to consider things from your guests' perspective. If there's something that your guests would reasonably want or expect, then it's in your best interest to equip your property with it.

Delivering on (rising) expectations

Airbnb is continually raising the bar on the guest experience, and the bar is already set high. Airbnb started as a simple air bed and breakfast. Guests had the expectation that they would be staying on an air mattress on the floor of an apartment. Back then, it was closer to an upgraded version of couch surfing. Today, many guests view Airbnb as an alternative to a hotel, and the expectations are clearly higher.

REMEMBER

In addition to what you've promised as their host in your listing, your guests will have certain baseline expectations. Meeting those expectations is a great place to start. As Airbnb grows and expands as a company, these expectations continue to rise.

Here are some baseline expectations your guests will have:

>> Your property is clean (see Chapter 15 for more).

>> Your Wi-Fi Internet is reliable (check out Chapter 5).

>> Your property is safe and secure (Chapter 15 discusses safety in greater detail).

>> Your property has adequate heating and cooling (refer to Chapter 15).

>> You quickly and reliably communicate with your guests. If you take hours or even days to respond to them, you can expect unhappy guests and negative reviews. (Refer to Chapter 10 for the lowdown on communication.)

As a new host or a host who wants to do better at hosting, you have to understand those expectations and be prepared to meet them. Even if you aren't in an Airbnb Plus/Airbnb Luxe space or aiming to reach Superhost status (which we dive into in Chapter 11), you should still aim to offer the great customer service and unique experience Airbnb promises its guests.

Setting up systems so your guests have a unique stay

Most hosts want to share their city with other people, and as a host that opportunity should excite you. If you set up systems to lighten your hosting load and delegate certain responsibilities, then you're much more likely to enjoy the hosting experience.

One of the most common examples is hosts putting a system in place around cleaning. Most hosts don't want another part-time job as a house cleaner, and needing to add that to your plate can be stressful. After you start hosting, you can set up systems around tasks such as cleaning so you won't get burnt out in the long term and can consistently deliver that personal touch as a host. Check out Chapter 10 for a full breakdown of all the ways you can use systems to maximize your hosting profit and minimize your stress levels.

Adding a touch of personal magic

What sets Airbnb apart most and the reason guests consistently choose Airbnb over hotels is the experience of living like a local. Guests have already experienced the same corporate hotel experience in different places around the world. With Airbnb they're getting the unique experience of living in a home or apartment.

Your touch of personal magic is about making sure you have the bandwidth to enjoy hosting, and that shows up in small and big ways. You communicate with your guests and answer their questions, which demonstrates you're excited about their arrival. This excitement can materialize both in person and through your messages.

You're passionate about hosting and really love what you're doing. Perhaps you give a small gift basket and are eager to hear how your guests are doing. You share tips about event and activities in the area with your guests. You may even leave something special for your guests during their stay. Compared to the burnt-out host who is just going through the motions about their guests being there, you're excited and do what you can to make their stay memorable and relaxing.

Before Becoming an Airbnb Host: What to Consider

This section focuses on what to think about before you make the decision to host. You may have reservations in the back of your mind that you aren't aware of but need to bring to the forefront. Ask the questions in this section to make sure you're ready to be a host. This is your chance to consider if hosting is the right fit for you.

Being aware of your hidden expectations

In order to realize your hidden expectations, first ask yourself what your expectations are for each aspect of hosting. How much money do you expect to make? What is your expectation for how much time you're willing to put into hosting?

What are your expectations for which parts of hosting you will and won't participate in? What do you believe a reasonable guest will be like?

TIP

Jot down any expectations you have and what you think hosting is going to look like for you. Then critically go through that list and ask how realistic each expectation is. Check out this book's table of contents for our advice on addressing your expectations and how reasonable they are. For example, expecting your property to bring in $10,000 per month may be realistic for you or it may be completely unrealistic. (Chapter 4 helps you determine what is realistic for you to earn.)

Be aware of some of the most common host misconceptions:

>> **Money:** People typically have a number in their head for how much money they'll bring in and a number for how much time it'll take to reach that amount.

>> **Time:** People often assume that they can just set up their listing on Airbnb and forget about it while the money rolls in. This isn't the case, and the truth is, hosting requires a fair bit of ongoing work to do well. You can put systems in place to reduce your workload, but hosting will always take more than a few minutes a month unless you decide to hire a property manager (we discuss hiring a professional property manager in Chapter 10).

>> **Effort:** This expectation is similar to how much time hosting will require. Oftentimes people believe that hosting doesn't require much effort and will be an easy way to pass the time while bringing in large amounts of money.

>> **How the guest will act and behave:** Some people expect certain guest behaviors such as whether or not guests will use the kitchen or the common space and how tidy guests will keep the bathroom.

>> **How the guests will interact with the host:** People have different expectations for the engagement of guests and interactions they'll have.

>> **What hosting a guest actually looks like:** People usually have an expectation or idea of what the experience of hosting will entail. They usually have a vision of what a typical guest stay will look like. For some people, they think, "Oh it's horrible. They'll burn down my property." That's quite extreme on one side of the spectrum, but on the other extreme are the people who expect that hosting will be a breeze. They may think, "I'll send their check-in instructions and never hear from them again. It'll be no work for me."

When you're aware of your own expectations, you can cross-reference them with the common misconceptions listed here to be sure that you don't have the wrong idea of what it takes to be a host. As long as your expectations are realistic, you'll be able to make the right call when deciding whether or not hosting is for you.

Inviting strangers into your home

An important detail to remember when considering being an Airbnb host is you don't get to control the personalities of the people staying in your home. Ultimately those people are strangers. All types of people with all kinds of backgrounds will be able to make a reservation in your home.

That's a tough reality for some people. You have to be nondiscriminatory and ready to welcome all guests regardless of their background or who they are as individual persons. As a baseline, be ready to be accepting of people from all walks of life because that's what you're going to get. You're going to have every type of person you can imagine.

TIP

Essentially, be ready to go in with an open mind and an open heart. You don't get to control the types of people coming into your space so plan on welcoming everyone the same way and appreciating everyone for who they are. If you're hung up on this point, then Airbnb isn't the right platform for you.

REMEMBER

Airbnb is serious about antidiscrimination. The platform is 100 percent inclusive, for both guests and hosts. It's absolutely against Airbnb's rules and policies to deny a guest based on race, religion, sexual orientation, and so on. Every host must formally agree before hosting to never discriminate against any guest.

Making the commitment

Consider that by choosing to host you're planning to make a commitment that can affect your time, money, and energy, which we discuss in the following sections.

The following money-related commitments especially apply if you're interested in hosting an entire apartment or home on Airbnb. Some people may have an apartment or home that's their vacation home or their former residence so it's already furnished. However, many other people are converting their long-term rental to a short-term rental and renting it on Airbnb. A huge deciding factor for those people is the return on investment (ROI) for hosting. Although you can make more money on Airbnb than through a 12-month tenant, ask yourself if it's worth the additional time and cost.

Time commitment

Ask yourself if you have the time to devote to hosting. Do you actually have the time? Is your lifestyle set up for hosting? For instance, if you know you're going to be partying Friday and Saturday nights, then you may need to choose not to host at your home those weekend nights. If you aren't able to message guests during the day or throughout the week, then you may need to consider getting someone to help you with communications. Consider your own lifestyle and figure out how much time hosting requires. Be realistic about whether you can actually host and do so in a way that aligns with how much time and energy you have.

Money commitment

You also need to consider money. Although you can control how much money goes into hosting, be aware that a portion of your Airbnb income is going to cover expenses, such as the extra toilet paper, hand soap, and dish soap you'll need. If you do it yourself or hire an outside cleaner, you're also going to spend money (and time) cleaning your property and doing the laundry. You need to invest in your hosting so consider to what extent you're comfortable doing that. Then get realistic about what your hosting will look like.

These expenses range from buying the day-to-day items like paper towels and hand soap to fully stocking your kitchen with cooking supplies to the larger and more costly requirements such as furniture. For example, if you have a spare bedroom that you need to furnish or an entire property that you need to furnish, it'll cost money. Consider what kind of financial investment you need to put into your property before you decide to host (check out Chapter 5 for more guidance on what you'll need to have or add to your property to make it guest-ready).

Energy commitment

When you make the decision to become a host, you're essentially making the commitment to put your best foot forward even when you don't necessarily feel like it. Your guests are going to have needs and you need to be ready to meet those needs with a positive attitude.

Especially when hosting space in your own home, make sure you're ready to make the commitment to be positive and energetic when guests are around. Having a bad day at work isn't going to be an acceptable excuse for being rude or short with guests.

Looking at how technologically savvy you are

Although Airbnb is an easy and user-friendly platform, when getting started you still need to make sure you're comfortable with technology. Two technology-related considerations for host are as follows:

>> **Consider if you have access to technology.** You need a computer and ideally a smartphone. You use your smartphone to respond to guests and

complete tasks on the go rather than needing to constantly be near a computer.

>> **Make sure you're comfortable with technology.** Generally, anyone can host because the platform is user friendly. The best way to get accustomed to technology is by going on the Airbnb site and setting up a listing without making it live. You can use this book as a guide on how to use the Airbnb platform and create your listing (in Chapter 6 we walk you through exactly how to create the perfect listing).

Familiarize yourself with the back end of the platform, including how everything works in terms of setting your pricing, responding to guests, and seeing how your listing performs. Don't overlook the technology, but also don't be overwhelmed by it. Fortunately, the technology is fairly easy to pick up. Essentially, the more you understand and integrate this technology as a host, the better the results for you and your guests.

Being aware of how your decision to host affects others in your life

You don't live on an island. Your decision to host can affect others as well. Consider these two factors when deciding to host on Airbnb:

How your hosting will impact others

When you decide to host you're taking on a commitment that will potentially impact those around you. The most extreme impact will be on other people who are living with you when you decide to host guests in your personal home. Suddenly, you'll have people living in that space, making noise in that space, and using the amenities of that space such as the bathroom. Bringing another person or people into your space will have a definite impact on your family or roommates, and you need to be mindful of that reality.

In a less direct way, hosting means that you're giving your guests the space that you list. You won't be able to offer it to your sister or parents or friends when they come to town. Unless you plan in advance, your family or friends can't come last minute and crash at your place. Your decision to host potentially changes that expectation for them.

This doesn't mean that if you experience any of these situations you can't host, but it's important to be mindful and consider to what extent hosting will change your lifestyle. You may need to say no to your friends about going out or have them plan on crashing somewhere else.

How your decisions in life affect your guests

You must be mindful of how your everyday decisions as a host impact your guests. For example, going out late at night and returning early in the morning, hanging out until midnight with friends in the living room, or being noisy isn't going to be acceptable when you're hosting guests and they're trying to sleep. Doing so is going to have a huge negative impact on your guests. For example, your sleeping guests who may be on vacation aren't going to appreciate your decision to use the blender at 5 a.m. to make a smoothie. Suddenly, your decision to not flush the toilet, take a long shower, or leave your hair in the sink or shower is impacting the people staying with you.

These decisions all impact the guests who are staying in your home. However, even if they're staying in your vacation home or an additional property you have, you're still going to be impacted. You can't have a family vacation at the last minute if your home is already booked with guests.

Determining the type of host you want to become

You need to figure out what type of host you want to be. Fortunately there is no one set way. If you do want to be an Airbnb host, you now can figure out what makes you unique and offer that personal touch to your guests.

REMEMBER

When figuring out who you are as a host, the good news is you have so much flexibility. You can really make hosting whatever you want it to be. You have the freedom to decide how you host, when you host, what space you host in, and what space you don't host in. You can map out what best suits your current goals and lifestyle and what you want to get out of hosting.

For example, maybe you have spare bedrooms in your own home as well as a vacation home. After examining what you want from your Airbnb experience, you find you don't want people in your own home because it's not conducive to your lifestyle, but you still want to host your second property. On the other hand, you may decide that you want guests during the week, but on weekends you like having more privacy and keeping your space to yourself. You can choose to host for just one week a month or just when you leave town for the weekend. You may work a seasonal job and don't want people there in the summers, but in the wintertime when everything is a bit quieter you do want guests there.

No matter when you decide to host, you need to understand what the baseline requirement for hosting is. Choosing to host for the additional income and not realizing the rest of the expectations and requirements — in other words hosting for the wrong reasons — is when you can run into issues. Chapter 12 addresses the basics of good hosting to help you be the best host you can be.

Chapter 3

Buying or Building a Property for Airbnb

B y the summer of 2020, the pandemic had all but shut down travel across the world to a halt. Hotels and short-term rental units in cities big and small sat vacant with little to no future bookings to look forward to. Would Airbnb survive? Would the travel industry survive?

It may seem silly now looking back but the widespread fear was palpable. Previously high-flying Airbnb hosts who took on second or third mortgages to quickly acquire more properties for their short-term rental business suddenly found themselves overstretched and with zero rental income to cover their mortgages. This forced many to sell off parts or all of their Airbnb businesses, including many of the most lucrative listings pre-pandemic.

But today as we're writing this, heading into our fourth-year post pandemic, the sentiment has entirely shifted. What was initially doom and gloom has turned into one of the best windows of opportunity for new and experienced hosts to secure prime Airbnb properties in prime Airbnb markets, just as pent up travel demand is set to explode.

In this chapter, we explore the new travel reality today and how that has created an opportunity to buy or build for Airbnb ready for the right hosts to take on.

Understanding the Opportunity Today

When Airbnb the company shelved its IPO plans, few thought they could IPO so quickly, let alone so successfully less than a year into the pandemic. From initially seeing their revenue fall more than two thirds between 2019 and 2020, with losses of over half a billion dollars, and having to resort to a massive layoff of its workforce, Airbnb and its hosts are thriving today.

What changed? The new post-pandemic world created a post-pandemic travel reality:

» **Constrained travel created new travel habits.** Early in the pandemic, with very limited flights and many destinations requiring mandatory multi-day quarantines upon arrival (some even imposing $10,000 fines and up to six month prison terms for travelers who break quarantine), travelers sought out easier local destinations rather than international or out of state destinations requiring long flights and costly quarantines.

» **More local travel demand.** More local travel during the pandemic led to people discovering and developing a taste for previously ignored travel spots within driving distance from their homes, particularly outdoor and rural destinations within a few hours' drive outside of major metros to get away from the crowds. For example, Big Bear, Joshua Tree, and Palm Springs all saw increased bookings beginning the summer of 2020 as accessible weekend destinations from the greater Los Angeles area.

» **Overall pent-up travel demand unleashed**. For most people, the pandemic meant millions canceled and delayed vacations and major life events such as weddings. But with widespread vaccinations and quarantine fatigue well established by mid 2021, governments and business around the world have relaxed travel restrictions, opening the floodgates for millions just itching to get their "revenge" travel in to make up for experiences lost during the pandemic. What people initially spent purchasing at home gym and entertainment early in the pandemic, they are now spending far more on airline tickets.

» **Longer average stays.** As we close out 2022 and head into 2023 at the time of this writing, not only are people traveling more often, at nearly pre-pandemic levels, they're staying much longer for their trips. For hosts, this means higher occupancy with fewer guest turns.

>> **Inventory in previous Airbnb hot spots still below pre-pandemic levels.** Although Airbnb began seeing record bookings again in early 2022, the supply of listings in major cities are still well below pre-pandemic levels, meaning the markets are in a host friendly state of having high demand and lower competition resulting in high occupancy rates and high nightly rates. While inventory is expected to recovery eventually, a high interest rate environment and a potential recession may keep inventory below pre-pandemic levels for at least several more years.

As we enter into 2023, the Airbnb space is entering an ideal opportunity window of fast-growing travel demand with depressed and slowly recovering inventory, which will continue to put upward pressure on occupancy and nightly rates in strong Airbnb markets.

Previously popular travel destinations are popular again but with less competition. Previously unknown destinations are now permanent draws for local travelers, providing a pocket of opportunity to acquire listings with strong profit potential but without the big city premiums for acquisition.

Renting Versus Buying or Building

When it comes to securing a property for your Airbnb listing, you have three options: rent it, buy it, or buy *and* build it. Each have their advantages and disadvantages involving tradeoffs that you must weigh for yourself. In this chapter, we compare each option to help you make a more informed decision.

The primary tradeoff between these options is risk versus reward. Renting has the lowest upfront capital required and the lowest overall complexity. The unit is typically listing ready minus the furniture. You won't need to make any major repairs or remodeling. And your startup capital is often a few thousand dollars to cover the first month's rent, the security deposit, and the cost of furnishing. The biggest challenge with renting often is finding a unit whose landlord allows you to rent on Airbnb. They are becoming more and more difficult to find. On the flip side, renting also comes with certain risks that buying or building do not. When you rent a property, the owner of the property still has the final say and if they want you out, your business could be shut down overnight. With renting, you also don't own any tangible assets (aside from some soon-to-be-used furniture) so if matters take a turn for the worst, selling isn't really an option.

With buying, and especially with renovating or building after buying, the level of complexity and overall financial investment increases. You need to come up with more capital, often in the hundreds of thousands of dollars for the purchase. The property will require extra time and money to bring its state up to rental readiness. On the easy end, it may require repainting, new carpets, and some resurfacing. On the extreme end, it may require a full tearing down of the old structure and a complete rebuilding of a new structure with all new fixtures and appliances. Figure 3-1 shows the relationship between these three options that show the tradeoff between taking on more risk with higher profit potential versus taking on lower risk with lower profit potential.

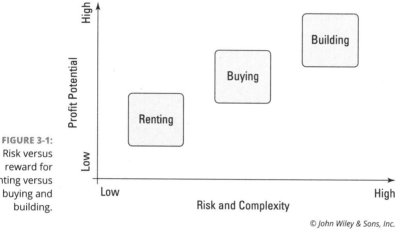

FIGURE 3-1: Risk versus reward for renting versus buying and building.

It's important to note that buying or building an Airbnb is typically a pretty serious financial decision. Naturally, if you don't have any experience investing in real estate or short-term rentals, then specific training and expert guidance such as the training and guidance that I (James) offer in BNB Inner Circle can be quite helpful to avoid mistakes.

REMEMBER

Renting to explore a market

Although renting a property for Airbnb means less control and generally lower potential profit expectations, you have situations where it is the more attractive approach.

>> **When you're exploring a market:** When you're exploring market where you're hopeful but still uncertain with respect to the long-term viability of running a consistently profitable Airbnb listing, renting gives you a low risk way to dabble in the market. After you gain clarity, either way, you can get out of your lease or look for a property for purchase in the same market.

>> **When you're saving up for purchase:** Even with access to financing, you can still expect to come up with a nontrivial portion of the purchase. For a typical

property in and around a major metropolitan market in North America, this amount can easily be in the low to mid six figures. Renting and listing provides a way to earn an Airbnb income while you save up funds for your purchase.

>> **Have worked out a rent-to-own arrangement with the seller:** Although uncommon, some sellers of properties may be willing to initially rent out the unit to you as part of a potential purchase agreement in what's called a lease option. It typically involves paying an above market rental rate for the right, but not the obligation, to be able to purchase the property at a predetermined price before an agreed to expiration date. This option is great if you're both saving up reserves for a purchase and feeling out the market.

However, without ownership, renting can put your Airbnb business and income at the whims of your landlord, especially when your original lease term has reached maturity. For greater control, you must own the property for your Airbnb listing.

Buying or building to realize full long-term profit potential

When you're convinced of the long-term Airbnb potential for a market, then buying or building a property for Airbnb can be the path to consistent long-term Airbnb income.

The following scenarios are ideal for buying or building a property for listing on Airbnb.

>> **You find an underperforming property in a great Airbnb market:** Even in the strongest markets, you find properties performing well under market standards due to it lacking key amenities or needing a simple refresh, whether minor or major. For example, a studio listing in a business traveler market can underperform simply because it lacks a proper workstation that would attract the mobile, work-from-anywhere travelers seeking a cozy place to both unwind and work remotely.

>> **The property requires easy and economical upgrades to get to listing readiness:** Ideally, the updates or upgrades you need to make are simple and affordable. Updates such as new paint, new rug, or linens are easy and won't hurt your wallet unlike major renovations such as a kitchen or bathroom remodel or new roof.

>> **The market can clearly support major renovation or a new build:** In this scenario, you find a property that is not listed due to major deficiencies requiring costly renovations or a complete rebuild. However, existing listings are showing occupancy and nightly rates that would more than cover the financing of the costs of the project.

If you've never bought a short-term rental property before, then you're going to need to spend a lot more time and effort to gain expertise and ensure you don't run into any costly mistakes. You can check out a company such as BNB Inner Circle for additional training, which gives a full overview of how to invest successfully in short-term rentals and get a great return.

TIP

All things equal, seek first to minimize unnecessary renovations or construction whenever possible. The purpose of any renovation or construction must be necessary to bring the property to market standards for capturing the bookings. Otherwise, you are only increasing your initial capital requirements and spending unnecessarily. The right renovations can transform an otherwise underperforming property into a market leader. See the following for a detailed case study of how James did just that, by taking a property from underwhelming to a market leading Airbnb.

RENOVATING AND BUILDING FOR SUCCESS: THE PERFECT PROJECT

James recently bought a cottage just a few hours outside of Toronto, Canada. When he bought it, the previous owner had kept the property in decent shape but had neglected a few mostly cosmetic renovations. The previous owner also lacked an eye for design, so the property appeared generally underwhelming.

With a few thousand dollars of renovation work, James was able to give the place a really nice face-lift by freshening up the paint, redoing some flooring, and refacing some cabinets. In addition to the renovation, he spent a bit more money furnishing the place nicely and adding amenities that guests really crave in that area, such as a hot tub, some board games, and a projector so that guests could watch movies on the big screen.

Lastly, James added a "build" phase to his project. The property was on a large lot that backed onto a forest, so James added a geodesic dome in the backyard so that more adventurous guests could do some "glamping" and sleep out under the stars.

Notice that all of these renovations and additions were done with one notion in mind: the guest. Everything that James spent money on was something that would attract more guests towards booking his place for their next getaway. As a result, when James launched this property on Airbnb for the first time, it quickly became one of the top performing properties in the market, which lead to some serious profits.

Choosing the Right Market

Don't try to get travelers to go where they're not already booking and going to. It's an uphill battle and a waste of your time and money. Instead, go to where they are already making bookings, where you can find, acquire, and list a new and attractive listing in an area where demand is outpacing the inventory of available listings.

This concept can occur in two types of markets: 1) Airbnb hot zones, existing high demand markets in major urban or tourist destinations, and 2) up-and-coming markets with fast growing demand outpacing existing, limited inventory. In the first, although ample competition is already there, the strong and consistently high travel demand means consistent profits for a well-positioned new listing. For the other, such as two-hour away weekend destinations outside of major cities, there are fewer and weaker competing listings vying for the growing demand.

Searching for Airbnb Hot Zones

Even within the same zip code, the difference between the income potential of near identical listings in an Airbnb Hot Zone versus one outside of it can mean more than three times the revenue potential.

For example, a near identical unit could be only a few blocks away where one can only achieve $1000 per month in Airbnb revenue while the other achieves over $3000 per month. These pockets of areas with high Airbnb travel demand are ideal places to search for your properties first.

So how do you find the Airbnb Hot Zones? You have two options: a do-it-yourself path or an easier done-for-you option.

OPTION 1: You can do it on your own but it is more time-consuming and less accurate.

>> **Pick some neighborhoods to target:** Choose a few neighborhoods and narrow down at least by zip code, but even better if you can get down to specific blocks.

>> **Get long term market rental rates:** Get asking long-term rental rates for similar listings in the market. For example, if evaluating 1-bedroom units, get rental rates for 1-bedroom units in the area. You can find asking rates on sites such as rent.com, apartments.com, or Zillow.com. In major cities, you can find plenty of listings for your research. In more rural markets, you may need to look at local classifieds or drive around looking for "For Rent" signs to inquire.

>> **Find Airbnb rental rates:** Go to Airbnb.com and search for the same types of listings for short term rental rates for both weekends and weekday rates. Take an average of at least 8 to 12 listings. Because some markets can be very seasonal, it's best to get data points up to six months in the future for six months, thereby allowing you to collect data for a 12-month period.

OPTION 2: Utilize a third-party data provider to provide you all of the information you need.

Third-party short term rental data providers such as AirDNA.co, MashVisor.com, and AllTheRooms.com all collect market data for most Airbnb markets, often with hundreds or thousands of comparable listings. Although they are not free, the data they provide for a modest fee is well worth the accuracy you get and the savings in time and effort.

The markets that provide you the biggest discrepancy between short term rental rates and traditional long term rental rates, the stronger the Airbnb demand in that market. For example, if you see average Airbnb revenue of $3000 per month versus an average of $1000 per month for a traditional lease rate, that is a 3:1 ratio.

As you compare different markets using the data you have, either acquired on your own or through data providers, you can see big differences between hot markets and cold markets. Hot markets can see a revenue ratio difference of 2:1 or even 3:1 whereas in cold markets, you can see ratios closer to 1:1, meaning all of the extra effort of running an Airbnb listing can be avoided by simply renting your unit as a long-term rental instead because you can expect to earn the same with just a single long-term tenant instead of many dozens of short-term tenants.

Understanding and Securing Financing

When it comes to buying and building a property for Airbnb, it is rare for someone to pay for the property and construction with all cash without any financing. Financing, often in the form of loan from a lender or investment from investor partners, typically helps fund from 40 percent up to 100 percent of the total project cost, with the most common financing in the 50 percent to 75 percent range.

For many aspiring Airbnb investor hosts, financing is necessary to make their projects a reality. Besides increasing your purchasing power by many folds, financing enables an Airbnb investor to buy more or better property in the same way a mortgage loan enables a homebuyer to buy more house than they otherwise could have.

Sources of financing

While many immediately think of funding from personal cash reserves and loans from banks, many other sources of financing are available for short-term rental businesses. Here are some more common financing options available to short-term rental entrepreneurs and investors.

TIP

>> **Self-funding:** Your first and easiest option are funds you already have available for your investment. You don't need anyone else's approval. You won't need to apply or make an investment pitch. It's entirely up to you. Taking out a second mortgage or a home equity line of credit (HELOC) or a cash-out refinance is not technically considered self-funding because you need to apply and qualify for these separately.

However, even if you have all of the funds for your project yourself, you want to explore other options to limit the cash outlay from your own funds to keep some funds on hand for other purposes or to do more investment projects.

>> **Friends and family:** As with most entrepreneurial ventures, friends and family funding is the next most accessible source of funding. However, there are plenty of reasons why many choose to seek elsewhere to avoid mixing business and personal relationships, chiefly among them to avoid situations that could permanently damage relationships with friends and family.

>> **Conventional loans:** A fixed rate investment property loan will be the most common and best option for many. And unlike government backed loans such as the FHA or the VA loans, you're not required to reside on the property to qualify. These come in conforming, when the loan amount does not exceed the threshold limit of $647,200 in most markets for a single unit property ($970,800 in high cost of living markets) as of 2022, or non-conforming when it exceeds that threshold.

>> **Secondary home loans:** Having had a long run of record low interest rates and rising home values, folks have had access to record levels of home equity as sources of funding for buying investment properties either through a HELOC or cash-out refinance. The interest rates will be higher than their primary mortgage rates but often will be more favorable than a standalone conventional investment property loan.

>> **Government backed loans:** If you qualify for FHA loans or VA loan programs (eligible only for military borrowers), which require you to reside on the investment property, you should prioritize these options over others as the terms are often quite favorable in comparison with much lower down payments (3.5% for FHA and 0% for VA). These options are ideal situations where you're investing in a multi-unit investment property where you are living in one of the units while renting out the others.

As interest rates go up and lenders tighten their lending, you may need to explore some less commonly used financing options available for a short-term rental investment should the previous options not be available to you for your investment or in your market.

>> **Hard money loans:** While more commonly used by fix and flip investors looking for very short-term loans to fund their short term renovations, some are willing to fund short-term rental projects. These loans often require a higher down payment, at least 25 percent, with higher upfront fees, interest rates, and prepayment penalties. However, hard money lenders operate in nearly all markets so it'll be worth shopping around to find the best terms. Due to the short loan terms of typically 12 months, these loans are meant to be repaid through a refinancing to longer term loans after the investment property has established a six to twelve month record of consistent rental income.

>> **Seller financing:** Also known as owner financing or a seller's note, this is essentially an agreement with the seller of the property to act as a lender. Most sellers are not open to this option but some can be convinced by offering a sizable non-refundable down payment, which they keep even if decide not to or fail to follow through on the rest of the purchase. Seller financing is worth exploring when buying an unusual property and/or requiring special expertise or execution for the project where the seller is unlikely to see a traditional buyer with access to conventional financing.

These arrangements can get tricky and unless both the buyer and the seller have prior experience with seller financing agreements, it's best to bring in third party legal expertise to review the agreement before committing.

>> **USDA loans:** Another government backed loan with no down payment requirement that require the borrower to reside on the property. These low interest, fixed rate mortgages, while intended to help low to moderate income borrowers in rural markets, can also be used for multi-family units as long as the borrower resides in one of the units. If you're exploring in a rural market, this is an option worth exploring.

>> **SBA 504 loans:** Although primarily used by small businesses to fund improvements for commercial real estate, these loans can sometimes be used to buy property or land and pay for improvements for a rental property investment. The biggest limitation being that it requires 51 percent of the property to be owner occupied.

This was not meant to be an exhaustive list but to provide the options that are most commonly available and used by short term rental investors. For example, although crowdfunding or private equity from professional investors are options, they're well beyond the scope of our intended reader audience.

Explore government backed and conventional loans first, then look at other options if those are not available to you.

Considering Other Investment Factors

With your intended market determined and financing options figured out, it's now time to find the right property to purchase. However, what is well suited for an Airbnb in one market may not work very well in another. You have some additional considerations to account for when searching for a specific property to purchase for the purpose of renting on Airbnb.

>> **Closer to attractions and conveniences.** Being within walking distance to an attraction or conveniences such as a lake, restaurants, subway station can make your property more attractive than those that are just outside of walking distance. If walking distance is not possible, short 5-minute drive is always preferrable to longer drive.

>> **Dedicated parking.** Not an issue in more rural markets but in more urban markets, this can make all the difference in bookings, especially if the area requires guests to have their own cars to get to local attractions and solid mass transit or ride sharing is not available or reliable.

>> **Local government friendly or neutral to short-term rentals.** With more and more cities adopting limitations, some even bans, of short-term rentals, it is crucial to get a clear idea of the current and likely future sentiment of the local government on short term rentals. A future ban or limitation could seriously turn a profitable venture into a money-losing venture overnight. If you're looking in an area that straddles different zip codes and city boundaries, look for the most short-term rental friendly city. If the city is planning on requiring permitting or licensing for short term rentals, would the property qualify? Is the property in the intended allowed areas for short term rentals?

>> **Having no neighbors or minimal potential for conflict with neighbors.** Is there limited street only parking? Guests using up parking is one of the most common complaints from neighbors next to short term rental aside from noise. The less potential guests have of running into neighbors the better the odds of avoiding conflict with neighbors. An angry and nosey neighbor can turn your Airbnb dream into a nightmare fast.

>> **Has or can easily add target traveler specific amenities.** This consideration varies quite a bit by market as each market may attract a different type of traveler. Does the market attract business travelers or remote workers? Can you easily add an attractive work station or office? Travelers enjoy catching or digging up oysters at the local stream? Look for properties with a nice yard that has or can add a fire pit for grilling oysters. Identify the core attractions and activities for your target travelers and look for properties that have or can easily add matching amenities.

>> **Strong short-term rental alternative backup plan.** If you had to turn your Airbnb rental into a traditional rental with a long-term tenant, would your investment still work out profitably? Would this property and specific location attract long term renters? Would it attract corporate renters if you had to turn it into corporate housing?

>> **Secondary or alternative income sources.** Similar to the previous backup plan, can the property be used as an event space? Does it have a big lot with a great view that could be used for small parties or weddings? Could it be used for filming? Does it have other spaces that can be rented out? Extra garage rented as storage for example or extra land for creating glamping sites for additional income. All things equal, a property with more alternatives can give your investment a good backup or secondary source of rental income outside of Airbnb.

Accounting for additional time

Unlike Airbnb hosts turning their existing homes into Airbnb listings, buying or building a new unit and getting it ready for Airbnb takes additional steps. The more complex the renovations or build, the longer the time you need to factor to going from purchase to listing your property, and from listing to ramping up your Airbnb listing to full profitability.

With little to no major renovations, a property that needs only minor updates for a refresh may only need a couple of weeks to get to listing readiness. However, for projects that involve building permits and hiring contractors, it could add months to even a year or more in time to go from purchase to listing readiness.

Depending on the nature of your project, what renovations or construction, if any, are involved, you can expect to add additional weeks or months to your overall project timeline. In Chapter 5, we take a deep dive into all the steps needed to fully prepare your property for Airbnb.

Chapter **4**

Determining Your Profit Potential

Before you invest significant resources and energy into becoming an Airbnb host, you first need to determine the profit potential for your future Airbnb listing to make sure all that effort will be worth it — in other words, you want to make sure you make money hosting. Far too many aspiring hosts jump into hosting with blindfolds on and don't understand whether their expectations are realistic and achievable. When reality and expectations don't match, disappointment results.

Not all properties and markets can perform well on Airbnb as short-term rentals. By doing a bit of research and analysis before you host, you can set realistic expectations and ultimately decide whether hosting on Airbnb still makes sense for you, with your property, in your market.

In this chapter, we provide guidance on how to determine the profit potential of your future Airbnb listing before you host. You can conduct proper market research and analysis to determine the "size of your pie"— how much you can reasonably expect to make as a host on Airbnb.

Decoding How Much You Can Really Make on Airbnb

Aspiring hosts will quickly discover that when attempting to estimate their Airbnb profit potential, where they gather the relevant information can have a big impact on their calculations.

Looking at broad national averages can give you a rough sense of how an average host is performing, but it may tell you very little about what you could expect in your specific market with your property. To get an accurate gauge, you need to gather the right kind of information and make sure they're directly applicable to your situation. The following sections explain the basics.

Starting with national averages

When Earnest.com, a student and private loan refinance provider, analyzed tens of thousands of loan applications from applicants who reported earnings from working on sharing economy platforms, such as Airbnb, they found the average Airbnb host earned approximately $924 per month from hosting.

However, because a small fraction of hosts earned disproportionately higher income than their peers, the median earning for hosts was much lower. Figure 4-1 shows that only half of Airbnb hosts earned more than $440 per month (approximately $5,280 per year).

According to Earnest.com, about one in two Airbnb hosts earns less than $500 per month and nearly three in every four earns less than $1,000 per month. Only one in ten hosts will earn $2,000 or more per month.

Your location mostly determines your Airbnb profit potential

The profit potential of your Airbnb listing is primarily determined by the property's exact location. That is, how much you could expect to make from your Airbnb is mostly out of your control and can't be changed after your listing goes live on the platform.

So, asking yourself questions, such as: "How much should my one-bedroom Airbnb listing earn?" doesn't help. Even if you're asking within the boundaries of your specific city, listings that are a minute walk from each other can experience significantly different levels of Airbnb travel demand.

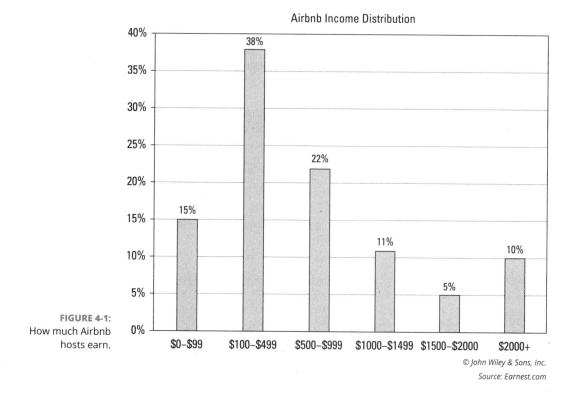

Airbnb Income Distribution

FIGURE 4-1:
How much Airbnb
hosts earn.

Some markets have very high Airbnb travel demand with a limited supply leading to high occupancy rates and high nightly rates. For example, a one-bedroom entire apartment listing in downtown Los Angeles, located immediately across the street from the Los Angeles convention center and walking distance to the Staples Center where the L.A. Lakers and Clippers basketball teams play their home games, will significantly outperform an identical listing only two blocks away. Figure 4-2 compares two properties and looks at how a three-minute walk could potentially impact your earning potential.

FIGURE 4-2:
Two blocks away,
a world of a
difference.

	Listing A	Listing B	Difference	
Avg Occupancy Rate %	86.7%	73%		13.4%
Avg Occupancy Rate (days/mo)	26	22		4
Avg Nightly Rate	$126	$105	$	21
Avg Monthly Revenue	$3,276	$2,309	$	967
Avg Annual Revenue	$39,312	$27,707	$	11,605

Just two blocks away, these two near identical Airbnb listings could see nearly a $1,000 a month difference (or almost $12,000 for the full year). Airbnb travel can become hyper local in some markets, especially if travelers care about immediate walking distance to points of interest.

In other words, the performance of Airbnb listings can vary drastically even across a short distance because of the high variability of demand across markets, which is more pronounced in dense urban markets. In more spread-out rural markets, the radius of a local market is larger.

The demand for Airbnb rentals in your specific market, whether it's a one-block radius in a downtown area or a five-mile radius in an open rural area, determines the profit potential of your Airbnb listing. However, just because you could expect to earn a certain profit doesn't mean you'll automatically achieve it. You still must earn it by being a great host.

Researching Your Airbnb Market: Earning Statistics

Picture yourself running a nice one-bedroom Airbnb listing in your city. After all the operating expenses that include supplies, utilities, and cleaning, say you're able to pocket a tidy $1,000 per month in profits. Should you be happy with your performance? Are you doing well as a host?

What if we told you that the other one-bedroom Airbnb listings in your market are making only $500 per month in profits on average? That would mean you're earning twice as much as your competition! You should feel good about that because that means you're executing well as a host.

But what if, instead, your competition is earning $4,000 per month in profits on average? You wouldn't be feeling too good about that information. If hosts with similar listings in the same market are earning three times as much as you are, you're doing some facets wrong as a host.

The best way to estimate your profit potential on Airbnb is to find out what similar listings in your neighborhood are already earning on the platform. But how do you find out? You gather *performance statistics* — the occupancy rates and nightly rates — for existing listings in your market that you'll be competing with.

In the early years, you would have to gather and estimate these statistics manually, a painfully laborious and inaccurate exercise that took hours to complete only to be outdated immediately. However, the growth and maturation of short-term rental data providers in recent years have provided fast, accurate, and up-to-date statistics to aspiring hosts for a nominal starting at just $20 to access local market reports. Some providers offer free limited reports or free trials occasionally, so make sure to search the web for a recent offer before making a purchase.

For a list of our currently recommended data providers, go to our online resources at www.learnbnb.com/airbnbfordummies.

Get the free reports and trials to see which one you like and then get a one-month subscription for full access to the market data in your market. You can't get the statistics on your own, and even if you tried, doing so would take you many painful hours to days to put together an inaccurate data set. Don't waste your time! You can always cancel your subscription after the first month. However, we recommend ordering the reports at least once a year to keep a pulse on your market and to gauge how your listing is faring against your competition in the market.

You need to look beyond the published asking nightly rates of similar properties on Airbnb — just because a few listings ask for $250 per night doesn't mean guests are paying that much nor does it mean that these listings are able to fill their availabilities at this rate.

And what the performance is like during one part of the calendar may look entirely different during other parts of the calendar. So, in addition to understanding the nightly rates, you need to look at other market metrics and considerations to access your profit potential accurately.

Finding the crucial market statistics

Regardless of which data provider you ultimately go with, you want to pay attention to a few key statistics when assessing the viability of hosting your property in your market. Here are the statistics to get and why pay attention to each:

>> **Daily rates:** The best way to know what you'll be able to charge is to find out what identical or similar listings in your market can currently charge guests. Although obtaining market averages is better than having nothing, getting a range of daily rates is more useful because a few very high performing or very low performing listings can artificially inflate or deflate the average figures in the market. For example, AirDNA market reports will also give you the 25th, 50th, 75th, and 90th percentile figures (see Figure 4-3 for an example of this data). Most hosts should use the 50th percentile figure (median) for their initial estimate unless they have reason to place their listing as more or less attractive than competitors to use the 75th or 25th percentile figures instead.

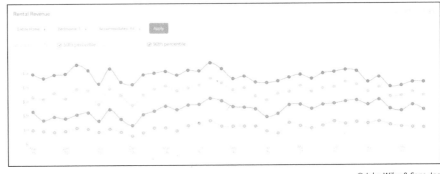

FIGURE 4-3:
Average monthly
rental revenue.

These numbers are the average monthly rental revenue for one-bedroom listings in a select city in Los Angeles, shown at the 25th, 50th, 75th, and 90th percentiles. For example, to achieve rental revenue rates at the 90th percentile line, your listing would need to be among the top 10 percent of listings in the market.

>> **Occupancy rates:** *Occupancy rates* are the percentage of available nights that are booked. For example, an Airbnb listing that is made available for rental for 100 days out of the year and is booked 65 days has an occupancy rate of 65 percent (65 divided by 100). Just knowing the daily occupancy rate isn't enough if you don't know how many nights are being booked in the market. Similarly, obtaining a range of occupancy rates rather than just an average is more useful.

REMEMBER

Take an honest assessment of your listing compared to the existing listings on the platform that are your competitors. Compare your listing to this entire set of direct competitor listings, ideally at least ten. Is your listing in a more attractive location versus the others? Does your listing look newer, more modern, or luxurious? Does your listing have more appealing amenities? Where does your listing place among this set? For an older property farther away from points of interest than competition, you may need to use the 25th percentile figure for your estimate because your listing will likely attract fewer guests. Alternatively, for an attractive new listing located immediately adjacent to the top performing listings in the market, you may use the 75th or 90th percentile figures instead because you can reasonably expect similar levels of performance to the top performers.

>> **Rental revenue:** The top data providers calculate the rental revenue figures for you and often present them in the same way they present the daily rates and occupancy rates data. Again, looking at the range is more helpful than the simple average. Brace yourself when you look at these figures the first time because many prospective hosts often have mismatched expectations from reality. For example, a prospective host whose expectations are colored by

the news articles covering the new breed of six figure Airbnb hosts might be sorely disappointed to discover he'll likely earn far less than six figures in his market. Better to know the truth early even if disappointing than to find out later after investing significant time and resources.

TIP

Although getting annualized figures are useful to understanding where your average daily rates, occupancy rates, and annual rental revenues may fall, you want to look at the monthly figures as well for the prior 12 months. Why? Some markets may have pronounced seasonality where the demand is much higher or lower during some months than others. Having this knowledge can better help you prepare for both the high and low travel seasons in your market. Refer to Chapter 8 for a detailed discussion of seasonality and how it impacts your pricing strategy.

Understanding the market deeper

Each data provider can provide the three basic statistics for their users that we mention in the previous section. However, to stand out from their competition and to further entice their potential customers to choose them over others, the top listing data providers offer many additional statistics about the market.

Here are some other useful details you may find:

>> **Market mix:** The *market mix* is basically a relative ratio of different types of Airbnb listings in a given market. For example, the market mix for Airbnb listings by a large lake may skew toward cabins whereas in a downtown urban market it may skew toward one- and two-bedroom apartments. This information lets you determine what the current composition of active Airbnb listings is, including whether more studio and one-bedroom units are being reserved compared to larger units with three or more bedrooms.

Knowing the respective performance of the different subsets of listings can tell you what the travelers to this market are demanding. For example, if the top performing listings are all private room and studio listings whereas the few large big house listings are mostly unoccupied, you may want to explore turning your five-bedroom house into multiple private room listings instead — you can't rent what people don't want.

>> **Long-term trends:** Understanding recent statistics tell you where the market is today, but those stats doesn't tell you how the market got where it is. Is the market growing or shrinking? Only by looking at several years of data can you spot this trend. With Airbnb increasing in popularity, more listings are coming online in more markets. However, in some markets, the influx of supply without a complementary growth in demand means more hosts competing for the same number of guests, leading to higher competition, lower pricing and occupancy, and ultimately lower profits for hosts.

- >> **Amenities statistics:** To understand how your property stacks up against your competition you need to know what your competition is offering. By looking at the amenities that everyone else provides and what only the top performing listings offer, you can determine exactly what amenities you need to compete and what you can aim to have to stand out.

- >> **Future statistics:** Some data providers have a direct data feed of hundreds of thousands of listings that allow them to know future occupancy and rates of competing listings. With this information you can price your future available dates to remain competitive.

- >> **Top listings:** Being able to see the performance of the top listings in your market based on actual performance data provides a target to aim your performance. With this information you can scrutinize every aspect of these top listings from their photos and title to their descriptions, pricing, and policies. You can't emulate the best without first being able to identify the best.

- >> **Rating statistics:** How guest ratings are distributed across property types and among your direct competitors can tell you how competitive your market is. The higher the ratings for existing hosts, the more competitive the market and the less margin for you to make hosting errors with your guests.

- >> **Granular seasonality:** Even though monthly figures help you spot broad seasonality trends in your market during the calendar year, having access to market performance for each day can help you spot and prepare for unusual spikes in travel demand. For example, an annual conference that brings in thousands of travelers can lead to overbooking during those specific dates. Refer to Figure 4-4 for an example to see the full year seasonality for a market. For a full discussion on planning for and adjusting your pricing strategy for special events, refer to Chapter 7.

  In some markets, Airbnb travel demand is seasonal and varies significantly depending on the month of year. In addition, certain recurring special events can also create unusually high demand during specific days of the year. Knowing when they occur and how much impact they have on demand allows you, the host, to price your listings appropriately.

- >> **Traditional rental statistics:** For investors who want to purchase property for renting them on a short-term basis on Airbnb, comparing the traditional rental market statistics in that market to short-term rental statistics is crucial to making a sound investment decision.

- >> **Other statistics:** If it's an attribute you must decide on for your listing, chances are the data providers are tracking and sharing the results to their users. This information includes how others are handling minimum stays, security deposits, cleaning fee rates, cancellation policies, and more.

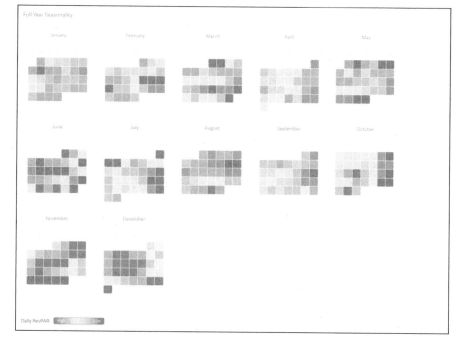

Full Year Seasonality

January February March April May

June July August September October

November December

Daily RevPAR

Source: AirDNA.co

FIGURE 4-4: Seeing market seasonality.

From our experience and those of our readers and students, hosts in different cities and countries find different data providers to be more or less accurate for them individually, so first exploring several options is worth it to see which works best for you.

ON THE WEB

Each data provider presents its own data, and none has all the metrics you want. So, take advantage of the free trials and then purchase a subscription for the one you find most useful for your goals. For the latest list of recommended data providers, go to www.learnbnb.com/airbnbfordummies.

Determining the Size of Your Pie

Getting the market statistics can help you form realistic expectations for rental revenue, but you won't get to keep that amount of money. Unlike owning a traditional rental property, operating an Airbnb listing involves higher operating costs so for every dollar that you collect through Airbnb, you only get to keep a fraction of that.

Knowing what data and metrics to gather is the first step. Turning those findings into a profit estimate require additional work — for every dollar in booking revenue, you only get to keep a part of it because you incur expenses while operating your Airbnb listing. Additionally, it's important to compare your projected earnings against the expected time commitment required to host successfully.

Factoring operating expenses

To estimate how much profit you get to take home, you need to understand and estimate the operating expenses involved in running your Airbnb rental.

REMEMBER

Operating expenses are the recurring expenses that happen monthly and exclude one-time expenses, such as fixtures, furniture, and appliances that you need to set up your listing initially.

Although each Airbnb listing may differ, here are the most common operating expense items to factor into your analysis:

>> **Rent:** If you're renting a property and then subletting the entire unit on Airbnb during the full calendar year, then the rent that you pay is a rental expense. However, if you're renting a portion of the property on Airbnb, such as a spare bedroom, or if you're only making the property available for rent for some of the days, then you will need to divide the total rental expense between the parts of the property used for Airbnb and those for personal uses. You need to pro-rate the rental expenses by the percentage of the property used for Airbnb (by area or by the number of rooms) and by the ratio of days made available as an Airbnb rental out of total available days. Pro-rating expenses can get tricky depending on your jurisdiction and situation, so be sure to consult with your accountant.

>> **Management fees:** Management fees include commissions paid to others to take over the day-to-day operations for your Airbnb listing. For the many property owners who want to profit from Airbnb without hosting themselves, they need to set aside a portion of their rental revenue to pay a property manager or co-host to manage their Airbnb listing on their behalf. (Refer to Chapter 18 for more about co-hosting.)

>> **Utilities:** Guests staying in your property want lights to see, running water to bathe, heat when it's cold, and air conditioning when it's hot. As a result, you need to pay the gas, water, and electricity bills. You also need to add any other regular fees paid to the city, including sanitation or sewage fees here. And due to the higher usage typical for short-term renters, these bills will be higher compared to that for long-term renters.

- **Internet/cable/satellite:** High-speed wireless internet is a required amenity in practically all Airbnb listings. Some hosts may even elect to provide cable or satellite television. These services aren't free.

- **Cleaning:** For the many hosts who elect not to do the cleaning themselves, they hire outside cleaners. Although most of the cleaning fees are passed directly to guests, some hosts may subsidize the cost to charge a lower cleaning fee to their guests to encourage more bookings. Don't have a washer and dryer on the unit? Add laundromat fees. To see a full discussion on cleaning-related best practices, refer to Chapter 15.

- **Repair and maintenance:** Operating an Airbnb listing means having more people come in and out of your property, adding more wear and tear on your property. Plumbing can leak or clog, furniture can become damaged, and appliances can break. And it's your job to make the repairs needed to keep your listing in pristine shape for the next guests.

- **Permits:** More and more cities are requiring Airbnb hosts to obtain and maintain valid permits to operating their listings. Unfortunately for hosts, these permits aren't free, and more than likely they're an annual expense.

- **Third-party tools:** From automated pricing to automated messaging and scheduling, third-party tools can help hosts simplify their operations and save them hours of manual work every week. But these tools come with monthly subscription costs. Refer to Chapter 9 for a full discussion on automation tools and best practices.

- **Consumables:** You need to keep your listing well stocked of items, such as toilet paper, soap, shampoo, and snacks and beverages. Although these items make up a small fraction of the operating expenses, you need to replenish them after each stay so the expenses do add up over the course of a year.

- **Other supplies:** Some items don't need replenishment after each stay, but they still need regularly replenishment over the course of a year. You may need to replace towels, linens, and sheets every three to six months due to wear or stains. Even the gas needed to make all the supply runs is an operating expense.

WARNING

This list isn't exhaustive or applicable to all hosts. Your specific operating expenses depend on factors specific to you, such as whether you own or rent your property and how you ultimately choose to run your listing. For a deeper discussion on operating expenses and how they impact your tax exposure as a host, refer to Chapter 17.

Estimating time commitment

To determine whether hosting on Airbnb is worthwhile economically for you, just knowing the likely profit dollars you can make isn't enough. You also need to estimate the number of hours it can likely require of you to earn that level of profits.

How attractive it is to earn $1,000 in profits during the month are entirely different stories between putting in 20 versus 200 hours of work where you'll earn $50 per hour versus $5 per hour. How much time does it take to host? It depends on several factors:

>> **DIY versus outsourced cleaning:** Cleaning is one of the most time-consuming and physically draining aspects of Airbnb hosting. Whether you do it yourself or outsource drastically determines your hours of input as a host. The larger the property, the larger the group size, and the longer the stay, the longer it takes to clean and turn the space for the next guest. Check out Chapter 15 for a full discussion of cleaning.

>> **Number of units you're hosting:** The more units you have, the more hours you must put into fielding inquiries, communicating with guests, making supply runs, coordinating with cleaners, updating listing pricing and calendars, and monitoring your performance.

>> **Manual versus automation:** The more tools and technology you use to automate operations and remove yourself from manual work, the more time you save. This includes decisions, such as setting up remote check-ins and check-outs rather than doing them in person and using automation tools for pricing, messages, and scheduling. Refer to Chapter 10 for a more detailed discussion on automating your Airbnb operations.

>> **Self-managing versus outsourcing:** The biggest factor in time commitment depends on whether you can manage your listing by yourself or hire someone else to do it for you. Whether you self-manage or outsource your Airbnb operations largely determines both the up-front commitment, the time it takes initially to set up your property and put together a winning listing, and the ongoing commitment, the time it takes to run your listing on a day-to-day basis.

Figure 4-5 shows the estimated hours per week a host can expect to spend on hosting-related activities. These estimated time commitments assume a listing that gets approximately eight to ten bookings a month with guests staying on average two to three nights. During the initial months of ramping up, hosts may spend more time adjusting and improving their listing and operations.

USING THE AIRBNB POTENTIAL PROFIT CALCULATOR

To determine your overall profit potential and your profit potential for the hours you can expect to put into hosting, run a financial analysis with assumptions for rental revenue, operating expenses, and time commitment.

To make it easier for you, we include a companion Airbnb Profit Potential Calculator you can access online to make your own analysis. Go to www.learnbnb.com/airbnbfordummies. Look for the Airbnb Potential Profit Calculator and follow the instructions to download the file and access the video demonstration to complete your own analysis. Here is a screenshot of the calculator.

Source: LearnBNB.com

We provide this calculator as a free online resource you can use to make all your assumptions and get an accurate estimate of the profit potential for your future Airbnb listing.

The calculator can help you estimate your startup costs, rental revenue, operating expenses, and your time commitment as a host. By going through the exercise, you can gain an intimate and more realistic understanding of your Airbnb market and what you can expect to achieve with your listing.

	Self-Manage Self-Cleaning	Self-Manage Outsource Cleaning	Outsource Hosting
Room	4–6	1–2	<1
Studio/1 bedroom	6–10	1–2	<1
2–3 bedroom	8–12	2–3	<1
4–5 bedroom	12–16	2–3	<1
6+ bedroom	16+	2–4	<1

© John Wiley & Sons, Inc.

FIGURE 4-5: Estimated time commitment required per week for hosting.

As you can see in this figure, the time commitment required for each host is different, depending on their property and the choices they makes on how they manages the property.

Comparing the Big City versus Rural

If you live outside a large city away from the epicenters of Airbnb travel, you can still profit as a host. Although the local travel demand largely determines the profit potential of your listing, you can increase your profit potential even in less popular Airbnb travel destinations with the following strategies in these sections.

REMEMBER

In more remote markets, the revenue potential for one Airbnb listing is probably lower than for one equivalent listing in or near the city. However, this doesn't mean you can't make a profit in these areas.

Earning a profit in any market

When the limited travel demand reduces the revenue potential of a single Airbnb listing in an area, the cost to acquire the properties and operate them as Airbnb listings is also lower, making the path to Airbnb profits simple: operate more units.

For example, a one-bedroom property in a very high demand part of Los Angeles may average $200 per night and achieve 85 percent occupancy, helping it achieve rental revenue of $5,100 a month. But an equivalent listing an hour outside of downtown may only average $100 a night and a 60 percent occupancy, achieving only about $1,800 a month. However, the first unit likely requires a monthly rent of $2,500 or more a month whereas a host may be able to lease the second unit for about $750.

The city listing may achieve a gross profit of $5,100 – $2,500 = $2,600. After additional operating expenses, the final profit to the host may be closer to $1,500. For the more remote listing, it may achieve a gross profit of $1,800 – $750 = $1,050. After additional operating expenses, it may pocket only $500 in profits, one third of the city listing. Figure 4-6 breaks down the economics between the urban and remote listing.

	Urban Listing	Remote Listing
Occupancy Rate	85%	60%
Avg Nightly Rate	$200/night	$100/night
Monthly Revenue	$5,100	$1,800
Cost to Rent	($2,500)	($750)
Operating Expense	($1,100)	($550)
Monthly Profit	$1,500	$500

© John Wiley & Sons, Inc.

FIGURE 4-6: Comparing an urban versus a remote listing.

Even though the remote listing likely earns a lower overall profit compared to its urban counterpart due to the lower Airbnb travel demand in the remote market, it nonetheless can still be profitable for a host. But if you want to make the same dollar profit, you need to operate more listings.

Adding more Airbnb listings without purchasing property

To list more properties, you must first get the permission to do so. Although you could purchase more properties, doing so is a time-consuming and cost-prohibitive strategy for most hosts. Instead of having to put tens of thousands of dollars toward a down payment in a purchase, here are two easier strategies if you want to add more Airbnb listings:

>> **Rental arbitrage:** Rent the property at the long-term rental rate from the owner, get explicit permission to sublet on Airbnb, and then earn your profit from the difference. Often, just one month's rent and a security deposit are often enough to secure the unit. This method is the Airbnb equivalent of "buying low and selling high." However, most landlords are still weary of subletting to an Airbnb host, because it may expose them to neighbor complaints and additional liability risk. Refer to Chapter 5 for additional discussion on managing landlord relations.

>> **Co-hosting:** More and more property owners want to reap the benefits (profits) of Airbnb hosting without hosting themselves. To do so, they either must hire a property management company or partner with a local Airbnb host to co-host their listing on their behalf. As a co-host, you can earn a percentage of the booking revenue from a property without having to purchase or lease the property. Check out Chapter 18 for a detailed discussion on why co-hosting is a great growth strategy.

Determining the Legality of Hosting in Your Market

As the regulatory landscape for Airbnb and short-term rentals continue to evolve, one city at a time, you need to identify and understand the local regulations in your city that may impact your Airbnb operation if you're thinking of creating a listing.

Being aware of the short-term rental laws, whether current or just on the horizon, can help you avoid costly fines from your city and consider how they may impact your earning potential.

Being aware of the potential risks of Airbnb hosting

Increasingly, new and pending local regulations move toward requiring licensing or permitting and adding limitations to short-term rentals. Cities around the world are implementing or contemplating more severe punishments for hosts of illegal short-term rental listings. To avoid facing potentially hefty fines, we encourage all prospective hosts to find out the local short-term regulations in their market.

How local regulations affect your profit potential:

>> **Permitting or licensing:** You may need to apply and pay for a license or permit to operate an Airbnb listing in your city legally. Many cities permit only properties in certain parts of the city and set a maximum number of permits they issue.

>> **Fines:** Operating an illegal listing without a proper permit or license could subject you to hefty fines. In 2018, Paris fined hosts more than $1.5 million over illegal listings. That same year, San Francisco fined a couple for $2.25 million dollars for operating 14 illegal Airbnb listings.

>> **Revenue potential:** Ultimately, the local laws regulating Airbnb hosting could significantly reduce your Airbnb revenue potential. For example, if there is a 120-day limit for using your property as a short-term rental, then you need to decide whether that's long enough to still make Airbnb hosting a worthwhile effort.

REMEMBER

It's not a question of *if or when* your city will regulate short-term rentals, but a matter of *how* your city is regulating or will regulate short-term rentals. The specific regulations that govern your market will have a significant impact on the overall profit potential and hurdles to getting started for your Airbnb listing.

Finding out what laws or restrictions apply to you

Although cities have historically struggled to enforce their restrictions, matters are changing as cities step up their enforcement efforts. For example, San Francisco forced Airbnb to remove 50 percent its listings in the city as new laws came into effect in 2018.

To find out where your city stands regarding short-term rentals today, you can try the following methods:

>> **Airbnb Help Center:** Airbnb is continually adding more resources to help both prospective and current hosts stay in the know about their cities. To see the latest materials from Airbnb about your city, go to www.airbnb.com/help/home. Then type the name of your city into the search bar titled "Search help articles."

>> **Search engines:** A simple search engine query for "Airbnb law (Your city name)" produces results in most cities that have recently passed or working to pass new short-term rental regulation. If you live in a major city anywhere in the world, start here. You can also try combinations with "home-sharing," "short-term rental," "ordinances," and "regulations."

>> **Local hosting groups:** Find a local Airbnb or short-term rental hosting group on Facebook or Meetup and ask current hosts in the city where you can find the latest information on local regulations. Many hosts are eager to help fellow hosts but be sure to consult group posting rules or seek permission from group administrators before posting questions to the group profile pages.

- >> **City hall website:** Go to your city's `.org` website and make the same query because municipal webpages often rank low on search engine results.

- >> **City hall offices:** If you still have trouble getting the information, call your city hall's offices and ask them to direct you to the latest information. As a last resort, you can pay them a visit during normal visiting hours to get help.

WARNING

Given the potential for significant fines and operating limitations, don't start hosting your property on Airbnb, or on any other short-term rental platform, until you fully understand how to operate legally in your city.

2

Putting the Spotlight on Your Listing

Prepare your property for Airbnb by having all of the essentials and extras that make staying at your property a delight for all guests.

Determine what amenities your guests want in your market to make your listing a no-brainer for guests to book.

Manage relations with neighbors and landlords to avoid costly misunderstandings and headaches in the future.

Become a guest to be a better host to learn what it takes to please guests by putting yourself in their shoes.

Build the perfect Airbnb listing for your property by writing an effective heading and a detailed description so prospective guests can understand what your listing is about.

Take great photos for your listing to showcase your property in its best light and get more bookings.

Chapter **5**

Preparing Your Property for Airbnb

Making sure your property is set up and ready to host guests on Airbnb is more than just putting a bed in a spare room. In this chapter, we walk through everything you need to do to set up your space for success. Maximizing your space creates an exponential impact on your overall results. Consider that by increasing the value of your property by just $10 per night, you'll have the potential to earn an additional $3,650 every single year.

The first step is making sure your property is ready for guests and second is making sure you as the host are ready for this new commitment. In this chapter we also talk about taking your property from its current state to where it needs to be in order to be successful on the Airbnb platform. Whether your property is furnished or unfurnished or has the required amenities, we're here to help you get it ready for guests.

Figuring out what you want to list, whether it's your whole space or just an extra room, is another important decision that this chapter examines with simple instructions on all factors you need to consider.

Equally important is making sure you maintain good relations with your neighbors and your landlord when hosting. This chapter gives you the lowdown on maintaining good relationships with your neighbors and landlord. We cover just what you need to know so you can be an Airbnb host and avoid upsetting anyone or breaking any rules.

Creating Profit Potential with Your Property

Your property ultimately dictates your maximum profit potential. There's a ceiling on what any given property can earn. However, most hosts don't reach that maximum potential for their property for a wide variety of reasons. In these sections, we help you figure out what that number is for you and how you can make sure your space is optimized so you actually hit that ceiling. We explain how you can increase your property's monthly maximum potential through a number of different methods.

For example, a one-bedroom apartment in Boise, Idaho, doesn't have the potential to earn $50,000 per month. No matter what you do to optimize your pricing or how much you spruce up the space, not enough people are seeking a one-bedroom apartment in Boise to generate that much income. Although you won't reach $50,000 per month, you do have the potential to turn a $1,500 per month property into a $2,000 per month property.

Maximizing the potential of your listing by optimizing your space

Maximizing the potential of your listing is all about taking advantage of all your property's current features to provide the highest value. Consider your property as it currently exists, whether it has furniture, amenities, or nothing at all. It has a current maximum potential, and there are ways you can increase that potential. Our goal is to show you all the ways that you can maximize that potential.

This way, you aren't wasting any opportunities but instead taking advantage of all the potential your space offers. Taking the necessary steps to maximize the potential of your space enables you to earn much more money in the long run and have much more satisfied guests.

For example, an addition on your house would include more bedrooms and therefore increase your listing's earning potential. On a lesser extreme, maybe you could renovate or decorate your space and make it nicer. If done correctly, it's likely to lead to happier guests and more bookings.

Here are a few ideas to consider when looking for easy ways to further maximize your listing's potential:

>> **Don't block off any rooms.** The whole place should be accessible to guests. If you have a whole house listing and one bedroom is blocked off, you want to unblock that room. If you have a one-bedroom listing that's in your personal home, then make sure the closet in that space isn't being used by you. Guests should be able to use that space for their clothing and belongings.

>> **Make sure your sleeping arrangements are maximized.** Have properly sized beds in every bedroom and ensure your property is equipped to sleep as many people as it comfortably can. If you have a bedroom big enough for a king bed but you have a twin, then you can sleep one more person by upgrading to a king size. As long as the rest of your property can comfortably accommodate the extra person, making that investment is a no-brainer.

>> **Keep your property properly decorated so that it looks inviting in your listing photos.** Your space needs to include more than just a bed with sheets and a mattress. Make your space feel like home for the people staying there.

REMEMBER

If you can't take action right now, save some of your Airbnb earnings so you can upgrade and get a better return on your investment. How exactly you can optimize your space differs for each individual host. Take inventory of all opportunities you may be missing out on to maximize your potential even further. Make a list and execute the ones that make the most sense for your own situation.

Starting your listing off strong

You always have room to improve your listing by further upgrading your space and offering more and better amenities to your guests. When you're first starting, the goal is not to invest as much time and energy as possible into your listing, but simply to grab all the low-hanging fruit. This way, you'll maximize your returns while minimizing your upfront investment. Consider the following sections when starting.

Ensuring the maximum is as high as possible right now

You first want to ensure that the maximum nightly rate you're able to charge is as high as possible for right now. Although you want to do as much as possible to maximize your listing's potential before you welcome your first guest, you can also do other elements to continually improve and increase your listing's potential all throughout your hosting journey. At some point however, you may find that the return on your investment isn't necessarily there.

For example, consider if right now you aren't in a place to upgrade your single bed to a queen bed. Don't stress about it. You don't need to perform that upgrade right away. However, it makes sense to make note of that upgrade and keep it on a to-do list. Then, after you reach X amount of income from your listing, you can make the investment into the queen bed.

Having the appropriate amenities

You want to make sure you have the important amenities for your listing that guests are going to expect. If your property can sleep eight people but only three of them can stay there comfortably, then you're wasting a big opportunity.

Consider if you have a pullout couch in the living room but lack bedding for that pullout couch. In this case, guests can't use the pullout couch so including it in the listing doesn't make sense. Cover your bases and make sure any additions or amenities are properly set up and ready for use by your guests.

Steering clear of money wasters

A mistake hosts tend to make is buying more items or nicer additions haphazardly in an attempt to raise their prices and generate more income. Consider buying a nice TV or similar amenity. If your listing tends to attract business travelers who rarely watch TV during their stay, that investment is unlikely to yield a good return. Keep your guests' needs and wants at the forefront and start by focusing on the items that are sure to bring in higher returns.

Determining the Amenities Guests Want in Your Market

When guests stay in your listing, they expect basic amenities. When you set up your Airbnb listing, you need a clear idea of which amenities to include. A great way to determine what amenities your guests want to have is by looking at other listings in your area that have great reviews. Look at what amenities they have that stand out or frequently get mentioned in reviews, and then make sure you add those similar amenities to your property. Doing so will increase your listing's desirability and overall potential. Offering guests the amenities they need for a comfortable and enjoyable stay is essential if you want to be a responsible Airbnb host and ultimately get great reviews.

In the following sections we discuss how you can make your listing competitive with the types of amenities you offer while also giving your guests a pleasant stay.

Identifying the types of amenities to include in your listing

Some amenities are basic and you need to include them, no matter what, whereas other amenities are upgrades that improve the quality of guest stays and their reviews. These amenities increase your listing's potential. We discuss the basic must-haves later in the section, "Focusing on the must-have amenities."

In order to provide more value to your guests, you can include more amenities that guests want, that make your listing shine above your competition. Here are a few examples of upgrade amenities that can wow your guests:

- » Fireplace
- » Hot tub
- » Board games
- » Local touches

These examples of amenities attract more guests depending on your market. They are the above-and-beyond amenities that tie into maximizing the potential of your listing. Local touches that are quintessential to your area can also provide a more authentic experience to guests, which is sure to delight them. We discuss specific types of amenities you should include in your listing in the section, "Focusing on Which Amenities, Furniture, and Appliances to Include," later in this chapter.

Each market has different types of guests staying at your property. Consider whether your listing is in downtown Toronto and specifically appeals to business travelers. In this case, adding a gaming console probably doesn't make a big difference in your bookings. However, if your listing appeals to families, then a gaming console may be a drawing factor. Hence, you need to understand who your guests are and what kind of experience they want, which we discuss more in the next section.

Looking at your competition to better gauge what guests want

By understanding your market and your ideal guests, you can decide how best to move the needle forward on your listing's potential. Examine similar listings on Airbnb and determine which are performing best and what they offer. With that information, you can discover how to improve your own listing.

TIP

Focus on the listings with higher nightly rates and the best reviews and see what types of amenities those listing have. For example, if you have a ski chalet, you may discover that all the best-performing properties have a fireplace and a sauna, so you may want to consider adding a fireplace or sauna in your listing.

Here are a few other examples of amenities to give you an idea:

>> If you're in a family-friendly market, look for a gaming console or other types of games, such as a dartboard, foosball, billiards, or ping pong.

>> If you're catering to larger groups, search for a big dining room table so everyone can sit and eat together.

Make note of the properties most similar to yours and see what amenities they have, which can give you a better glimpse at what guests in your market want.

REMEMBER

Make sure to compare your property with properties that are your direct competition and comparable in the same level of luxury, size, and amenities. Comparing your cozy one-bedroom listing that prices around $80 a night to a luxury three-bedroom apartment that lists at $250 a night won't give you the types of results you're looking for.

Focusing on Which Amenities, Furniture, and Appliances to Include

Features that really impact a guest's stay are your furniture and appliances. Determine what furniture, appliances, and other amenities you want to include and then make sure you maintain them so your guests can utilize them.

REMEMBER

Different items provide different levels of value for your guests. As a host, you want to determine which items deliver the greatest return on your investment (ROI). Pay attention to your reviews and the ways your guests respond to the amenities you provide so you can offer even greater value. Items such as the fridge, beds, and Wi-Fi offer a much greater ROI because those are the must-haves for every guest's stay.

With furniture, appliances, and other amenities, certain items are must-haves, others are nice to have, others are outstanding to have, and others still are a waste of your money. Within these groups, you want to identify which is which for your property. It varies a bit from property to property, but generally the must-haves are quite similar. In these sections we go through each category so that you know how you can avoid wasting time, money, and effort on unnecessary amenities and pour more into the must-have and nice-to-have features.

REMEMBER

Issues that may not be a concern for you can really affect your guests' stay. To offer the best experience for your guests, make sure that everything in your space is in top condition, and if not fix it or replace it. For example, if your oven breaks, even if you rarely use it, you need to fix that promptly. If your guest's bed is lumpy and outdated, then replace the mattress or invest in a new bed altogether. If you don't take care of them, you risk guests having a poor stay and those misgivings later appearing in their reviews. And if something is showing wear and tear, replace it.

Focusing on the must-have amenities

Here is our list of must-have furniture, appliances, and other amenities. If you want to list a property on Airbnb, then make sure you have these items:

>> **Bed:** Your guests need something to sleep on. It can be a mattress with box springs, a sleeper sofa, or an air mattress.

>> **Nice towels and sheets:** Both make a huge difference on your guests' stay. When your guests arrive to your property and get into a scratchy bed, they won't feel good about the quality of the bedsheets. Furthermore, provide more than one towel per guest, especially if your guests are staying longer than a day.

>> **Coffee maker:** Most people consider a basic coffee maker as a must-have. Along with this, include some fresh coffee available that will last at least the first morning of your guests' stay.

>> **Fully stocked kitchen:** Make sure your kitchen is ready to use and fully stocked with a frying pan, utensils, proper cutlery, plates, and cups. The greatest area where hosts miss the mark is in the kitchen by not having the necessary amenities.

I (James) was recently in a property that had a frying pan without a spatula. Unfortunately, I didn't realize the lack of a spatula until I was cooking eggs and couldn't flip them. I had to go buy a spatula in order to make my breakfast, which was a pain and super inconvenient. At another property, hosts only provided two glasses and two plates so guests had to wash their dishes after every meal. For vacations and holidays, guests don't want to be forced to do dishes after every meal or leave the property to purchase cookware.

» **Refrigerator:** Most listings also need a working fridge, whether it's shared or not.

» **Oven, stovetop, or microwave:** You generally need to offer a way to cook food by including an oven, stovetop, or microwave.

» **Water:** You need drinkable water. If you're hosting in an area where you can't drink the tap water, you must offer bottled water or a water cooler for your guests so that when they arrive, they have something to drink.

During a trip to Thailand, I (James) arrived at my Airbnb late at night with no water to drink. The host didn't provide a water cooler or any bottled water. In Thailand the tap water isn't safe to drink so I had to go to a convenience store in the middle of the night and carry a bunch of water back with me. I was thirsty and just wanted to go to bed, but instead I had to schlep to get water. To not have access to a glass of water was a miserable way to start my stay, and it set a bad first impression, "Oh, I don't have water." As a basic necessity, you need drinkable water at your space for guests.

» **Wi-Fi:** Your space should include an Internet router that reaches your entire house with no dead spots. Your guests should get a signal from anywhere in your space so that they aren't in their bedroom unable to access the Internet. Unless your listing is a remote cabin in the woods with the allure of being off grid, it needs Wi-Fi.

International guests rely on Wi-Fi. They often don't have cell service, so the only way they can keep connected is through reliable Internet.

REMEMBER

TIP

Furthermore, make sure your Wi-Fi speed is fast enough so multiple devices can stream. If you have 25 Mbps speed, you can tout that in your listing.

» **Toilet paper, paper towels, and tissues:** Be sure to leave enough toilet paper for all your guests and for the duration of their stay. Leaving just enough to get them through the first couple hours is simply poor hosting. If your guests are forced to leave the property to resupply the toilet paper, that's a hassle and overall a failure to meet a basic requirement.

A lot of hosts get stingy and think guests will steal the toilet paper. The reality is that some may, but you must accept it. What you stand to lose if you overstock the place is a couple dollars. However, you stand to lose hundreds of potential dollars in income when you get poor reviews for only leaving one roll of toilet paper in the space.

>> **A shower curtain, bathmat, properly working sinks, and running hot water:** These items may seem basic, but depending on your situation, you may overlook them.

Sometimes people list a spare space in their own home and they neglect certain amenities that they themselves don't often use. For example, your oven may be broken and you don't care because you're always eating out. That doesn't mean your guests will be okay with your broken oven. You need to get it fixed. This issue is more evident to people who are hosting their entire space. They realize they need to get their oven fixed whereas when people live in the place, it may not occur to them.

For example, I (James) stayed at a listing where the oven was broken. The host told me that she never used it. Instead she was storing boxes inside. Using it as an oven just wasn't part of her life, whereas to me I thought it odd to have boxes stored in the broken oven.

TIP

Take inventory of all your basic appliances and ensure they're usable, accessible, and functioning so that you have all the basic amenities people need. Monitor furniture and if it starts to show wear and tear, consider replacing it. Just as important, make sure you don't overlook anything relatively obvious that your guests will need.

Remembering the often forgotten

Hosts often forget a few important amenities that impact their guests' stay. Remembering these items sets you apart quite a bit from your competition:

>> **Bedside table with a lamp:** You'd be surprised at how many hosts forget the bedside table when setting up their listing, which is essential to have. When your guests get into bed, a bedside table is the ideal spot for their phone charging, glasses, or glass of water.

>> **Plants:** Including plants in your space is important. Any homey space has some kind of greenery or plant. Even a faux plant is okay.

>> **Sharp knives:** Many people keep the typical butter knives in their homes but forget to include steak knives or a paring knife. If your guests prepare a meal and require a sharp knife, not having one is a huge inconvenience.

>> **Salt, pepper, and basic condiments:** Oils, salt and pepper, and a couple condiments are essentials for most guests. If you're someone who eats out for most meals and doesn't cook at home, you still need to provide these cooking essentials for your guests. You risk leaving a bad taste in their mouths if they can't properly season their food.

Stuck between a must-have and a nice-to-have

Some scenarios fall in what we call the ambiguous zone between a must-have and a nice-to-have, depending on your area and type of property. Here are those items you may have to figure out whether they're must-have or nice-to-have, based on your competition:

>> **Dishwasher:** A dishwasher, for many properties, is a nice-to-have. As long as you have a sink to clean the dishes, you're fine. However, if you have a higher-end property, then a dishwasher is widely considered a must-have.

>> **Air conditioning:** In some locations, AC isn't negotiable. It's a must-have, whether it's central air or a window unit. (Imagine staying in a stuffy New York City apartment in July or an Atlanta bungalow in September with no AC.) And, if you're trying to attract a higher caliber guest, then AC is a no-brainer.

However, AC may be nice-to-have but not essential in other types of listings. Take a city such as Toronto that has a ton of old homes without central air. They may just have fans.

Be conscious of your own property and your competition and the type of guests booking your listing so that you can better determine what items are nice-to-have and what items are must-haves.

Providing a bonus: The nice-to-haves

Sometimes nice-to-haves become must-haves, especially if you want to stay in line with what your competition is offering. Here are some examples of nice-to-haves:

>> **Smart TVs:** Smart TVs with some type of Internet connection to allow for streaming are generally always nice-to-have and often not a must-have. Maybe you don't have a cable to connect their computers to your TV, but your guests can still access features such as Netflix or other online shows with your Wi-Fi.

>> **Higher-end coffee maker:** Although a basic coffee maker is a must-have, a higher-end coffee maker is a nice-to-have.

>> **Wine glasses:** Even if you aren't a wine drinker, the odds are high that one of your guests will want to enjoy a glass at some point. If you try to think about hosting from your guests' perspectives rather than from your own perspective, you'll have a much easier time including all desired amenities.

>> **Water filter:** As long as tap water is potable and people can drink it, tap water is a must-have. A water filter is a nice-to-have.

>> **Toaster oven:** Although a toaster is a must-have, a toaster oven is a nice-to-have in most cases.

Check out your competition and identify the nice-to-haves in your own area. Depending on how high end the market is for your listing and your listing's competition, a gas range stove may be considered a standard nice-to-have. For most properties, investing in an expensive gas range oven doesn't make sense, but many high-end properties probably have them, so it makes sense to invest in one.

Surprising with the outstanding

This is where you get the opportunity to go above and beyond for your guests. When the above-and-beyond elements are performed well, you see the guests' satisfaction reflected in their reviews. To determine what these are for your listing, note attributes that aren't expectations but are really nice for guests to have. These are the elements that surprise and delight your guests and leaves them with a great feeling. As a guest, this is the experience that makes you go "Wow, that's so smart" and "Why would someone not have that?" Consider the following:

>> **Universal phone chargers:** Having a universal phone charger in each bedroom and in the main living space is key. How many times have you gotten to a space and haven't had your phone charger out and ready to go? If there's a phone charger that's both compatible and convenient that goes a long way for people. It's an unusual item that's not very common but goes a long way for your guests.

>> **Speakers:** Another amenity that's unusual but goes far with guests is having a speaker on your property that people can easily connect to and use. Most people want to play music. It may not be a baseline expectation and they won't come in and expect that it's there. However, it makes quite the difference when people have access to that amenity.

>> **Games:** If you're welcoming groups or families into your space, then having some games to play is a great way to win them over. Whether you're providing cards or board games, guests are often delighted to have those options. Especially if your market is heavy in groups, it's yet another way to set yourself apart from your competition.

A common concern with items such as the ones mentioned is theft. However, guests stealing your universal phone charger or board game happens rarely. Here are a few reasons why you shouldn't worry about your guests taking advantage of you as host:

>> **When you maximize the property potential, you appeal to the upper tier of guests who aren't looking for a cheap stay.** These are the guests with the highest income and who don't see the value in stealing a phone charger or bottle of soap.

>> **As a host, you go above and beyond, which creates reciprocity.** The guests don't want to take from you. Instead, they're super grateful to be staying there. It's highly unlikely that you lose your phone charger, speaker, or rolls of toilet paper.

>> **You have a security deposit and you can use that security deposit if a guest does take something more substantial in value.** If a phone charger or speaker gets taken, then you can present a claim against your guests and be compensated for anything high in value. Chapter 6 explains the security deposit in greater detail.

What you're really doing when you opt out of providing these types of amenities for fear of having them stolen is stepping over dollars to pick up pennies. You save $15 on a phone charger and then lose out on bookings at your property to the tune of several hundred dollars. Furthermore, you can't be skimpy on filling up your soap dispensers and body care products. Nothing is worse than having some cheap host who only fills them a little bit because they don't want guests taking it with them. The reality is that they likely won't. Even if your guests do snag a bottle of your shampoo, it's a $1 or $2 risk you must be willing to take as a host.

Avoiding the wastes of money

Determine your must-have and nice-to-have amenities and avoid these complete and total wastes of money. For example, spending $15,000 on a massage chair is a complete waste. Even if you get the odd guest who books your property for that reason, the likelihood that the stay adds $15,000 to your bottom line is very low.

Another example of an unnecessary cost is having the highest-end satellite TV. In many cases, the satellite TV package is a waste of money. In reality even if you have basic cable, which is oftentimes still unnecessary, people typically prefer a smart TV or HDMI cable that they can use to connect their computer to the TV and stream their favorite shows. Overall those alternatives are more than enough. Most guests booking an Airbnb want to connect their computers or Netflix account if they're going to watch TV at all. Generally, they're still fine with local television or basic cable if those are the only options.

Very few people are going to stream a sports event happening halfway across the world. And if they do, they usually have the ability to do so online if it matters that much to them. Investing in a top-of-the-line satellite package is more often than not a total waste of money.

In terms of furniture and appliances, obscure items that are a complete waste include anything from a panini press to a pancake griddle. Having a frying pan and stove is sufficient.

Figuring Out What Space Is Accessible to Guests in Your Listing

Determining what areas of your space are accessible to guests is an important decision, depending on the type of listing you have. Keep these points in mind:

>> **If you're listing bedrooms in your personal home:** Be specific about the bedrooms and bathrooms your guests can use. You need to figure out whether they have access to all the bathrooms in the house or just one as well as whether they have access to the kitchen or the living room. If the answer is yes, you must maintain those spaces and keep them ready for guests.

>> **If you're listing a whole house:** Figuring out what space is accessible to guests is simple: Keep all areas in your house available to guests. Ideally, you don't block off any space other than maybe a closet if you want to lock something away.

>> **If you're listing an auxiliary space such as a guesthouse:** Be intentional about only listing the parts of the space that are actually available to guests. Be clear in your listing about the areas that guests have access to and which areas are private versus shared.

Make a conscious decision on which spaces you're maintaining and keeping in guest-ready condition and then list only those spaces that you're willing to share with guests at any time. These sections give you more details, room by room.

Bedroom and bathroom

Especially in shared spaces, be clear on which bedrooms guests have access to and which bedrooms aren't available to them. Determine whether they have access to all the closets in their bedrooms. Be crystal clear in your listing so there is no room for confusion.

Be just as specific with bathroom usage. If you have one bathroom that you specifically use to get ready in the morning and you don't want to give guests access to it or don't want to keep it guest-ready, then don't list it.

For both bedrooms and bathrooms, make sure that any locking doors don't require a key. It will only be a matter of time before guests lose a key or lock themselves out of one of the rooms, so avoid the issue entirely by using manual interior locks rather than keyed locks.

Kitchen

If you offer access to the kitchen, leave space in the fridge for guests to use. If you aren't sharing the kitchen, then you can't list that space on Airbnb. If you want to allow access to your kitchen but don't plan on leaving any room in your fridge, then you can't list that guests have access to a full kitchen. More than likely, a guest at some point will want to put something in the fridge and be upset when there isn't room.

If guests don't have access to your kitchen in its entirety, be clear on whether they can use any of your kitchen materials such as the fridge, microwave, dishware, or blender.

Access to living room, outdoor spaces, and other rooms

Concerning other common areas inside or outside your house, communicate what you want from your guests so they know your expectations, which can cause fewer problems down the line. If your guests have access to your living room, game room, or other common room, be specific in your listing.

If you have a guesthouse in your backyard, be clear on which parts of your backyard your guests can access as well as whether they can use your kitchen inside the main house. If your guesthouse doesn't include a kitchen but you plan on providing access to your kitchen in the main house, specify in your listing that the kitchen is in a separate building.

Managing Neighbors' Relations

Hosting on Airbnb can potentially impact your neighbors, so communicating with them is important. You want to inform your neighbors that they'll see different people coming and going from your property.

Furthermore, maintaining a good relationship with your neighbors is important because you want them as allies. You want your neighbors to be friendly toward your guests if they pass them rather than treating them rudely. The last problem you want is for your guests to disrupt your neighbors or your neighbors to disrupt your guests.

REMEMBER

Most importantly, you want to avoid a situation where your neighbors are angry and hostile toward your Airbnb guests, which can lead to complaints and issues with your landlord or the city. In order to avoid any such situation, communicate clearly with your neighbors from the start. These sections help ensure you're a good neighbor when you're an Airbnb host.

Being a good neighbor: Why doing so is profitable

Having a positive relationship with your neighbors can be profitable to you. In any situation, your neighbor either adds or subtracts value for your guests. More than likely, an unhappy neighbor may have a conflict with your guests, which can lead to a poor review. If a neighbor is adamantly opposed to your hosting, he can also cause issues with the city. On the opposite end of the spectrum, if your neighbor is thrilled with your hosting, he can be exceptionally warm and inviting toward your guests and add to their overall experience when they encounter each other.

REMEMBER

What you're providing to guests is more than just a place to sleep. You're providing your guests with an experience, and your neighbors can play a large role in determining whether that experience is positive or negative.

For example, if your neighbor passes your guests on the street and acts super welcoming and offers directions or recommendations to a local coffee shop, that's very helpful for your guests. Those are the comments that often come up in 5-star reviews. Guests write that they had a great time because everyone was so friendly.

Consider the alternative: unhappy neighbors who look for any reason to complain about you, whether it's to the city, your landlord, or whoever else. There's the potential to have your listing shut down if your neighbor is persistent enough. Overall, they can do a lot of damage to your hosting business.

Investing in neighbor relations before you start

As soon as you start thinking about hosting on Airbnb, you want to run the decision by your neighbors. The more advance notice you give, the better for your relationship. Ask them if you can provide them anything to keep them updated and to make the experience better. Your neighbors may not be impacted by every single one of your guests, but they will be affected sometimes. Explain to your neighbors how your Airbnb listing will bring guests to the neighborhood and that you want to make sure they're on board with having Airbnb guests as their neighbors.

Keeping your neighbors updated can set the tone for your relationship, so do what you can to be a great neighbor. Generally, people love hosting because they like meeting new people, and many people enjoy having Airbnb guests as neighbors. They reap all the benefits without doing any work. They get to meet new people without having to do any of the grunt work. If you come in with the right attitude and start as early as possible, your neighbors more than likely will be much more receptive.

On the flip side, if you wait to receive a complaint before informing your neighbors that you're hosting on Airbnb, more than likely they'll be unreceptive to your hosting. From your neighbors' point of view, your hosting will be nothing but a nuisance to them. Waiting to tell your neighbors after your hosting becomes an issue is never the right call.

Communicating with your neighbors

The best way to be a good neighbor is to treat others the way you want to be treated. Treat your neighbor in line with what you would want if your neighbor started hosting their space on Airbnb. Take your neighbor into consideration in everything you do as a host. In order to put this into practice effectively, the most important task to do is communicate clearly with your neighbor about what's going on at your property and why.

Maintaining an open line of communication is ideal. When you do this, you have someone with whom you have a good relationship and who lives next to your property at all times. If you've ever had bad guests at your property, you can understand why that's so appealing. Your neighbor can let you know what's going on at your property and you can avoid potential damage from your property being abused. Here are some important points to remember when communicating with your neighbors:

> » **Give them your contact information and let them know the best way to get in touch with you.** Inform them whether you have a preferred mode of communication, such as text, phone call, or email. By sharing your contact details, your neighbors have a clear and easy way to get in touch with you whenever a question or concern arises.

>> **Set clear expectations on when and how you like to communicate.** Tell your neighbors how to most effectively contact you for different situations so that nothing gets missed or forgotten.

The greatest issues concerning your relationship with your neighbors aren't when something happens at your property but rather when something happens that doesn't get promptly and effectively handled by you or someone on your team. For example, if your cleaners forget to take the trash out to the curb, your neighbors won't care that they forgot as long as you let them know and get it taken care of another way. It won't cause an issue unless the trash remains out at the side of your house for a week or two and starts smelling and attracting animals. Then it's a big issue.

If your neighbors complain about noise at the property, but you deal with it immediately and the noise goes down, it's not an issue. However, consider if your neighbors try communicating with you and don't hear back. Then they aren't able to sleep and wind up having a miserable next day at work. Now, it's an issue. Instead, having that open line of communication is the best way to both prevent any negative situation and to make sure your neighbors' needs are fully met.

Managing Landlord Relations

You have a few considerations when managing a relationship with your landlord if you rent the property you plan to list on Airbnb. In this section, we touch on how to manage this relationship, how to get permission to host your property, and why that permission is important. Dealing with your landlord is an ongoing process. Effectively navigating the relationship makes hosting your space that much easier.

Being aware of the risks of hosting without consent

The bottom line when planning to host an Airbnb listing out of your rented property is to get permission from your landlord. We can't stress this enough. Most standard lease agreements prohibit you from subletting. Many contracts now explicitly prohibit renters from hosting on Airbnb unless they reach an agreement with their landlord.

WARNING

The risk of hosting without explicit permission is that you violate the terms of your lease agreement. When your landlord finds out that you're hosting, they has the authority and grounds to evict you from the property. Depending on your area and the specific laws, they also can impose different fines on you for violating the terms of that agreement. Hosting without the consent of your landlord causes more headache than it's worth.

Asking your landlord if you can host on Airbnb

The process of requesting permission to host isn't always as simple as just asking your landlord. The best time to have the conversation is before you sign the lease agreement. At this point, you have more leverage than after you sign.

Landlords or property owners who rent their properties on the long-term rental market typically desire security and consistency. If they already have you as a tenant who's locked into a 12-month lease, when you ask about hosting, they'll less likely say yes. Essentially, there's no real benefit to them. You're already signed on for a year.

REMEMBER

If you ask before signing your lease, you tend to get better results due to the higher leverage you have. The change is a change in initial terms, before an agreement has been reached. If you try to negotiate after signing a lease, your landlord is likely to feel as though the initial agreement is being violated and that you're making an unreasonable request. However, no matter when you ask, ultimately your landlord wants to know what benefit hosting on Airbnb offers them, which we discuss in the next section.

What landlords want to know when it comes to hosting

Landlords want to know what's in it for them to allow a tenant to list his property on Airbnb. The best way to go about this is to ask your landlord. After you find out how your hosting can benefit them, you can ask your landlord why they're hesitant or what worries they have. It could be any number of concerns, depending on your landlord and their specific needs.

Your landlord may wonder what types of guests are coming in and what risks that presents. They may ask what protection they have in the event of any damage. The questions are wide and far ranging.

When you answer their questions, keep the following in mind:

>> **Show your landlord what's in it for them.** If you make a simple request without showing them benefits, they have no reason to change or loosen the terms. Most people continue to do matters the same way unless they see a

reason for change. After your landlord knows the reason, they may be more open to the idea. The next section discusses these different benefits during your pitch.

>> **Ask what would be reasonable or desirable for your landlord.** Discuss their concerns so you can better address the specifics.

Pitching your landlord

You have a few ways to show the benefits when pitching your landlord. Tell your landlord any combination of the following during this conversation:

>> **Be transparent and offer to share a link to your listing so your landlord can see how you're maintaining it.** You'll clean the place more often because it must be in pristine condition for your guests. Plus, the landlord doesn't have to worry about tenants trashing the place or using it for something illicit because you want to be a responsible Airbnb host. Your landlord can even check your guest reviews to see how you're cleaning and maintaining the property.

>> **Explain that hosting can financially help you so you're able to rent the space for longer.** Now, you're a more reliable tenant.

>> **Offer to personally take care of any minor maintenance at the property.** If you have money from hosting that affords you the ability to fix the clogged toilet, for instance, you won't call the landlord anymore, which can be a huge benefit and take some burden off the landlord or their property manager. You call your own maintenance person for the small stuff.

>> **Mention Airbnb's $1 million host protection.** This added insurance can reassure your landlord that they don't need to worry about potential damages because the property will likely be even better protected than with another tenant.

>> **Offer to pay rent further in advance, pay more rent overall, or pay a bigger security deposit for any potential damages.** This option is the last and least ideal one for you.

On the note of paying more rent, the amount doesn't have to be a lot. Typically, the value of a property is based on the rental rate. Increasing the rent payment by even $50 per month makes a difference because the landlord can sell the property for more money down the road. People are willing to pay more to buy a property because it can earn them more money. In other words, the rent increase doesn't have to be a lot to make it financially worthwhile to the landlord.

Getting Proper Insurance Protection

You want to protect yourself from any potential liabilities because you don't want the scenario where you aren't insured and the worst possible scenario occurs. Although Airbnb provides its own insurance, we recommend multiple channels for protecting yourself and your property, which we discuss in these sections.

Grasping the importance of being properly insured

Buying insurance is about protecting yourself in the case something happens at your property. You can take a few actions to minimize or eliminate your risks of issues such as property damage or personal injury. However, you still want a backup plan in the event that an issue does occur so that you're always fully protected against the worst-case scenario.

WARNING

Be aware that if you don't get the proper insurance specifically covering you for short-term rentals, you risk paying out of pocket for any issues or damages. What's important is that you're protected.

Understanding AirCover for Hosts and not relying on it alone

Airbnb does have a $1 million host protection policy called AirCover for Hosts, that protects you as a host and covers any damages that occur on your property as the result of a guest staying there. The policy can cover you as a host for anything from damages (including pet damages), to messes that require additional cleaning, and even income loss. It's a great policy, essentially offering third-party insurance from Airbnb to you for damages caused by a guest. Plus, it's good for up to $1 million. As an added layer of protection, AirCover for Hosts works.

TIP

If you ever find yourself needing to use AirCover for Hosts to make a claim, remember to take lots of photos of the damages, only communicate with guests via the Airbnb platform, keep all your receipts, and file your claim within 14 days of the guests checking out. If you fail to do this, you risk having your claim denied.

WARNING

However, you shouldn't rely solely on it for the following couple of reasons:

>> **You don't have control.** If you go the route of only using Airbnb's policy, then you rely on Airbnb to submit those claims successfully and get you paid. To have full control over protecting your property, you want to steer the car and

maneuver where it goes. However, consider the fact that Airbnb is balancing a couple conflicting incentives when using that insurance policy to protect its hosts:

- Whenever a guest causes damage that hurts the company's reputation, Airbnb wants to make sure the host is protected. The company has the incentive to show that the liability policy does pay out and the host gets covered so that the hosting community at large feels safe and protected.

- However, Airbnb also knows that if the company uses the policy too much, then the premiums will increase. The company has a financial incentive to use that policy as little as possible.

>> **It only covers damages that are caused by guests during their stay.** This means that personal injury or any issues that occur outside of a guest's actual period of stay aren't covered. Such issues may be unlikely, but you want to be covered against them, nonetheless.

Hence, you want to make sure you have full control over your insurance.

Buying your own insurance to ensure you're fully protected

To ensure you have full control over your insurance coverage, we suggest you purchase your own liability insurance policy that covers your property for damages. Your policy should clearly specify that it covers you for use of the property for short-term rentals. Then, if a guest does cause damage, you have three lines of defense:

>> The first line of defense is your guest's security deposit.

>> The second line of defense is Airbnb's liability policy.

>> The third line of defense is your own personal insurance plan.

This way, you know you're fully protected because you hold an insurance policy that protects your property from all damages. If you have all three of those pieces to protect yourself, more than likely you're covered for even the worst-case scenario.

TIP

To purchase your policy, start with a broker who is the most qualified person to help you get the right insurance policy. A broker looks at different options for you, given your property, the level of protection you need for your area, and the use of your property.

The price of an insurance policy and the level of protection varies, depending on if you're insuring your home up to $100,000 or $1 million as well as where your property is located and which company you choose.

Other pertinent issues are how often you host and whether you live in an urban area with high rates of crime or a small-town suburban neighborhood. Your broker evaluates all the options and has access to several different companies and plans.

Brokers receive a commission from the insurance company for selling the policy so as the consumer you won't pay anything extra to use an insurance broker. Your broker also helps you understand the plans and break down the policies to show you exactly what coverage you receive in different scenarios. Make sure to ask as many questions as needed to fully understand your plan.

TIP

To find a broker in your area, ask around for referrals. The best people to help guide you in this matter are other hosts in your area, especially hosts with similar properties. If you're unable to find a broker through referrals, a quick online search for "short-term rental insurance [your city]" should yield some good recommendations. You can also consider joining an Airbnb host Facebook group for your city and post the question there.

Being a Guest First to Better Understand Hosting — Walk in Your Guests' Shoes

"Walk a mile in your guests' shoes to understand them," said some wise Airbnb host. In 2016, we surveyed nearly 1,300 active hosts through our LearnBNB blog and discovered nearly one in three had never been an Airbnb guest before, including many hosts who have been hosting for more than a year!

The best way to understand Airbnb and your competition is to experience it for yourself, so book an Airbnb listing or two in your locale and consider each component of the stay: from browsing to booking to checking in and checking out and to the actual visit. This practice takes you from being a mediocre host to a truly great host who knows what your guests want and who can deliver on it.

TIP

To truly appreciate the entire experience that guests go through to search, choose, book, check into, check out of, and rate Airbnb listings for their travel, you must become a guest first at an Airbnb.

Here's how to get the most out of your educational Airbnb stays:

>> **Book at different levels of listing.** You can discover a lot from the pros by staying at the most popular and best performing listings in the markets hosted by Superhosts (we discuss Superhost status in more detail in Chapter 11). You can also discover just as much from average or even underperforming listings. Your goal is to gather as much about what to do and what not to do.

>> **Take notes of every high and low point.** Pay attention to how you feel, especially whenever you're either stressed or grateful during your stay. Note the moments when you had questions, when you felt unsure or uncomfortable, or where something could have made the experience better. Keep track of the moments where you were pleasantly surprised by a thoughtful amenity or interaction with the hosts.

REMEMBER

We strongly suggest you stay with a Superhost during one of your stays. If you have the ambition to become a Superhost, then staying with one gives you an idea of how a Superhost differs from a host who isn't.

During your research, ask yourself these following questions:

>> What captures your eye to make you click on the listing: the cover photo, the price, or the listing headline?

>> Why did you select that specific property?

>> When you clicked what did you do next?

>> Why did you not select a listing? Maybe it had great photos and a great description, but there was one bad review. Maybe you still booked anyways because there were other good reviews. Maybe it had two or three bad reviews. If the description didn't answer specific questions you had, such as parking situation, would that have mattered?

>> When you finally booked the Airbnb, how was the experience?

>> Did the host message you right away or did he wait awhile?

>> Did the host get back to you in a reasonable time if you asked any questions?

>> When it was time to check in, did you feel stressed out because you didn't receive check-in instructions or did the host send instructions well in advance?

>> How easy was getting into the property?

>> Is there anything you wished you had at the property?

>> How attentive was the host during your stay? For example, did he touch base with you to see if you needed anything? How quickly did the host respond to your questions?

>> Did the host have a house manual with detailed instructions about commonly asked questions?

>> Were any basic amenities missing that you needed?

>> Was the listing description accurate to the property?

>> What would have made your stay more pleasant?

>> Did the host provide check-out instructions?

>> When you write your review, what review are you writing and why are you writing it?

>> At what point did you decide to give the host a 5-star review if you decided to do so? Or, at what point did you decide you wouldn't give more than 4 stars? What was it that triggered those decisions? What would have caused it to be a higher or lower review?

TIP

After you've been a host for a few months, go through this process again and treat yourself by booking a weekend getaway or staycation at an Airbnb and experience different levels of hosts, properties, and approaches to hosting, which can do wonders for your own hosting style. Again, take notes and find the areas you can improve and do differently. Experiencing different approaches to hosting and using them to figure out how to continue adding value for your guests is an effective hosting practice.

Chapter **6**

Building the Perfect Listing

B efore you can start hosting guests, you first need to showcase your property on Airbnb with a listing. Your Airbnb listing is the page where potential guests can find information about your property and how to book it. Elements of your listing include your property photos, your listing description, and your headline.

This chapter walks you through how to build each piece of your listing so you can show off your space in the best light. After your listing is complete, you can go live on Airbnb. This chapter explains in greater detail other aspects of your listing so you can start getting bookings.

Making a Strong First Impression

Putting your best foot forward is important when it comes to your listing. Doing so means you didn't rush anything or rationalizing that your listing is just "good enough." The trap many hosts fall into is quickly setting up their listing so they can go live and later realizing they didn't get the right photos, their property wasn't staged the way they wanted, or they didn't spend time drafting their property's description.

For example, you ordered a new couch, which is a significant update to your listing. However, the couch won't be delivered for two weeks, and you don't want the property sitting vacant for that period. Rather than wait for the couch and then update the photos on your listing, you set your listing live now so you get some bookings during those next two weeks. Unfortunately, that's often a terrible plan.

Starting strong is important for a few reasons:

>> **It ensures that you'll get great reviews from your first guests.** This will help you out substantially in the long term.

>> **It makes your initial experience of hosting much less stressful.** If you constantly need to run around fixing and adding updates to your property during your first few weeks of hosting, the hosting experience is likely to become quite overwhelming.

>> **It helps you with Airbnb's search algorithm.** Airbnb's search algorithm is ultimately what determines how many people actually see your listing. When you first launch your listing, Airbnb will send lots of traffic to it to give it a shot. If your listing isn't optimized and you don't turn that traffic into bookings, you'll notice that the amount of traffic your listing receives will slow down drastically. Refer to the nearby sidebar for more about Airbnb's search algorithm.

Include any items or amenities now, such as a desk for business travelers or your new couch, before you go live with your listing. Add whatever amenities you can from the beginning and take the time to perfectly craft your listing now to give yourself every possible advantage.

Remember to take your time going through the process of setting up your listing. Ask yourself, "Is this listing as good as it can be?" If you already know your listing can substantially improve at the get-go, then make those improvements first whenever possible. Wait for the couch, lose the potential bookings during those two weeks, and then go live.

Returning to the couch example, don't rush making the listing live with items you plan to change or improve later unless you need to for financial reasons. Optimize every aspect of your listing, including everything from your photos and cover photo to the headline and description.

HOW AIRBNB'S ALGORITHM WORKS DURING THE INITIAL LAUNCH PERIOD

Airbnb's algorithm tests your listing during the initial launch period. That's another reason why it's so important to make a strong first impression. When listing on Airbnb it's not only about the number of bookings you get during those first few weeks, it's about all the additional bookings that they will lead you down the road. When you first start, you're setting the pace for all future bookings. When first launching, Airbnb's algorithm is designed with a low barrier to entry for new hosts to come onto the platform.

In the first two to four weeks as a host you'll likely see a bunch of traffic on your listing. You can check out your listing on the back end and see the number of people viewing your listing in a day, week, or month. Initially, that number is likely to be quite high. Then, it's up to you to have a great listing and turn those views into bookings.

If you create a strong listing from the start and a lot of your views turn into bookings, here's what will happen:

- Airbnb will give you more views long term, and those views will turn into more and more bookings and consequently more and more dollars.

- You get even more reviews from all your bookings. With these reviews, assuming you've done an excellent job and they're positive, Airbnb further rewards you. You get even more views and credibility.

- Airbnb sends you even more traffic. You then convert more of these views to bookings. Suddenly, Airbnb gives you even more traffic because you've shown you can consistently turn bookings into dollars.

You can easily see how this becomes an ongoing positive feedback loop. The better host that you are, the better you fare. It feeds back in and continues. Remember, everything starts with that great first impression. After you take that initial traffic that Airbnb offers you and you convert it into bookings, you continue getting more views and start the ripple effect.

However, also realize that there's another side to the equation. If you take Airbnb's initial views and do a poor job of converting them into bookings, then the algorithm will do the opposite. If you quickly slap together a subpar listing, here's what the opposite feedback loop looks like:

- You're not going to get many bookings when you first launch.

- You'll start receiving far less traffic to your listing.

(continued)

(continued)

- You then drop to the second, third or fourth page. You fall in the search rankings so that fewer people see your listing at all.

- You end up with fewer reviews on your listing, giving it little credibility in the eyes of potential guests, and causing it to be even harder again to climb back up the mountain.

Now you have no traffic, the listing is underperforming and there isn't much to do about it. Turning that listing around becomes more difficult. Even if you make drastic improvements down the road, you still won't have the traffic to convert into bookings. Now you're at the bottom of the hill trying to make these improvements. Slowly over time the algorithm will give you more traffic again, but your road to success will be much longer than it needs to be.

For this reason, it's so important to make a strong start even if it takes a couple more days, weeks, or months. Do whatever you can to get your property to 100 percent and list it strongly with great photos, a great listing description, and a great headline. It pays off massively in the long run.

Creating a Listing That Gets Attention

Your listing needs to draw in potential guests so they click and later book. This is your chance to win them over by featuring the best photos, descriptions, and guest reviews.

The following sections guide you through how to set up all the elements of your listing in a way that attracts attention and generates bookings.

Winning at Airbnb search engine optimization

Airbnb search engine optimization (SEO) is about adapting your listing to help it improve in the search rankings. Airbnb is relatively clear in stating how to optimize your search performance on the platform.

REMEMBER

The most important factor is your listing's *bookability*, or in other words how likely it is to be reserved by guests. Basically, the more bookable your listing is to guests, the better your SEO. In plain English, if guests are more likely to book your place and can do so easily, your listing will get more views, which will put more dollars in your pocket. As a rule, winning at Airbnb SEO means doing everything you can so guests can easily book your property. Here you can find some of the best ways to do exactly that.

To improve your SEO actually isn't too difficult. Make sure you do the following with your listing to see SEO improvement:

REMEMBER

>> **Turn on Instant Book.** Instant Book is a setting on Airbnb that enables guests to book your place right away, without needing to contact you first. Consider if guests can book your property in one click versus reaching out to you, requesting to book, getting approval, and finally booking. The former is clearly easier. Guests can book instantly without needing to communicate with the host.

In fact, turning on Instant Book is the top way to improve Airbnb SEO. Consider the greater context of a guest booking your place when Instant Book is turned off. In the buying mind-set of this day and age, people want the ability to instantly reserve their accommodation and complete their travel plans.

We give you the ins and outs of Instant Book in the "Turning on Instant Book: The Pros and Cons" section later in this chapter.

>> **Respond quickly to guests' questions.** If you respond quickly when they reach out, that tells the algorithm that your property is more bookable, and you perform better in the search ranking.

>> **Have a well-structured, complete listing.** Add more photos to your listing so guests are more likely to book and don't have as many questions for you. Keep a detailed and well-organized listing description that answers all the questions that potential guests may have. That way, guests can book right away versus having to reach out with questions before booking.

>> **Have your listing priced effectively.** If it's priced too high, it won't be bookable and performs worse in the overall search rankings. If guests do really want to book, they may ask for a discount. More than likely, prospective guests will book another listing priced more competitively.

>> **Have your friends and family wish list your listing.** This function enables users to add different properties that they want to visit to a wish list. As an Airbnb user, you mark it as being on your wish list and that signifies that you want to stay there.

By executing on all of these items effectively, you then continue to ascend higher in the search ranking.

Identifying the most important pillars when setting up your listing

When setting up your listing, three fundamental elements will have the greatest overall impact on your bookings. If you set these three elements up properly, guests will visit and book your listing drastically more often than if you rush through these elements and neglect to do a good job of setting them up.

Those three pillars are your listing's:

>> **Photos:** Your photos are at the forefront with your cover photo having a disproportionate impact on the rest of your listing. The first detail prospective guests see before clicking on your listing is your cover photo. If you mess up on your cover photo, substantially fewer people will click through to your listing. The rest of your photos are important as well, because most guests will look at your photos before checking out other elements of your listing. In fact, photography is so important that we devote Chapter 7 to it.

>> **Headline:** Your listing's headline is nearly as important as the cover photo because it's one of the first items prospective guests see. A bad headline has the same effect as a bad cover photo, so you also need to nail your headline. We explain how to ace your listing headline in the section, "Writing a Strong Headline," later in this chapter.

>> **Description:** Your listing's description is a longer written description of your listing and all that it has to offer. This element's job is to answer any and all questions that a potential guest may have before they decide to book. We give you the lowdown on ways to write a winning description in the section, "Drafting a Great Description," later in this chapter.

Your cover photo, headline, and other photos are what get people to your listing and then keep them there to give you a chance. Your description, pricing, cleaning fee, and your reviews are what make the prospective guests decide they like your property enough to book or whether they'd rather abandon it.

Understanding how to play the long game to perform better

Long-term performance on Airbnb is quite different than short-term performance. Getting some initial bookings is great; however, it's worth very little if you do a bad job of hosting and get a bunch of bad reviews.

Ultimately, you want to perform exceptionally well over several years of hosting. To do so, you must focus on getting great guest reviews. This means overdelivering to your guests who are staying at your property. That's the most important factor. As a great host you're consistently satisfying your guests and making sure they leave with a great experience. At times, this will mean sacrificing some short-term gains in favor of long-term gains.

For example, you may be hosting guests and your furnace breaks down in the middle of the winter. Focusing on creating long-term success means you get it fixed immediately. You're attentive and make sacrifices on your time to deal with it right away. You may also make sacrifices on your monthly financial goal by compensating their stay at a hotel or giving them a free night (after you buy space heaters and set them up in your listing). We dive into how to deal with these types of issues in more detail in Chapter 14. For now, know that you want to be a phenomenal host in every situation and do what's best for your guests.

The result will be the great reviews you receive as a phenomenal host. Those sacrifices enable you to perform well in the future versus simply during the current guest's stay. You get outstanding reviews, you get more bookings, and that feedback loop keeps going.

On the flip side, getting a bad review negatively impacts that feedback loop. You may have a bunch of traffic, but that one bad review means less of that traffic converts into bookings. Even if one fewer person books with you, that equates to money lost for you and your future listing potential.

If you get three or four bad reviews in a row, then you get two, four, or even ten people who leave your listing page without booking who may have if you had strong reviews. Now because your listing isn't converting the traffic it gets into bookings, Airbnb's search algorithm will provide it with fewer views.

It's a downward spiral until you increase your positive reviews. You're ultimately always going either upward or downward. Your listing is never truly stagnant with Airbnb unless your listing is getting no bookings. Unless your listing is dormant, you're either improving or declining, so you want to make sure your listing keeps improving rather than declining.

Writing a Strong Headline

Your *headline* is a crucial part of making a strong first impression. Your headline is essentially the title of your listing, which guests see when they initially search for properties. Initially, your headline and your cover photo are the only reference points for your guests. A strong headline gets potential guests to click through to your listing.

Whatever you can do to get more people to click through, as long as you're being completely truthful, is a positive matter. Ask yourself what information makes people come visit your listing. Don't think about what information you want to tell people or how you can best describe your property. Think about what will get people to click through.

The following sections walk you through the specific goals you need to achieve with your listing headline and exactly how you can create the perfect listing headline for your space.

What makes a great headline

A great listing headline engages potential guests and offers descriptive information about your space. In other words, speak to the main appeal of your listing. What is the main reason people want to book?

The best listings identify desirable features and amenities that prospective guests want. Address the following types of information in your headline that guests are looking for:

>> **Main accommodations:** Guests want to know how many bedrooms and bathrooms you have.

>> **Location:** Guests typically care a lot about where your property is.

>> **Feeling the property evokes:** Guests want to know what type of space they're booking, whether it's modern, cozy, romantic, or something else.

>> **Local events:** Guests may want to stay in close proximity to an event, such as a concert or festival (see the nearby sidebar, "Gearing your headline to events near your space" for more information).

TIP

To address these items, find one or two key descriptive words. For example, to address the feeling your property evokes, you can use charming, quirky, modern, spacious, or cozy — or whichever other adjective is relevant. Concerning the location, use words such as "near Central Park" or "oceanside." Refer to the next section for more in-depth advice about using descriptive words in your headline.

What you need to know to draft a top-notch headline

Although writing your listing headline is important, it's not rocket science. In order to write a headline that attracts potential guests, you want to capture their attention. Keep the following tips in mind:

GEARING YOUR HEADLINE TO EVENTS NEAR YOUR SPACE

If an event is happening close to your listing, more than likely prospective guests are looking to stay at your place so they can attend. As the event nears, reference that event in your headline, especially if you're located close to it.

Consider if you're right outside Coachella. Most prospective guests looking for an Airbnb in the California desert during those Coachella weekends will visit your listing when you add "perfect for Coachella" to your headline. By doing this, you're speaking exactly to what's important to those guests.

If you update your headline, then you can get a bunch more people clicking through to your listing because you told them the important information they wanted to know. You can even add a paragraph to your listing with important information relating to staying at your place for the festival. Sharing that information with your potential guests is crucial.

» **Understand that you only get 50 characters to use when writing your headline.** As a result, be intentional on how you use those characters so you can give as much info as necessary, so guests click through to your listing. The more info that leads them to click through the better. Wording it the right way isn't as important as giving them the right information in a limited amount of characters.

» **Use abbreviations.** Abbreviations are a great way to maximize space as long as your potential guests understand them. Here are some great abbreviations to use in your headline:

- BR for bedroom
- BA for bathroom
- AC for air conditioning
- DT for downtown
- APT for apartment
- w for with
- 5 min to rather than five minutes to

For example, rather than writing "Five-bedroom, two-bathroom luxury apartment in walking distance to downtown with fireplace," you can save space and characters by abbreviating: "5 BR, 2BA lux apt, 5 min to DT, w fireplace." Including those details, where many listing headlines contain all the same info and fail to stand out, can help your listing stick out and improve its click-through.

>> **Utilize descriptive words that succinctly tell prospective guests what your space is like.** Figure out what one or two words best describe your space and are most likely to resonate with your target guest who's looking to book your property. Be sure to use these words in your listing headline to grab people's attention. Examples include romantic, cozy, spacious, and so on.

>> **Mention one or two amenities that guests are going to love.** For example, if your listing has a hot tub (or fireplace or swimming pool), make sure you include that information in the headline because those words make your listing more desirable. If guests are looking for a cozy place with a fireplace, suddenly they click your listing.

TIP

Capitalize these amenities in your headline in order to draw more attention to them. Consider the flip side to this point: If you don't highlight the plusses about your listing, then you miss guests who want to stay in a cozy place with a fireplace. Even though you have that amenity, they may not realize that you do.

Writing your own headline

You may feel pressure to write a perfect headline. Take a deep breath. We're here to help. In this section, we present some great proven formulas for Airbnb head-lines along with examples so you can model yours using these templates.

Table 6-1 shows three formulas and examples of optimal headlines. You can use these formulas to create or improve your own headline. Note that each formula begins with a key adjective and the house (or apartment) type. Pick the one that works best for you, depending on what features are worth highlighting most in your space.

TABLE 6-1   **Airbnb Headline Formulas**

Formula	Example
[Adjective] [House Type] with [Valuable Amenities]	Spacious Apt with PARKING & Queen Beds
[Adjective] [House Type] [Proximity] [Popular Destination] + [Amenity]	Charming Cottage 1 Min Walk to Lake + JET SKIS
[Adjective] [House Type] great for [Type of Experience]	Private Guest House Great for Quiet Getaway

We take a closer look at the formulas here:

» **Formula 1:** This formula uses an adjective for your house and the house type. Pair that one descriptive word with whether your space is an apartment, three-bedroom home, or condo. Then, add in the valuable amenities such as whether you have parking, king beds, a fireplace, or swimming pool. Select the most unique amenity or the amenity most desirable to guests and include whatever features offer the most value.

» **Formula 2:** Another headline format uses an adjective, house type, the proximity to a popular destination, and then the amenity. This headline tells potential guests a bunch of information in one title. For example, you could write "Charming 3BR Cottage 1Min Walk to Lake + JET SKIS" or "Cozy 2BR Condo 5Min Walk to Central Park + Fireplace." Prospective guests know the type of property: a charming 3BR cottage. They know the distance to an important location: 1min walk to lake. Finally, they know a valuable amenity you provide: jet skis.

» **Formula 3:** This headline format gives guests that are looking for a specific type of stay all the information they need. If your property appeals to a very specific type of traveler who wants a particular experience, such as a "quiet getaway," this format can be perfect. For example, a headline appealing to business travelers may say "Quiet Condo Perfect for Business Travelers." With this type of headline, you call out a specific guest or a visit that a guest can experience at your property.

WARNING

Be careful with using language that could alienate other guests who may also want to book. If you put "great for business travelers," make sure that primarily business travelers are the types of guests booking properties like yours. If your property is well set up for business travelers and couples, when you say "great for business travel," you send the wrong message to the couples, running the risk of turning ideal clients away.

Drafting a Great Description

Your listing's description needs to answer all guests' questions so that they're not left wondering anything about your property. Give your guests the details they need to book your property right away. Make sure you organize all the details so that guests can easily scan and find the information they need. The following sections give you the nitty-gritty details you need when writing your description.

What to include in your listing description

A great listing description catches your prospective guests' attention and keeps it. To do so, a strong listing description has the following information:

>> **Sleeping arrangements:** Guests need to know how many beds there are, what sizes, and how they're laid out.

>> **Amenities:** Let guests know what special amenities they have access to.

>> **Rooms guests have access to:** You also want to include details on what each room has to offer for guests.

>> **The neighborhood:** Inform guests on what to expect they can do nearby.

Organizing your listing for success

As far as the overall flow of your listing description, prioritize from the most important information to the least important information. Apart from that, you need to maintain a good amount of structure. Focus on the following:

>> **Organize your listing description into different sections with headings to signify different rooms.** Create actual headings for the kitchen, the bathrooms, the bedrooms, the patio, and any other rooms in your space so readers can more easily access the information. This way, prospective guests only need to search through the "kitchen" header when they know the amenity they seek is in the kitchen. It's also helpful to add a heading for "Amenities" where you can add all the desirable amenities such as Netflix, a fireplace, or a billiards table. Using headings is more inviting so guests don't have to scan through multiple paragraphs for what they're looking for.

> You can provide more specific information under the headings, especially for larger properties with multiple bedrooms. Clarify to prospective guests exactly which amenities are in each room. For example, under the heading of "Master Bedroom" list the amenities "Queen bed, attached full bathroom, 42-inch TV, private entrance."

>> **Use bulleted lists.** You can utilize hyphens, plus signs, stars, or arrows — basically anything that defines a bullet point. Listing with bullets is a great way to organize your listing description and make it easily digestible for potential guests.

>> **Don't hesitate to include information twice.** Even if you already wrote "Netflix" in the amenities section, add it into the specific room where it applies. Guests can easily find the information this way and are less likely to overlook it.

>> **Be succinct.** Avoid rambling or including too much filler. Instead, include the necessary information in an easily digestible way and as efficiently as possible. Be engaging, too. People don't like to waste their time.

>> **Be complete.** More of the right information is always better. If you have too little information, then some prospective guests will book another property. Others may also reach out to you because your description doesn't give them the information they need to make a reservation. If you have a lot of information, just make sure you organize it to help guests find what they need.

>> **Make it flow.** The best way to organize all the information in your listing description is from what is most important to what is least important in the eyes of your guests. For example, a family of four traveling to your two-bedroom home is likely to care more that the second bedroom has two twin beds than that it has Netflix. For that reason, under the heading of "Second Bedroom" you'll want to make sure that "2 twin beds" comes before "Netflix."

Keeping the goal in mind (more bookings)

Your goal at this point is simple: Get more bookings. Hence, you want to make sure that people actually look at your description. If you put too little information in your description, guests won't be wowed by it, and you'll lose out on bookings. They'll find the information they need on someone else's listing and book that one right away.

TIP

Give them everything they need to book your property instantly. Offer up any potential benefits of your property and answers to foreseeable questions. Put your-self in your guests' shoes and think about what kinds of questions they may have about your property. Furthermore, make sure you include all the relevant information they may want. If they have to reach out to you to ask a question, more than likely they'll lose interest by the time you respond to them and not book.

For example, when you welcome business travelers, they'll want to know how fast the Wi-Fi is. Be prepared: Run a quick test and put your Wi-Fi speed in your listing description. You've answered that question before they had to ask. Here are other types of questions prospective guests may have while perusing your listing description before booking:

>> Does it have a hair dryer, iron and ironing board, desk (fill in the blank)?

>> Is there a gym onsite that we can use?

>> How close is it to public transportation?

>> If it's an apartment or condo, does it have an elevator, or is it a walkup?

>> Is parking provided? If not, is there free parking nearby?

>> How close is the property to Attraction A or Venue B?

Location questions are especially important. When guests book your property, they don't know the exact address before booking. Airbnb only provides a nearby radius, which doesn't provide anything specific to guests concerning how far the property is from where they want to go. Telling them what locations, attractions, and amenities are close by is super useful information. For example, in your listing, say "5 min walk to subway line 1" or "10 min car ride to amusement park." Providing that information can make the difference, especially if they're making that walk or drive multiple times per day.

Consider why the guests are coming and what type of group they are in. This practice sparks a lot of questions you can foresee those guests having about your property, the location, and amenities. The more questions you can answer in your listing description, the more likely these potential guests are to book. Answer all the questions you can, even if they don't specifically relate to your property.

The types of questions may differ depending on the type of guests. Some may be more common for a specific type of traveler, such as a business traveler versus a family. The family may ask about the stair situation, whether you have a backyard and play space, and how child-proof the space is.

CAN YOU DELETE YOUR LISTING AND START OVER?

Although you can delete your listing after a poor start and create a new one, we don't recommend it. Re-creating your listing is a ton of work, and Airbnb often doesn't give you the same initial boost in traffic the second time around. Airbnb has your property information stored in its database. When you create a new listing for a property that's already had an unsuccessful launch, you'll initially get some additional traffic, but it likely won't be as much traffic as on the first initial launch. Airbnb realizes it's the same address so to an extent the company knows what to expect. Airbnb still gives your listing additional traffic, but it's not nearly as substantial. Furthermore, replacing your listing with a new one takes a significant amount of time — as much as six hours.

Rather than starting over, we recommend you focus on improving individual parts of your listing. Start with your reviews above all else. If you have negative reviews, correct the issues and respond to the reviews so that other potential guests can see that you care and that you've resolved the issue. From there, work through your listing headline, photos, and listing description as per this chapter to ensure that everything is set up properly. Finally, make sure your listing is as bookable as possible.

Some details aren't specific to your property, but guests still want to know the answers. Proximity details, such as if there's a swimming pool or movie theater nearby, can be huge drawing factors for guests. Be thorough and include answers to those questions in your listing description.

Sometimes, your description offers answers to questions guests haven't yet considered. It never hurts to include more details rather than less. The more information guests know, the more confidence they have and the higher the chance they will book instantly.

Setting House Rules

House rules cover anything about your property from whether you allow pets to how many guests are permitted. Some rules are more general that every host should have. Others may be more specific and geared toward your property. When writing your listing description, you want to set house rules and make sure you cover whatever is specifically important to you as a host and clearly convey that information to your guests. A more direct and clearer list of house rules leads to fewer issues with your guests.

The house rules are a part of your listing that enables you to indicate specific rules that your guest must agree to follow prior to booking. Airbnb requires guests to explicitly agree to whatever you put in your house rules.

REMEMBER

Make sure you put your house rules in the house rules section on your listing and then Airbnb takes care of the rest. If you put your house rules in the listing description and not in the house rules section, your guests may not see your rules, thus not agreeing to them when booking your property.

WARNING

If you don't put your house rules in the proper location, you may have a difficult time enforcing them if there is a dispute. Airbnb won't let you enforce them because the guests didn't expressly agree to them. Include a physical guest handbook in your space with your house rules to further remind your guests of anything you deem important.

TIP

When going through the initial, guided listing creation process on Airbnb, you won't immediately be shown all the adjustable settings, such as your check-out time and minimum night stay. Be sure to go back into your listing after completing the initial creation and review all your settings to ensure that everything is set exactly the way you want it.

It's important that your house rules cover all the necessary information so that you as a host are fully protected. This also helps to set clear expectations with guests as to what is and is not allowed so that both you and they can avoid any potential issues.

Knowing what to cover and why

When drafting your house rules, take the time to figure out what's important to you. Then draft a list of any rules you plan on enforcing. You want guests to know how they need to behave while staying in your property. If there's any ambiguity for guests on whether or not a rule is in place, it's almost impossible for you to enforce that rule through Airbnb. That's why you want to specifically include any rules you plan on enforcing in the house rules section.

House rules are set in stone so that all guests must follow them with no exceptions and no wiggle room. Here are some house rules you may want to include in your listing:

>> **No parties allowed.** Add the note about parties into your house rules so you can make sure there are no parties. We suggest you add a rule that states even if there is no damage caused by a party, the guests will still be charged a fine. This way, even if a party causes no damage, you have a deterrent in place, so people still won't throw one. Most property owners and landlords know that if you have a party at your property it's not just the material damages alone that cause a negative impact. More than likely, a party will upset your neighbors because of the extra noise. Some neighbors may even feel unsafe.

>> **No extra guests allowed.** Make it clear to guests that only the number of people specified in their booking are allowed at the property. If they reserve your property for 6 people, they're not allowed to show up with 16. You can also choose to charge an additional fee for extra guests, which we discuss later in this chapter in the "Additional guest fees" section.

>> **No smoking.** Make it clear that guests are charged the full security deposit in the event of smoking regardless of any damages. Even if you're a smoker, you'll likely want to have a nonsmoking listing because most people want to stay in nonsmoking units. If you have a smoking unit, you close yourself off to a large pool of potential guests who would otherwise book with you.

>> **Quiet hours.** Clearly state what time guests need to be quiet to avoid any potential noise complaints from neighbors. Adding a house rule such as "Quiet hours after 10 p.m." is an easy way to let guests know the specifics. This way, if ever there is a noise complaint, guests are far more likely to be agreeable to following the pre-laid out rule.

When you make your house rules, make sure you're clear on the repercussions for a broken rule. For example, rather than saying "No parties allowed," expressly state that "Guests will be charged the full security deposit in the event of any parties." Provide that deterrent so you can avoid the possibility of unwanted parties. This specific rule around parties applies to nearly all hosts, unless you're an Airbnb host who plans to allow parties. However, the majority of hosts want to keep that house rule in order to have guests respect their neighbors and their space.

Don't allow any ambiguity. Make sure everything is clearly stated so the guests aren't worried about a potential misunderstanding that could make them lose their security deposit.

REMEMBER

Only add house rules that you actually plan on enforcing. Rules such as "Please remove your shoes upon entering" are worth mentioning to guests, but the house rules section isn't the place to have them. You can message your guests before their stay for this type of request. The house rules section should be succinct so that there's no chance of guests overlooking a more important rule, such as "no smoking."

Enforcing your house rules successfully

You have two ways to respond and take action against guests who have disobeyed your house rules. Here they are in a nutshell:

>> **First method:** Reach out to your guests politely via the Airbnb platform. Inform them that they've broken or are breaking a house rule and request mediation. If they're disobeying your stated quiet hours, this can be as simple as asking them to quiet down. If they have extra guests, this could mean asking them to leave or charging them an additional fee.

REMEMBER

Whenever guests break the house rules, it's essential to communicate with them through the Airbnb platform. You may want to also call them on the phone, but it's important to also communicate through the Airbnb platform so that if you need to enforce any penalties, Airbnb is able to see a record of the communication.

>> **Second method:** If you can't resolve the situation using the first method, you resolve the issue by going through Airbnb's mediation process. Airbnb handles the issue directly with your guests. If you end up needing to go this route, follow these steps:

1. **Document the issue.** Take pictures of any damages caused to your listing as well as any proof that one of your house rules has been broken, such as an ashtray to serve as evidence of smoking.

2. **Contact Airbnb's support team as soon as possible, before your next guest checks in.** If you reach out to Airbnb after your next guest checks in, you'll have no way to prove which guest broke the rule and Airbnb will therefore be unable to resolve the issue.

After you reach out to Airbnb, Airbnb will request all the needed information to resolve the issue. Follow the company's instructions and your issue should be resolved in no time.

Going through the mediation process is a very rare situation, and most of the time it's an agreeable process. If you do have a guest who causes more serious damage and isn't cooperative, then keeping good documentation is your best bet to keep the process streamlined and avoid running into any issues with it.

Choosing a Cancellation Policy

Airbnb offers a wide range of cancellation policies to fit each individual host. In the following sections we examine the six different cancellation policies and explain why a stricter policy is generally the best option for hosts.

Identifying the six cancellation policies

At publication Airbnb has six cancellation policies. You can select one of the following:

REMEMBER

Note that Airbnb constantly changes and updates these policies. These policies shift and adapt so stay up-to-date and understand your options and the policy you selected. Airbnb alerts you whenever it makes changes so be sure to pay attention so that you aren't surprised by cancellations.

>> **Flexible:** Free cancellation until 14 days before check-in (time shown in the confirmation email). If booked less than 14 days before check-in, free cancellation for 48 hours after booking, up to 24 hours before check-in. After that, guests can cancel up to 24 hours before check-in and get a refund of the nightly rate and the cleaning fee, but not the service fee.

>> **Moderate:** Free cancellation until 14 days before check-in (time shown in the confirmation email). If booked less than 14 days before check-in, free cancellation for 48 hours after booking, up to five days before check-in. After that, guests can cancel up to five days before check-in and get a refund of the nightly rate and the cleaning fee, but not the service fee.

- **》 Strict:** Free cancellation for 48 hours, as long as the guest cancels at least 14 days before check-in (time shown in the confirmation email). After that, guests can cancel up to seven days before check-in and get a 50 percent refund of the nightly rate and the cleaning fee, but not the service fee.

- **》 Long term:** Automatically applied to reservations of 28 nights or more. Guests can cancel before check-in (3 p.m. in the destination's local time if not specified) and get a full refund, minus the first 30 days and the service fee.

- **》 Super strict 30 days:** Guests can cancel at least 30 days before check-in and get a 50 percent refund of the nightly rate and the cleaning fee, but not the service fee. This policy is by invitation only to certain hosts under special circumstances.

- **》 Super strict 60 days:** Guests can cancel at least 60 days before check-in and get a 50 percent refund of the nightly rate and the cleaning fee, but not the service fee. This policy is by invitation only to certain hosts under special circumstances.

Selecting the policy that's right for you

The cancellation policy you select is more important than you may think. The general rule is for whatever cancellation policy you choose just ask yourself how you would want to be treated as a guest. By having a cancellation policy that's stricter, you end up giving yourself more options.

We recommend you set a strict cancellation policy, or super strict 60 days or 30 days if possible. Note that at the time of this writing, Airbnb doesn't make the super strict 60 days or 30 days cancellation policies available to all hosts. With this type of policy, you get maximum flexibility. You won't always uphold the strict cancellation policy because you always have the option to refund your guests. However, using a strict policy gives you more options, which is ideal.

REMEMBER

If you set a more flexible or moderate cancellation policy, then you enable people to opt out of their visit even after booking. This policy means that your returns and your guests are less locked in.

Understand that with a more flexible cancellation policy, you pay an opportunity cost. The *opportunity cost* is if guests decide to cancel one month from their visit when they booked three months before their visit, then for those two months when they had your place booked, no one else was seeing it.

All the people who could have seen your property couldn't book it. The closer you get to the arrival date, the less chance the listing has of being booked if someone suddenly cancels and the listing becomes available again. Booking someone else into your space is virtually impossible when someone cancels two hours before check-in. It's highly unlikely any of those cancelled dates will get booked at such short notice because prospective guests plan their travels in advance. On the other hand, if someone cancels three months in advance, you have a high probability of getting those dates booked.

REMEMBER

Look at a strict cancellation policy less as a way to hold guests hostage and force them to stay at your property and more as a safety net for yourself to ensure that you aren't taking on unnecessary risk that guests cancel last minute.

Put yourself in your guests' shoes. If you canceled three months in advance, would you want the host to insist on keeping 100 percent of the booking value? You'd feel fairly angry about it, right? So why would you consider doing the same to your guests if you're a host?

If you're using a stricter cancellation policy, you get more options as a host. You decide if you issue a refund to your guests. If guests ask for a refund, but they don't qualify under your policy, then you can override it and still issue the refund.

If you have your policy set to moderate or flexible, then you don't have the option to keep the money. Furthermore, guests get a 48-hour grace period to cancel after they book. If the visit is within 14 days, they don't get that grace period. Outside of that 48 hours they can get a 50 percent refund if they cancel within seven days.

You can determine on a case-by-case basis whom to issue a refund to. How long they had the property booked for makes a big difference. Having your listing booked for 72 hours and then cancelling a month before is very different to having your listing booked for four months and cancelling two weeks before. Potentially a few people saw your listing and could have booked within those 72 hours, but if your listing was booked for four months, that number of people who could have booked is much larger.

Keeping a strict policy enables you to treat each situation differently. Say they cancel seven days out, or 14 days out, or one month out. If it's fairly close to the date of their visit, then you offer them the 50 percent refund and they get the other 50 percent when someone else books the place. Choosing this type of policy enables you to recoup your lost booking revenue and the cancelled guest also gets compensated.

WARNING

Airbnb sometimes encourages or requires you to offer guests a discount in exchange for accepting a stricter cancellation policy. If you run into this while setting your cancellation policy, you likely are better off selecting a more flexible cancellation policy that doesn't require you to offer guests a discount. Alternatively, you can simply offer the discount and increase your prices accordingly.

Determining Appropriate Fees

Additional fees come into play when hosting on Airbnb. These additional fees include the cleaning fees, the security deposit, and the fees for an additional guest. We outline each of those fees and how to determine an appropriate amount depending on your own situation.

Cleaning fees

Cleaning fees are fees that you set to charge guests a one-time rate for their stay to account for your cost of cleaning the unit after they check out. The cleaning fee you set is added to their reservations on top of the nightly rates that they pay for staying at your place.

TIP

To determine your cleaning fee, figure out the cost of having your space professionally cleaned. Whether you plan on cleaning the space yourself or having professionals clean for you, you still want to base your cleaning fee off the professional rate. Doing so gives you the flexibility to have a professional cleaner help you out if need be. Have a couple cleaners give you quotes on how much a cleaning costs to help you determine your fee in your listing.

Add the cost of replenishing materials such as toilet paper, hand soap, dish soap, and paper towels. Figure out the approximate cost per stay. It's likely only a couple dollars per stay because most guests won't individually go through all your hand or dish soap and will likely only use a couple rolls of toilet paper. Add those numbers together and include any taxes and that's essentially your cleaning fee. Chapter 15 discusses more specifics on cleaning and why hiring cleaners is so important.

A common misconception people believe is that by having their cleaning fees too high or at a reasonable market rate, they deter guests from booking their property. However, that isn't true. You end up getting the same number of bookings and the same returns whether you set your cleaning fees well below or at the market rate. The time when you lose out on bookings is when you go too far above the market rate for professional cleaning.

Security deposit

Your *security deposit* is technically only a fee in the event that a guest causes damage or breaks a house rule and needs to be fined accordingly. A security deposit is a set amount that Airbnb authorizes on the guest's credit card. In the event that a guest causes damage to your property and you successfully mediate through

Airbnb, Airbnb will award you compensation for the damages from the guest's security deposit.

REMEMBER

In the unlikely event that a guest causes damage to your property that exceeds the amount covered by that guest's security deposit, you still have coverage under Airbnb's $1 million host protection as well as through your own insurance plan. We discuss Airbnb's host protection and short-term rental insurance in detail in Chapter 5.

For this reason, the security deposit you set should only be enough to cover any reasonable damages that guests could accidentally cause to your property. Setting your security deposit unreasonably high in an effort to protect your property from worst-case scenarios that your insurance is designed to cover negatively impacts your bookings.

Setting a price for your security deposit has more guesswork and ambiguity than other fees. Rather than a scientific, calculated formula, your security deposit should basically be enough to cover any reasonable damages at your property. That means you avoid going through yours or Airbnb's liability insurance.

For your average property you don't want to set your security deposit less than $150 to $200. That number is reasonable because $150 worth of damages can be caused at most properties through simple carelessness. For example, consider if someone bumped into your TV and knocked it over. Any piece of technology you have is easily worth $100 to $150 if broken. Such items can easily be broken by accident.

If you ever do need to make a claim on one of your guests' security deposits, refer to the section above, "Enforcing your house rules effectively: The how-to" where we walk through all the steps on how to do so.

Additional guest fees

Additional guest fees are fees that are applied when a guest's group exceeds a specified number of people. For example, if you set an additional guest fee of $15 for groups of more than four people, then a group of six would have an additional fee of $30. Hosting more guests than your property typically accommodates is the only time you should have an additional guest fee.

TIP

To set an additional guest fee, all you need to do is specify on Airbnb what you want your additional guest fee to be and after how many guests in a group you want it to be applied.

Overall, trying to stagger so your two-bedroom listing charges different rates for one, two, three, or four people creates problems and headaches for you. You won't get a better return. Instead, set your price at the optimal pricing without factoring additional guests into it.

REMEMBER

If you want to use this fee in your listing, only charge it if you had an additional cost to having that extra guest. The only time you have an additional cost is if, for example, you make up a pullout couch or need the cleaners to do that. If you bring in cots or air mattresses, that type of event warrants an additional fee. The last situation you want to do is make your guests feel as if they've been nickeled and dimed. All that does is leave a bad taste in their mouths.

Turning on Instant Book: The Pros and Cons

As a host you always want to have Instant Book turned on whenever possible to improve your SEO. Only turn it off if you have a specific reason for doing so.

Using the Instant Book feature, like a lot of things in life, has its pros and cons. Before you make the decision to use (or not use) this feature, make sure you understand the pros and cons so you can plan accordingly.

Here are the pros:

>> You get way more bookings. People are able to book your space more easily, and as a result more people will.

>> Your listing shows up higher in Airbnb's search results and gets far more traffic.

Meanwhile, here are the cons:

>> You get less control over who comes to your house and when. You can't decide on the type of guests you accept and when you accept them.

>> Your property needs to always be ready for guests because guests can book anytime on short notice. To alleviate this issue somewhat, as a host you're able to set a minimum notice period that you require for guests to book — in the form of a cut-off time for same-day bookings or up to 7 days of advanced notice. That being said, this period is fixed for all your bookings, and the more advanced notice you require, the fewer bookings you'll be able to get.

Although there are certainly downsides to having Instant Book turned on, by being proactive you can negate the impact of any of those downsides. Here are a few ways to mitigate the downsides of Instant Book:

>> **Keep your calendar up to date at all times.** As soon as you know there's a personal conflict with hosting at a certain date, block those dates off in your calendar. Rather than waiting until the last minute, be proactive and block off any questionable days in your calendar. Only open days on your calendar where you want people booking a stay.

>> **Clean after check-outs rather than before check-ins.** As soon as a guest checks out, have the cleaning team start the turnover. Even if you don't have another guest coming in right away, perform the cleaning proactively. This way, your property will always be ready for guests.

>> **Cancel reservations with guests who you feel uncomfortable about.** If you have Instant Book turned on, Airbnb enables you to cancel reservations with any guests who you feel uncomfortable about. You can cancel up to three reservations per year online, and after that you need to call in to Airbnb's support team.

You want to enable Instant Book anytime you can. The only reason to disable Instant Book is if you're not concerned about optimizing returns. Turn off Instant Book only if Airbnb is just a hobby for you and you value the control with having it turned off more than you value the financial return with having it turned on. In that case, go ahead and turn Instant Book off and regain your control.

AIRBNB AND INCLUSIVITY

You as a host can cancel any bookings without penalty if you feel unsafe accepting those bookings when you have Instant Book activated. However, Airbnb has clear policies around discrimination.

Due to this policy, there's a fine line when it comes to cancelling on bookings due to personal concerns. You need a legitimate reason for feeling uncomfortable with a guest, such as bad reviews that you notice on the guest's profile. If there's a legitimate reason for your concern, then Airbnb doesn't penalize you in the event of a cancellation.

Whether or not you have Instant Book turned on, after you sign up to host, you agree to let anyone stay at your space no matter their race, gender, age, sexual orientation, or whatever. Airbnb has zero tolerance for discrimination of any kind.

Chapter **7**

Making Your Listing Shine with Photography

We aren't overexaggerating when we say that photography is probably the most important component in your listing. Outstanding photos enable prospective guests to see inside your listing and can make it stand out above your competition (and boring photos can make your listing not show its true potential). Making sure you nail the photography is essential because guests primarily decide on whether to book your listing based on the photos. Having bad photos versus amazing photos can be the difference between occasional bookings or a completely full calendar.

Don't assume that all you need to do is take a couple good pictures with your smartphone. The difference between bad, good, and amazing photography is drastic. This chapter shows you why photography is one of the most make-or-break aspects of your listing. We explain how you can get great photos so your listing is operating at its maximum potential. Anything less than outstanding photography sells your listing short and doesn't enable it to reach its maximum potential.

Setting Your Photo Strategy

Your photos show off your space and encourage potential guests to check out your listing. However, you don't want to quickly take a ton of photos and post them on your listing. Instead, make a plan to present your space in the best light. Visuals are key. Don't overlook your listing photos. They're a crucial component to getting more views, which leads to more guest bookings and more dollars in your pocket.

In these sections we help you comprehend why photos make such a difference in your listing's potential and how to pick between your photos so you can feature the most attractive shots. We also share why hiring a professional photographer is the move that sets you apart from all your competition.

Understanding why photos are so important

For most guests, the photos are the first step in keeping or cutting places they want to book. If you want guests to give your space a fair shot, then you need the photos to do so.

When guests are searching on Airbnb, the first two features they see are a listing's cover photo and its headline. Those two elements, along with the price, are guests' only reference points when they click through to your listing. Naturally, your photography tells much more about your space than a simple headline or nightly rate offers. As a result, you want your photos to sing your listing's praises because they're a huge factor in drawing interested guests to click your listing in the first place.

Prospective guests want to book properties based on whether the photos are appealing or not and whether the space looks the way they imagine it. Only after they've combed through your listing's photos do they dive deeper into your listing's other elements such as the description. Photos are a quick and easy way for them to eliminate properties that they deem less desirable or that lack key features and amenities that they're looking for.

Analyzing which photos perform best and worst

Testing your photos is one of the best ways to determine which photos are doing better and how you can improve your listing. Initially, you make an educated guess at which photo will perform best as your *cover photo*, which is the photo that guests see on the main search page among all the other listings. However, after having your listing up for a few months, you'll likely want to test that cover photo against others. Your cover photo is the first detail prospective guests see and it's responsible for getting them to click through to your listing. Many factors impact whether or not guests book your property, but your cover photo is one of the top factors because it essentially forms a guest's first impression.

You can also check your listing's performance inside your Airbnb account to see how many people are clicking through to your listing. Doing so makes testing different photos easier. After you see a difference in the number of people clicking through to your listing and the number of views you're getting consistently, you can use that data to see which photo performs best as your cover photo.

REMEMBER

After you test several cover photos, keep the best performing one. You get more visitors to your listing in the long term, which makes an exponential difference on your returns on the property. Assuming you set up the rest of your listing properly, more views equal more bookings. It's a ripple effect. More bookings boost you in the search rankings, which lead to more views. Now you have a feedback loop where you experience better results and upward momentum.

Hiring a professional photographer: Why doing so is a smart decision

One of the most important decisions you make when creating an Airbnb listing is whether to hire a professional photographer. We recommend you don't skimp on your photos; instead, use a professional photographer for all your listing photos. Period.

What a pro can do for you and your listing

The difference between you taking your own photos or hiring a professional photographer to capture your listing can make all the difference in the number of reservations you get. A professional photographer who has experience in shooting for Airbnb has the following that you more than likely don't:

>> **They have the best equipment and the most expertise.** They have a mastery of elements, whether that's getting the best angles, shooting in different modes, capturing the right style, or correctly using the right lighting. Generally, a professional photographer handles all the nuances required for getting highly attractive and engaging photos.

>> **They know the difference between a good photo and a great photo.**
A great photo versus a good photo is the difference between just a few bookings and a fully booked calendar. Your photos are a fundamental part of getting people to click through and book your listing. Any difference you make is likely to equal huge returns. A pro knows what makes a great photo, and you're more likely to get the best photos versus doing it yourself.

TIP

Give your photographer the proper outline and instructions on what shots to capture so you receive the shots you need. The return on investment is huge.

>> **They know how to shoot an Airbnb listing.** Airbnb photographers shoot photos that enable guests to envision themselves in that space and feel a certain way about staying there. The photographer emphasizes not only the physical space but the amenities in the space as well. They capture the feeling of the couch and the beds and the warmth of the dining room and the coziness of the living room. Unlike traditional real estate photographers who typically showcase the shell of the property, Airbnb photographers showcase the heart.

Refer to the later section, "How to hire a pro" for advice on how to find an experienced photographer to shoot your listing.

Why shooting your own photos is a bad idea

Many hosts start out thinking they can capture good enough photos on their own. They may have the latest smartphone or even a DSLR camera. What could go wrong, right? A lot. Shooting a property for Airbnb is very different from shooting your standard photography in nature or portraits. Just because you're an amateur nature photographer or shoot high school students for their senior pictures doesn't mean you're equipped to shoot a property for Airbnb.

Many hosts make a mistake by trying to photograph their own spaces or hiring a friend or amateur photographer who isn't specialized in shooting an Airbnb listing. By taking the photos yourself (or using a friend or amateur photographer), you're not maximizing the potential of your own listing. Worst case, your photos can look amateurish and won't attract prospective guests to examine your listing in greater detail, resulting in fewer reservations for your listing, no matter how nice it is.

How to hire a pro

Make the nominal investment into professional photography when you first set up your Airbnb listing. You make massive gains in comparison to the hosts who don't realize this opportunity and go the seemingly less expensive route by doing it themselves or by using an amateur photographer friend.

Although Airbnb offers professional photography, using that service doesn't give you the control you want to advise what shots you want. To hire a professional photographer, quickly search online for Airbnb or real estate photographers in your area. You should find a number of options.

After you find some potential photographers, take a look through their portfolios to determine who the best options are and then request some quotes. Remember, professional photography is an investment that's likely to pay off tenfold. Don't skimp and just look for the cheapest option.

After you find the right photographer, you need to schedule a time for them to come out to the property and shoot it. You want to provide them with the shot list and guidance that we discuss in the following sections ahead of time. After the shoot, your photographer picks out the best photos, touches them up in post-production, and provides you with the final photos for your listing. You can expect to pay them anywhere from $50 to $300 depending on the area you live in, and the turnaround time on receiving your completed photos should be no longer than one to two weeks.

Staging Your Property for Photos

Before having a photographer come by to shoot your space, you need to make sure it's staged properly. If your property doesn't look amazing, there's no way your photos will look amazing. In these sections, we show you why staging your property prior to photos is essential and how to do it like a pro.

Realizing why property staging is key

Staging your property is essential to the guest experience. Guests should envision themselves staying at your place while browsing your listing. As a result, aim to make your guests excited when they see your listing photos. Staging is all about giving your guests a real taste of what it's like to stay at your property from the comfort of their own home.

Forget about the shell of your house. Instead focus on every piece and small touch that makes it feel homey. Most guests seek a place that aligns with the ethos of Airbnb, which is to live like a local. A hotel is the antithesis of Airbnb. Consider Airbnb akin to staying in a place that feels like home. Staying as a local has many small differences that show up in the way you stage your property to make it homey.

Staging your space like a pro

When staging your listing, keep the following tips in mind to help your listing stand out:

>> **Make sure your space is immaculately clean.** Your bathroom needs to be hygienic and well-presented. Hire cleaners to clean your space before photos are taken. Make sure the cleaners go above and beyond in their cleaning.

>> **Keep everything in order.** Make your space look like a magazine spread. Do the following when you stage:

- Make sure your chairs and rugs are properly aligned and overall nothing is out of place.

- Hide any cables so they're out of sight.

- Fluff pillows and position them just right on the couches and beds.

- Iron sheets, so they don't appear super wrinkly.

- Tuck away any tags on your bedding, towels, or pillows.

- Put down the toilet lid and close the shower curtain. If you have a nice shower, then you may want to open it for specific shower photos. However, mostly keep it closed so the bathroom appears nicer and cleaner.

These little touches bring your space full circle and result in phenomenal photos. That level of detail is what brings your space to 100 percent and leads guests to book your place over the competition.

>> **Zhuzh everything.** In other words, you're giving a little pizzaz to your space and making it stand out. For example, add inviting throw pillows on the bed. (If you don't have any, buy some with a splash of color.)

>> **Stage to the next level.** Set your space apart by staging it to feel like a home. Add a couple plants or flowers. Lay a newspaper out and set your table with a bowl of fruit and a mug of fresh coffee so guests can envision themselves sitting at your kitchen table, eating breakfast, and reading the news. After that, it's the nuanced and more detailed side of things that really bring it all together.

Getting All the Shots

According to psychologists, people remember beginnings and endings better than they do the middle of experiences, even if the middle parts were technically stronger than the whole experience. So, what are you to do as a host? Create strong beginnings and endings.

The first and last element that a prospective guest is likely to see when it comes to your listing is your photos. Moreover, the very first photo that your prospective guests sees is your cover photo, so it's crucial that this photo highlights your listing's best features.

For this reason, getting all the shots you need to make your listing stand out and set the right expectations for guests is exceptionally important. The next section walks you through the different types of shots your listing needs to achieve this.

Mixing it up: From wide to detailed to closeup shots

Planning out your shoot day is paramount because your photographer needs to take shots from different angles to showcase the space. Find unique shots for your photographer and offer suggestions about shots that emphasize different parts of your home. Have your photographer highlight all the important parts of your space so nothing is left up to the guest's imagination.

You want both wide-angle shots and close-ups for different reasons. Overall, you want to make sure your photos do three tasks:

>> **Show it all.** Let guests envision themselves in each room.

>> **Answer any questions guests may have.** Have your photographer use a mix of shots to help answer any questions guests may have, such as what amenities your listing offers.

>> **Help potential guests to envision themselves in the space.** By showing the heart of the property rather than just the shell, you enable guests to envision themselves in your space.

WARNING

One of biggest mistakes we see is people taking one photo of a space and then leaving the guests to wonder what else is there. Maybe they can't quite tell if there is a fridge in the kitchen or not. Maybe they don't understand if there is more space on one side of the room or if it's actually a wall. If potential guests are unsure about something while looking at your place, then that uncertainty could lead them to booking somewhere else.

Make sure your photographer takes the right photos so your guests can clearly determine what the space is and how it's configured. Ensure that your photographer captures shots of all the main amenities in your property as well. For example, if you mention your pullout couch in the listing description, be sure to have photos of the couch both set up as a couch and fully made up as a bed. This way, people can visualize where the pullout couch is, how big it is, and what it looks like. Your photos should eliminate any mystery for the guests.

Examples of wide-angle shots

Your photographer should use wide-angle shots to showcase the entire space. These shots help guests understand the layout of your property. If possible, include any shots that show multiple rooms in one photo. Your photos should highlight specific spaces as well, and any shots displaying the hallways give guests an understanding of the layout of the whole property. Where are the bedrooms, bathrooms, and kitchen? Showcase your outdoor spaces such as your backyard, barbecue, patio furniture, porch, garage, or parking spot. If you have attractions or hotspots nearby, such as a park, restaurant, or pool, add those photos to offer even more value to your guests.

Examples of medium-wide shots

Depending on your space, the medium-wide shots achieve the same as wide shots. In a large, open concept room you want a wide shot. However, in a bathroom you don't need a super wide shot. You want a medium or average width shot to show the full space.

Examples of closeup shots

To answer potential guest questions, have your photographer take closeup shots of the coffeemaker, the blender, or gas burner stove to offer more detail on the type of amenity. Those photos answer guests' questions if guests are interested in cooking. Have your photographer also take photos of your TV with Netflix on display. If you have a smart home or music speaker, then include those features in your closeup pictures. This way, guests don't need to read your whole description to know if you have certain desirable amenities.

Using a photography checklist

Make a property photography checklist to ensure that no shots get missed. Your plan should also involve the specific lighting, the mood setting, and the types of photos you want your photographer to capture. Walk throughout your listing, write down specific instructions, and figure out exactly what you want and then communicate your desires with your photographer. Looking at other listings on Airbnb, especially Superhosts, who have dynamic photos, can give you some inspiration. (Refer to the section, "Identifying Tips and Tricks Used by Top Listings and Superhosts," later in this chapter for more tidbits.)

Working with Your Photographer to Get Great Photos

If you hire a professional photographer to capture great shots, it's up to you to communicate what you want and then ensure that the final photos capture your property in the best way possible. In the following sections, we provide some insights that can help you to ensure that your photographer gets the exact shots that you need.

Lighting the shot

More than likely, your photographer will bring her own lighting equipment to shoot your property, but you can take care of the following to help ensure the lighting is right:

>> **First and foremost, schedule your photoshoot in the daylight.** All your photos should have optimal natural light wherever possible. Never shoot a property at nighttime because nighttime photos are the worst option for ambiance. Furthermore, you don't want darkness outside your windows.

Have all your exterior photos taken at golden hour when the sun is setting. These photos are even more beautiful than those captured during peak daylight hours.

>> **Open your blinds or curtains to include as much natural light as possible.** As much natural light as possible makes all your photos appear brighter and more appealing.

REMEMBER

>> **For any low-lit or underlit areas, ensure that your photographer has proper equipment, so all your spaces appear warm and well lit.** The only spaces that should have artificial lighting are those that don't have enough nature light, such as a windowless bathroom or a basement. Generally, anywhere you can get natural light, showcase that natural light.

No areas in your space should appear dark or mysterious. Dark and uninviting are the antithesis to a homey Airbnb space.

Composing the shot

When composing the shots, your photographer should capture your space in the best possible way. You want to present the most attractive version of your kitchen, bedroom, bathroom, and living space.

For the composition your photographer won't need too much guidance. They hold the professional expertise to do a great job on her own. What matters most is that you give them your requested shot list. Refer to the earlier section, "Getting All the Shots," where we explain what types of shots you want. When your photographer takes photos, look at them and evaluate the angles and compositions. Make sure the photos are answering potential guests' questions and providing your guests with the proper image of your space.

For example, consider you have a large, open-concept living room and dining room and you want your photographer to compose several shots featuring just the living room and several shots of just the dining room. However, at least one shot should show both spaces together. That photo answers questions your guest may have about the location of both spaces. By including the right composition, you make sure each side of your space is shown. If possible, include in your shot list a photo at an angle displaying more natural light or showcasing featured artwork.

Getting the proper exposure

Exposure is another element that your photographer should have a good handle on. They shouldn't need much guidance in this area because after all you hired a professional. That being said, if anything, make sure the photos are underexposed rather than overexposed. In post-production it's much easier to correct for under-exposure versus overexposure.

For reference, *exposure* refers to the shutter speed of the camera being faster or slower.

>> **Overexposed:** If the shutter remains open longer and too much light is allowed inside, the photo is overexposed. If photos are overexposed, then you end up with minimal color. All the colors will be so bright that they are lost and appear white.

>> **Underexposed:** If the shutter speed is faster so less light is allowed inside, then the photo is underexposed. You end up with darker photos, but no color is lost.

Your photographer can easily increase the brightness in those underexposed photos during post-production. However, if the photos are overexposed, the photographer can't bring the colors back.

Furthermore, whenever possible ask your photographer to shoot in HDR. HDR stands for high dynamic range, and your photographer should be familiar with what this style of photography is and how to shoot it. With HDR, your photos will come out looking much more vibrant, with a greater depth of color and better brightness. What results is a rich, crisp, and overall beautiful photo. In any space, in addition to utilizing HDR, having good lighting and color profoundly improves your photos.

Identifying Tips and Tricks Used by Top Listings and Superhosts

When figuring out what photos to use in your listing, refer to these tips that many Superhosts and other hosts of top listings utilize. Nothing is wrong with modeling your photos after theirs. If these types of photos work for them, the idea is they'll also work for you.

>> **Test your cover photo and see which option is the most effective.** Refer to the earlier section, "Analyzing which photos perform best and worst" for more information.

>> **Including more photos is better but avoid repetitive photos.** Aim to share details and answer potential questions through your photos. However, don't overshare and risk your potential guest losing interest after scrolling through the fifth photo of your dining room table from every angle.

The difference between 10 and 40 photos is massive. Remember, you need to show the space from all angles needed to answer questions guests may have. Sell them on all the features and advantages of your property.

We recommend 25 photos as an absolute minimum. However, oftentimes we recommend upward of 40 photos. Essentially, focus on your number of photos and the way those photos are lit and staged.

TIP

>> **Determine whether your photos are doing their job.** To do so, ask whether they answer all the questions your prospective guests may have, show the whole space, and help guests to envision themselves staying there. Let those intentions guide you.

>> **Start in one area and show photos as if the guest is walking through your property.** Begin on the main floor and then walk potential guests through the property in a logical order. Don't jump from the kitchen to the bathroom to the bedroom and back to the kitchen. Make sure the mood-setting shots line up with where the photos are within your space. For example, include a shot of a magazine and fresh cup of coffee on the dining room table with the photo of the dining room and include a picture of the coffeemaker with the kitchen photos.

FOCUSING ON A FEW PHOTOGRAPHY EXAMPLES THAT SHINE

A quick search for Airbnb PLUS and Luxe listings in your area reveals a large selection of listings with quality professional photography. Here are a few of search results you see using Colorado as an example destination:

- **"Contemporary Townhouse by Cucumber Gulch Preserve":** www.airbnb.ca/luxury/listing/29646897

- **"Renovated Log Cabin in the Woods":** www.airbnb.ca/rooms/53298442

- **"Fruita/Loma Guest House at the Perfect Day Getaway":** www.airbnb.ca/rooms/plus/47351409

You immediately notice that the photos on these listings do a fantastic job of answering all the questions that prospective guests may have as well as showcasing the entire space and allowing guests to envision themselves staying there. Chances are good that after seeing these listings you're compelled to take a trip out to Colorado and stay at one, which is exactly what photography can accomplish when done correctly.

>> **Pay attention to the aesthetics and mix your photos up in terms of your wide angles to close-ups.** Don't have ten closeup photos in a row. If a guest sees your close-ups of the TV, coffee cup, and coffeemaker all in a row, they don't get an accurate view of your space in its entirety. Instead, intersperse different viewpoints in your photo order. Doing so keeps guests engaged, and you don't risk boring them with a bunch of amenity photos. If guests are bored by your photos or disinterested, they may click out of your listing and onto another listing.

3

Uncovering Important Pricing Essentials

Set your baseline pricing for your listing so it is optimized to get you the most earnings during most of the season.

Factor in special events and seasonality to adjust pricing for both high and low demand seasons to maximize earnings.

Use automated dynamic pricing tools to take out the guesswork and ensure your listing is optimally priced at all times.

Set appropriate levels for other fees to minimize booking friction for guests.

Increase the profit potential for your listing by making simple adjustments to your listing.

Spend on smart purchases to reduce operating expenses and increase profit potential.

Go on cruise control with automation to free yourself from day-to-day hosting operations and maximize your earnings per hour spent hosting.

Understand what being a Superhost means, how you can increase your bookings as a result, and discover how you join this elite group of Airbnb hosts.

IN THIS CHAPTER

» **Understanding the factors in pricing**

» **Creating a ramp up strategy**

» **Factoring in seasonality**

» **Monitoring temporality and special events**

» **Utilizing dynamic pricing**

» **Comprehending and setting fees**

Chapter **8**

Setting Your Listing Pricing

A lot goes into setting the right pricing for your Airbnb, in fact, much more than meets the eye. Many new hosts choose pricing haphazardly and resort to a "set it and forget it" mentality with pricing, often leading to suboptimal listing performance.

Setting the right pricing requires understanding the different factors that impact Airbnb pricing. Neglecting even just one of these factors in your pricing strategy can lead to fewer bookings and lower profits.

We're here to help you stay on top of pricing your listing so your listing can both get off to a great start and stay competitive on Airbnb. This chapter examines each of the important components of pricing and shows you the tools and methodology to setting your own optimal pricing for your listing.

Focusing on Baseline Pricing

Determining a *baseline pricing* is finding the optimal amount you charge for your Airbnb listing under typical market conditions with average demand. Any adjustments you make to your pricing start from this baseline level.

To establish the baseline pricing, you analyze comparable listings on Airbnb to create a pricing strategy that works for you. The following sections help you start pricing your listing so it's competitive wherever you live.

Studying your competition: Gather comparable market data

The best way to establish your baseline pricing is by looking at what your competition is charging in your market. You can think of your *market* as the tightest geographic radius that allows you to gather data for at least a dozen comparable and competitive listings. For example, in an ultrahigh-density urban market, this could be just a one block or even a minute walking radius. In the sparse country side, it could mean more than 10 miles or a 30-minute drive radius. In a typical suburban neighborhood, a safe starting point is three blocks or a 15-minute walking radius. You need to adjust as needed for your specific area.

REMEMBER

Your *competition* includes the most similar Airbnb listings in your market — those similar in size (beds, bedrooms, bathrooms), amenities, and overall positioning in terms of pricing and target audience. For example, if your Airbnb listing is a one-bedroom unit targeting the budget-friendly traveler who doesn't mind being a bit farther out from the main attractions, then your competition is similar, economy-focused one-bedroom Airbnb listings. However, if your Airbnb listing is a two-bedroom luxury condominium in a downtown luxury high-rise residence, your competition includes other two-bedroom luxury Airbnb listings.

When studying the competition, gather at least a six (preferable a dozen or more) similar Airbnb listings and record the following information:

>> **Weekday rates:** For each comparable Airbnb listing and hotel listing, collect the average weekday rates (Sundays to Thursdays) for 4 weeks, 8 weeks, and 12 weeks into the future. Take the average of those five days for each of the three weeks for each comparable listing.

>> **Weekend rates:** For each comparable Airbnb listing and hotel listing, collect the average weekend rates (Fridays and Saturdays only) for 4 weeks, 8 weeks, and 12 weeks into the future. Take the average of those two days for each of the three weeks for each comparable listing.

TIP

If you're unable to find enough (at least six) comparable Airbnb listings in your market for your baseline pricing analysis, you can substitute with comparable hotel listings. For most hosts, comparing to economy and midrange hotel offerings make the most sense. Identify the nearest two- and three-star hotels to your property and compare your studio or one-bedroom listing to their lowest priced offering. For larger properties of two- or three-bedrooms, compare to the lowest priced hotel suites. However, you may need to adjust your findings down by 15 to 30 percent because average hotel listings are often priced higher than their Airbnb counterparts in the same market.

After you're done collecting this information, you have six data points for each of the listings you've identified for your comparison — three weekday averages and three weekend averages — resulting from 21 daily prices for each of the comps.

Taking the average again of the average weekday and weekend rates for these similar listings gives you a good baseline pricing for your Airbnb listing in your market. Figure 8-1 shows an example with 12 comparable Airbnb listings and their corresponding data points for their weekday and weekend pricing.

						Prices						Averages	
Comp #	Comp URL	Prop Type	Beds	Rooms	Baths	WD 1	WD 2	WD 3	WE 1	WE 2	WE 3	Weekday	Weekend
1	www.airbnb.com/room	Entire place	1	1	1	$70	$85	$74	$104	$115	$114	$76	$111
2	www.airbnb.com/room	Entire place	1	1	1	$76	$95	$71	$112	$117	$108	$81	$112
3	www.airbnb.com/room	Entire place	2	1	1	$66	$92	$79	$94	$135	$110	$79	$113
4	www.airbnb.com/room	Entire place	1	1	1	$69	$89	$77	$119	$125	$115	$78	$120
5	www.airbnb.com/room	Entire place	1	1	1	$68	$86	$81	$108	$131	$106	$78	$115
6	www.airbnb.com/room	Entire place	2	1	1	$75	$95	$80	$111	$136	$103	$83	$117
7	www.airbnb.com/room	Entire place	2	1	1	$67	$88	$75	$106	$113	$117	$77	$112
8	www.airbnb.com/room	Entire place	1	1	1	$76	$93	$81	$124	$141	$106	$83	$124
9	www.airbnb.com/room	Entire place	1	1	1	$71	$93	$71	$111	$123	$107	$78	$114
10	www.airbnb.com/room	Entire place	2	1	1	$67	$92	$79	$114	$114	$101	$79	$110
11	www.airbnb.com/room	Entire place	1	1	1	$78	$83	$75	$103	$110	$110	$79	$108
12	www.airbnb.com/room	Entire place	1	1	1	$69	$83	$76	$101	$126	$104	$76	$110
											Overall average	$79	$114

FIGURE 8-1: Baseline pricing exercise.

© *John Wiley & Sons, Inc.*

ON THE WEB

Tracking additional information for the comparable listings can help you understand the pricing dynamic in your market even better. Tracking additional information, such as the listing URLs, property type, number of bedrooms, number of bedrooms, and number of bathrooms can assist you to fine-tune your baseline pricing analysis. If you want to track many factors for your comparable listings, download a spreadsheet template at www.learnbnb.com/airbnbfordummies.

Choosing a baseline pricing strategy

After you gather your data and have a baseline weekday and weekend pricing rate that you feel comfortable with, you need to figure out how to use that information.

Here are three primary pricing strategies you can consider adopting to price your listing:

>> **Match market offering and charge less.** If you intend to match the amenities and overall offering of your competition, you can gain an edge by charging slightly less than your competition. By offering the same amenities at a discount, you can secure more bookings.

>> **Beat market offering and charge the same.** If you intend to clearly beat the offering of your competition, you can gain an edge by charging the same overall pricing as your competition. By offering better amenities at the same price, you can secure more bookings.

>> **Make unique offering and charge premium.** If your Airbnb listing offers something unique that guests value and the competition in your market can't match, then you may be able to charge a premium. By offering something unique and valuable, you can charge more than your competition.

Depending on which strategy you find most fitting for your Airbnb listing, your baseline pricing will be lower than, about the same, or greater than the baseline pricing you found from the comparable listings.

However, settling on your baseline pricing doesn't mean you just set your pricing to these levels for the entire availability of your listing. At various times you want to purposely price lower or higher than your baseline pricing. We explore each of moments in the following discussions.

Ramping Up to Baseline Pricing

The first such scenario where you price differently from your baseline pricing is during your ramping-up period, typically the first two to four months after an Airbnb listing first goes live on the platform. During these first months on the platform, your objective is to build momentum for your listing as quickly as possible, not to maximize the profits of any individual bookings.

TIP

To do so, get as many bookings and as many 5-star guest reviews as fast as possible. When a listing is fresh on the platform, it has no bookings and no reviews. All things equal, potential guests almost always book with listings that have more reviews than similar listings with no reviews.

During your ramping-up period, follow this pricing schedule to build momentum for your listing.

1. **Start at 20 percent lower than your baseline pricing.**

   Doing so underprices your listing relative to your competition right out of the gate.

2. **Wait for one week and check to see if your listing is mostly booked two weeks out.**

   - If mostly booked for next two weeks, then stay the course until your listing is mostly booked four weeks out — aim for 80 percent plus occupancy.

   - If not booked out, drop pricing by another 10 percent every week until you're booked four weeks out.

   - If more than four weeks are booked within the first week, then raise prices by 10 percent every week until you're fully booked for the next four weeks or until reaching baseline pricing.

3. **After you reach the baseline pricing, sign up for third-party dynamic pricing software to monitor and adjust pricing going forward automatically.**

   For more on dynamic pricing, check out the later section in this chapter, "Using Dynamic Pricing: Yes or No?"

TIP

Be sure to note in your listing profile title and description that your listing is "NEW." Doing so can help potential guests get comfortable with your lack of reviews and help them understand why your listing is priced so favorably versus competition — that it's due to your newness and not some defect.

Understanding and Adjusting for Seasonality

When setting your pricing, sometimes you need to adjust for seasonality. *Seasonality* means the overall Airbnb demand — the occupancy and average nightly rates for Airbnb listings in the market — may be much higher or lower than their typical rates when travel is correspondingly much higher or lower than average.

For example, Airbnb cabins by a popular ski resort may be booked almost every evening, even at much higher than average nightly rates during the high demand skiing season. However, these same cabins may have a hard time booking nights even at significantly discounted rates during low season when the snow has melted and far fewer guests want to spend their hot summer on these dry barren ski slopes.

For some Airbnb markets with well-defined seasonal attractions, you can easily know whether there is seasonality in the market. But for many markets without obvious seasonal factors for travel demand, you can verify seasonality by obtaining the relevant market data for the prior 12 months (a full calendar year). Check out Chapter 4 for details on how to obtain earning statistics for your market.

The seasonality of your Airbnb market falls into one of these four categories:

>> **Flat seasonality:** If the demand is the same all year around, then there is flat seasonality. In these rare markets, you can expect the occupancy and average nightly rates to stay about the same throughout the year. Often, flat seasonality is associated with low overall Airbnb travel demand for the market.

>> **High season only:** If the demand spikes high for a part of the year but stays flat the rest of the year, then the seasonality is said to have a high season. In these markets, you can expect the occupancy and average nightly rates to spike higher only during the high season but stay relatively flat the rest of the time.

>> **Low season only:** If the demand drops lower for a part of the year but stays flat the rest of the year, then the seasonality is said to have a low season. In these markets, you can expect the occupancy and average nightly rates to fall noticeably lower only during the low season but stay relatively flat the rest of the time.

>> **High low seasons:** If the demand drops lower for a part of the year and spikes higher for a different part of the year compared to a middle level the rest of the year, then the seasonality has both a high and low season. In these markets, you can expect occupancy and average night rates both to drop during low season and spike during high season.

Figure 8-2 shows what each of these four seasonality scenarios may look like if you plotted the average occupancy rates in these markets by month where 100 represents the annualized average occupancy rate. After you obtain the market data for a full calendar year for your market, you can notice that the average occupancy or nightly rates in your market will look like one of these scenarios.

Figure 8-2a shows a flat seasonality market, Figure 8-2b a high season only seasonality market, Figure 8-2c a low season only seasonality market, and Figure 8-4d a high and low seasonality market. For all examples, the average occupancy rate during normal season is at 80 percent.

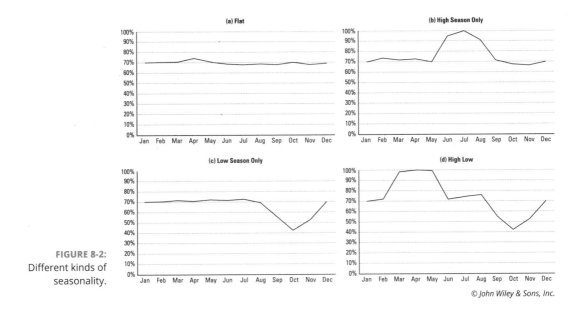

FIGURE 8-2:
Different kinds of
seasonality.

© John Wiley & Sons, Inc.

Factoring in Temporality and Special Events: Going from High to Low

When pricing your Airbnb listing, you need to consider *temporality*, or how far out in advance the guest is booking. Having a guest book your listing six months out may feel good, but not if you allowed a guest to book it at a far lower rate than you could have achieved.

Consider an example from the airline industry. According to a 2019 study by CheapAir.com analyzing 918 million airfares in more than 8,000 markets, the optimal time to book a flight for the best chance at the lowest possible airfare is about three months out. Booking far earlier, for those seeking peace of mind, or booking within the final weeks before the flight, often results in much higher airfares.

The prime booking window for airline tickets is somewhere between 20 to 120 days, with the best rates occurring around the 80 to 90 days from the flight. Booking earlier or later means paying higher prices for the consumers, but higher profits for the airlines.

Airbnb pricing has a similar dynamic when you optimize for temporality during dates with unusually high travel demand, such as when your city or nearby area has a special event that draws a sudden influx of travelers.

For example, the largest trade shows or conventions can draw hundreds of thousands of attendees, leading to booked hotels and Airbnb listings months in advance. Hosts who misprice their listings for these events by not increasing their prices can miss out on significant profits while hosts who appropriately price for the high demand by raising prices can achieve additional profits.

Unlike the airline industry however, you won't typically see a large price hike for Airbnb bookings within the final two weeks prior to a special event. As the event approaches, you should reduce your pricing to ensure a booking rather than risk having an empty listing during an otherwise busy weekend.

TIP

For pricing your Airbnb during special events, start high and then steadily reduce your pricing as the date of the event approaches. By using the following protocol, you can maximize your chances of earning more profits during special events:

1. **Start high.**

   For two months or further out from the date of the event, price your listing at the highest price you can justify from one to two nights prior to the final night of event. Finding the right price to start with takes some guesswork, because it can vary from being only 20 percent higher to more than 400 percent higher.

2. **Reduce weekly until booked.**

   Reduce the average nightly rates for those nights by an even amount such that by the final week prior to the event, you reach your normal rate. More than likely, you won't reach this pricing because your listing will most likely book beforehand. For example, if you're charging a premium of an additional $100/night for the event with eight weeks to go, reduce the premium by $12/night every week until it's booked.

3. **Reduce aggressively if within two weeks.**

   If you overpriced your listing and still not booked with two weeks of the special event, we recommend reducing your pricing more aggressively to ensure a booking rather than sitting empty. Pricing 10 to 20 percent lower than your remaining competition is typically enough to ensure booking at this stage.

BIG JULY EVENTS, BIG PROFITS

Over consecutive weekends every July, the San Diego Pride parade and the Comic-Con events both lead to booked hotels and Airbnb listings within a five-mile radius of the San Diego Convention Center.

Stretching over a 1.5-mile route, the San Diego Pride parade attracts more than 250,000 people from all around the world each year, making it one of the largest Prides in the United States. Meanwhile, Comic-Con attracts more than 130,000 attendees from more than 80 countries for a multiday celebration for comic book fans, cosplayers, pop culture lovers, and countless celebrities in disguise.

Airbnb estimates to have hosted approximately 41,000 guests during those two busy weekends. The average listing can double its average nightly rates during this period. Some listings are even able to charge up to five times their normal nightly rates, essentially earning in two weeks what normally took them two months.

But according to Everbooked, a data research firm that tracks short-term rental and Airbnb statistics, less than half of the listings raised their prices during this period. That means more than half of the hosts didn't adjust their pricing and were likely booked for those weekends several months in advance at well below what they could have charged.

Using Dynamic Pricing: Yes or No?

Although manual pricing is useful for establishing your baseline pricing and understanding adjustments for seasonality and special events, it's woefully inadequate to account for a major factor in *optimal pricing* — the current available supply and pricing of your direct competition.

That is, your pricing for any given available night for your listing should consider the overall availability of your competitors and their pricing for the same night. For example, if most of your competitors are also available the same night and their current pricing is low, you'd have a difficult time pricing your comparable listing at a premium. Similarly, if most of your competition is already booked leaving few alternatives for the potential guests, you're more likely to be able to charge a premium for that night.

For a typical listing mostly available two months out, that's approximately 300 available nights to track the occupancy and pricing of competitive listings. Doing so manually just isn't possible to do, let alone keeping it updated. That's why we highly recommend you use *dynamic pricing tools* that track the competitive market supply and pricing and automatically update their Airbnb listing prices in near real time.

These sections explore why you should opt out of Airbnb's own automated Smart Pricing tool and why a third-party provider is your best option.

Underperforming with Airbnb's Smart Pricing tool

Airbnb's Smart Pricing optimizes pricing to maximize the number of bookings across the platform not to maximize the profits for any individual listing, including yours.

After all, Airbnb is a business, and it's in business to make money by charging service fees from both the guests and hosts of all bookings made through the platform. But it doesn't charge both sides the equally.

Airbnb currently charges most hosts a flat 3 percent of the gross bookings and most guests about 13 percent of the subtotal (the nightly rate plus cleaning fee and any additional fees) in North America. In other parts of the world, the host and guest fees range from 3 to 5 percent and up to 20 percent, respectively.

Here's how that works out for a three-night booking for an average listing priced at $150/night:

>> $150 per night times three nights = $450 total nightly rate

>> 13 percent of $450 is $58.50 guest service fee

>> 3 percent of $450 is $13.50 host service fee

>> $58.50 divided by $13.50 = 4.33

In June of 2019, Airbnb began testing a host-only fee model in select markets in Asia, Africa, Europe, and the Middle East to better compete with peers who don't charge any guest fees on reservations. Although a future Airbnb may be without guest fees, guest fees are still being charged in most markets as of early 2023.

Airbnb makes more than four times more from guests than from hosts. In order to maximize their earnings from fees, Airbnb has incentive to get guests to book as many nights as possible by encouraging the listings to be priced as low as possible. And that's exactly what Airbnb's automated Smart Pricing does with its recommendations: it consistently recommends prices that are well below what the listings could often justify in their market.

Through our interactions with thousands of hosts from around the world, we've seen many hosts who tried but eventually stopped using Airbnb's Smart Pricing after they discovered that their listings were at times charging 40 percent lower than their optimal prices. That's a quite a bit of profits to leave on the table!

Aligning incentives with third-party dynamic pricing tool

Unlike Airbnb's Smart Pricing tool, third-party dynamic pricing tools don't earn a service fee from the guests. These tools only earn a fee as a small percentage of what their clients earn. The more that they help you earn, the more they earn. Their incentive is aligned with yours: maximize profits for both.

The typical fee for a third-party pricing provider is 1 percent of gross bookings. For example, for a two-night booking at $150 per night with total gross bookings at $300, the total fee for the booking is $3. The fee is often even lower for hosts with multiple listings.

Here are some advantages of using a third-party dynamic pricing tool to help you see why they're a smarter choice:

>> **Dynamic pricing for every availability:** Without an automated service, a host can't evaluate the large number of data points every single day and set the optimal pricing for every available night over the next 12 months. A dynamic pricing tool ensures low demand nights are filled with lower pricing and high demand nights are booked at highest profit nightly rates, often resulting in both higher occupancy and higher overall profits for hosts.

>> **Positive return on investment:** Although the top third-party pricing providers taunt that their clients can see revenue boosts of up to 40 percent (perhaps the host was coming from Airbnb's Smart Pricing), most hosts we talk to who have switched to third-party dynamic pricing typically saw revenue increases around 10 to 20 percent, which is still many times the payback on the nominal fee paid by the hosts.

>> **Market insight gain:** In addition to helping you set dynamic prices for your listing, the third-party pricing tools almost always include access to market statistics by letting you compare against similar listings in your market across the full calendar year. These insights can help you make manual adjustments in addition to the dynamic prices to account for factors not captured, such as major new events in the market.

>> **Cross-platform compatibility:** For hosts who want to list their property on other popular platforms in addition to Airbnb, most dynamic pricing providers provide full integration with other top platforms and hosting management and scheduling tools.

>> **Tools for other advanced tactics:** Besides options to fine-tune your pricing strategies to be more aggressive or conservative to suit your preferences, the top third-party dynamic pricing tools are constantly adding new feature sets to distinguish itself from competition. For example, Wheelhouse recently added features that allowed hosts to make fine manual adjustments for last minute discounts, weekend rate adjustments, seasonality adjustments, and dynamic minimum nights requirements.

Here are the disadvantages of using a third–party pricing tool:

>> **Initial setup required:** Although the process has become easier over the years, the early setup can be a steep learning curve for some hosts. We highly recommend you research your market to establish your baseline pricing and understand any seasonality before setting up third-party dynamic pricing.

>> **Ongoing cost:** The fee is just 1 percent, but 1 percent of every booking made through the booking tool can still add up. However, even a modest gain more than makes up for it. By doing your own research and setting your own prices manually for several months and then signing up and for a third-party dynamic pricing provider, you can quickly see just how much a boost your listing will get.

>> **Better functionality in major cities:** The pricing tool's recommendations are only as good as the data the provider gets to feed into its pricing recommendation engines. For listings that are well outside the popular markets in and around the major metros, the pricing recommendations can be less reliable. If you're in a less-populated area, establishing your own pricing first as a basis for comparison is vital.

>> **24-hours updates:** Although the third-party pricing tool is far better than the weekly, monthly, or never updates from hosts manually managing pricing, it still isn't frequent enough as supply and demand for certain travel dates can change significantly within 24 hours. Some providers allow manual update requests, but until tools start providing real time updates, these tools have yet to reach their full potential.

Figure 8–3 shows a hypothetical Airbnb listing that averages 15 nights booked per month at an average nightly rate of $150 per night. Thus, it's average monthly booking revenue, before any other fees collected, is $2,250. If this host signed up for a dynamic pricing provider, the host's revenue increases can range between 0 and 40 percent.

Revenue Increase	New Revenue	1% Fee	Net Gain
0%	$ 2,250.00	$ 22.50	$ (22.50)
5%	$ 2,362.50	$ 23.63	$ 88.88
10%	$ 2,475.00	$ 24.75	$ 200.25
15%	$ 2,587.50	$ 25.88	$ 311.63
20%	$ 2,700.00	$ 27.00	$ 423.00
25%	$ 2,812.50	$ 28.13	$ 534.38
30%	$ 2,925.00	$ 29.25	$ 645.75
35%	$ 3,037.50	$ 30.38	$ 757.13
40%	$ 3,150.00	$ 31.50	$ 868.50

FIGURE 8-3: Example of how a third-party pricing tool can benefit a listing.

© John Wiley & Sons, Inc.

As you can see from the figure, if this host sees a revenue increase between 10 to 20 percent, which is common among hosts that switch to third-party dynamic pricing, the hosts can expect to gain $200 to $400 per month in additional revenue. If the listing was severely underpriced due to Smart Pricing and saw a 40 percent increase, the host would have nearly $900 more per month in revenue!

ON THE WEB

For a current list of recommended third-party pricing providers, go to www.learnbnb.com/airbnbfordummies.

Setting Other Types of Fees

As an Airbnb host, you need to be aware of many other fees that you can set and charge guests. Get them right, and you could have more consistent bookings and profits. Get them wrong, and you could undo all the work you've put into your listing and pricing.

Here we explore the important additional fees you can charge guests and how to go about setting the right strategy for each.

Setting the cleaning fee

The cleaning fee is often the biggest fee charged to guests and can range from nothing when hosts decide not to charge for cleaning to several hundred dollars for larger and higher end listings.

When starting out, price at or slightly below the median rate of your competitors. As your listing gains momentum and as you build a competitive advantage versus your competition, you can adjust your cleaning fees higher.

During the ramping-up period, when you want to price very competitively, set your cleaning rate to match the rate of the lowest rates charged by any of your competition. As you ramp up your nightly rates, you can also adjust your cleaning fee.

These sections explore the different options you have as a host for pricing your cleaning fee.

Charge nothing

Few hosts choose this option because guests are generally used to paying a cleaning fee and the standard for cleaning an Airbnb listing is higher than ever before. This option removes the barrier to booking as the price that guests see is what they pay (outside of Airbnb's service fee of course), but not charging a cleaning fee means you lose out on profits.

The only hosts this option can potentially work for are

>> Hosts who operate small listings (rooms and small one-bedroom listings only) who enjoy doing the cleaning and turnaround themselves

>> Hosts whose listings allow them to charge a premium over their competition and thus pricing some portion of the cleaning fee into their nightly rate

Charge in line with competition

For most hosts, this option is the recommended starting point. It allows you to pass most if not all the cleaning cost to your guests while still presenting a cleaning fee that is in line with market rates. If you want to go with this option, identify a dozen of the most comparable competitive listings in your market and charge slightly less than the median fee.

Charging in line with your competition creates no additional barriers versus competition. However, a cleaning fee may not always cover your cost, especially if you're hiring outside cleaners. Some listings with competitive amenities and great reviews could pass that difference onto slightly higher nightly rates.

Charge for average length of stay

For many markets, the average booking is around three to four nights. Price your cleaning fee such that guests who are booking that most frequent length of stay in your market aren't turned off by the fee. This option is ideal for listings that tend to cater to longer stay bookings of five or more nights.

On one hand, this option discourages shorter stays because the cleaning fee often makes one- or two-night stays quite expensive. On the other hand, it may not always cover your cost to clean, especially if you're hiring outside cleaners.

Charge what your cost is to clean

You can also charge based on your desired minimum hourly rate times the number of hours it takes you to clean or the actual cleaning fee that you pay to hire an outside cleaner. This option works for established listings that have solid reviews in a strong market where their potentially higher cleaning fees aren't enough to significantly impact overall bookings.

Guests pay for the entire cost of cleaning for each booking. No out-of-pocket cost to you. However, using this option often prices you above your competition, especially for smaller listings, creating a barrier to booking.

Setting the extra person fee

Airbnb lets you set a nightly rate for your initial occupancy and then set a fee for additional guests above and beyond the initial figure you set. Of course, you can still cap at the maximum occupancy number your property can legally accommodate. For example, by setting a $15 extra person fee, a three-night reservation with an extra guest will collect an extra $45 in rent (3 nights times $15 extra per guest per night). Refer to Chapter 9 for a discussion on determining your maximum occupancy.

Although many hotel chains charge for an extra person fee, few enforce this rule at check-in. Most hotel travelers aren't even aware of this fee. For Airbnb travelers, even more so aren't aware.

Airbnb used to ask potential guests for their number of guests at the end of the search, which led to surprises when the guests saw the extra person fees added. However, Airbnb now asks potential guests to input their number of guests at the start of their search, so the extra person fees are added to the totals of the search results, thus eliminating that unpleasant surprise at check-out.

Charging an extra person fee: Why to do so

Here are some reasons you may want to include the extra person fee in your listing:

>> **Extra body means extra costs.** Having an additional guest often means higher utility costs, higher consumption of snacks and toiletries, more mess,

and more wear and tear of furniture and appliances. The fee can help offset those extra costs.

>> **You get extra profit.** With Airbnb making it easier than ever to charge for extra person fees, it could mean extra profits left on the table if you don't charge that fee. For an average listing available year-round, that could mean $500 to $1000 in additional annual profits.

Charging an extra person fee: Why not to do so

You may not want to add an extra person fee for these reasons:

>> **Guests still see the charge before booking.** Although the extra person fee is less of a surprise now than before, guests still see the extra person charge as an added fee at check-out. In very competitive markets, even little barrier for booking can mean fewer bookings and thus less profits.

>> **Average occupancy is max occupancy.** If the average occupancy of your bookings for your listing is the maximum occupancy for your property, then you can't add an extra guest fee because you have no physical space to accommodate the extra guest.

Calculating the extra person fee

You want to make sure your extra person fee isn't on the high side compared to your competition. Identify a dozen of the most comparable competitive listings in your market and charge slightly less than the median fee. If half of your competition isn't charging a fee at all, you shouldn't charge a fee.

If you don't have enough comparable listings to establish a starting point, start low with the following recommendations and then adjust by $5 increments as needed:

>> **Listings under $150 per night:** Start at $10.

>> **Listings between $150 per night and $300 per night:** Start at $15.

>> **Listings over $300 per night:** Start at $20.

TIP

During the ramping-up period, don't charge this fee to minimize barriers to booking. As your listing stabilizes and reaches your baseline pricing, then add the extra person fee.

Setting the security deposit

Whether intentional or not, valuables can disappear from your listing and guests can inadvertently damage your belongings. A travel companion could decide to take the coffee maker. A child may spill food and drink on the couch or mattress, requiring costly cleaning or replacement.

REMEMBER

To protect hosts and to discourage theft and careless behavior from guests, Airbnb lets hosts set a security deposit amount. Unlike traditional security deposits, it's more of a credit hold than an actual deposit of cash or credit. Guests aren't charged the value of the fee at booking.

Essentially, guests agree to place a hold on their credit card, in the amount of the security deposit, until the hold is released. In most cases, hosts never make a claim, and the hold is released 14 days after the guest checks out.

Charging the security deposit: Why it's a good idea

Here are a couple reasons why charging a security deposit is a wise idea:

>> **Most hosts require security deposits.** Guests are used to this and charging one won't create a barrier to booking unless the amount is glaringly outrageous. According to iGMS, a leading vacation rental software, 59 percent of Airbnb listings have a security deposit.

>> **It offers quick added protection.** Although the odds of you making a claim against the security deposit is extremely low, more than likely you'll need to do so at one point. Accidents happen. And if you host long enough, you'll eventually encounter a guest from hell. And for most incidents where the security deposit is enough, it's also the quickest way to get payment compared to making insurance claims or getting mediation through Airbnb support.

Calculating the security deposit

Just as with other fees, you want to set your security deposit fee in a way that doesn't cause a potential guest to pause before they are about to book with you.

TIP

We suggest you identify a dozen of the most comparable listings in your market and note the security deposit levels they set. Don't be the highest. Start with at most the median rate. If you don't have enough comparable listings to base your security deposit level on, use the 25 percent rule. Keep your security deposit at no more than 25 percent of your average total booking. For example, if the average booking for your listing is three evenings at $150, then 25 percent of $450 is $112.50.

For most listings, the ideal level is generally between $100 to $600 per booking, where the $600 levels are typically reserved for listings with average bookings well over $2,000.

Keep these two other considerations in mind:

>> **Set the fee lower than your average booking value.** For example, if your listing is a $150 per night listing and your average stay is three nights, then you'd want to keep your security deposit below $450. A $450 security deposit for a large listing with an average booking value of $2,500 is much more palatable than the same $450 fee for a $450 booking.

>> **Move unnecessary valuables.** If you have very expensive items, such as art or custom furniture that guests aren't likely to appreciate but may damage instead, remove those items from your property. Having fewer valuables that require costly cleaning, repairs, or replacement means you can get away with a lower security deposit fee.

REMEMBER

Yes, any incident that requires a claim against the security deposit likely will be time consuming and annoying. But incidents that require a claim are rare. So, don't let your fear of rare incidents influence your decisions that impact your listing's appeal to potential guests. The peace of mind that comes with setting a high security deposit can lead to costly missed bookings. For some hosts, getting additional insurance coverage is an option. Check out Chapter 5 for more on insurance.

Lowering the barrier to booking

When deciding on appropriate fees, your goal is not necessarily to maximize additional revenue, but to lower the barrier to booking as much as possible. Sometimes, asking for too high of fees can backfire and lead potential guests to book with your competitors instead.

Currently, Airbnb already has a challenge with respect to short guest stays where the total cost after adding fees is often more than double that of the advertised nightly rate. Figure 8-4 highlights what booking a one-night stay on Airbnb often looks like for guests — irritating!

Although this mockup example is extreme because the fees are only spread across one night, we can't overstate the impact of the fees on guests during the checkout process. Before making the final reservation, guests decide based on looking at the final cost per night after adding in all the additional fees.

$99 per night	
★ 4.81 (127 reviews)	
Dates	
04/15/2023 ⟶	04/15/2023
Guests	
1 guest	⌄
$99 x 1 night	$99
Cleaning fee ⓘ	$100
Service fee ⓘ	$26
Occupancy taxes and fees ⓘ	$23
Total	**$248**

Reserve

You won't be charged yet

FIGURE 8-4:
The fees can
add up.

The bigger the gap between the final price and the subtotal from just the nightly rates, the less likely the guest will end up booking. In setting your fees, you want to make sure your fees are no more than the middle ground of your competition.

Chapter **9**

Increasing Your Profit Potential

After the initial ramp-up period, your Airbnb listing's performance will stabilize — its bookings revenue and profits begin to fall into a predictable range. However, if you don't make deliberate changes to your listing or to how you host, your Airbnb listing's performance will stay about the same going forward.

Although it would be obvious that your listing has room for improvement if it were struggling to attract guests and achieve profitability, spotting opportunities when your listing is already getting consistent bookings and profitable can be difficult. You might leave money on the table and not even know it.

Ask any two randomly selected profitable Airbnb hosts on how they best can increase their Airbnb profits, and you almost always get different answers. Although you can try dozens of strategies, they all fall into two basic categories. That's right, you can only increase profits in one of two ways:

» **Reduce operating costs:** If you can spend less to operate your Airbnb listing, even if your revenue remains the same, you can increase your profits.

» **Increase revenue:** If you generate more revenue from your Airbnb listing disproportionately more than the increase in your operating costs, you can increase your profits.

Even though both seem apparent and easy to understand, they can be quite difficult to implement. Doing so requires thoughtfulness to determine what costs to cut and not to cut as well as which strategies are most likely to grow your revenue and increase your profits. Not to worry. This chapter helps you with these two and examines how to implement them with different tactics. Furthermore, this chapter explains how you can determine if your listing is performing to its full potential.

Leaving Money on the Table

You can't determine the true performance of your Airbnb listing by looking at it in isolation. You can only judge the performance your Airbnb listing by comparing it to those of its direct competitors, the similar-sized listings with the same amenities targeting the same travelers in the same market. If your listing is performing above that of its competition, then you're likely leaving little to no money on the table. If your listing is performing below that of its competition, then you're leaving money on the table. If you're somewhere in between, your listing may still have some opportunities to improve.

For example, imagine that you're hosting a cozy one-bedroom Airbnb listing in a good part of your city and you're able to pull in $2,500 per month in bookings. Would you be happy with that performance?

Considering that the average Airbnb host is achieving less than $500 per month in bookings, you may shout, "Yes!" But what if a dozen nearly identical listings in the same neighborhood (in other words, your direct competition) are averaging $5,000 per month in bookings? That would mean you're leaving $2,500 per month ($30,000 a year) in booking revenue on the table!

Here are the three different scenarios when comparing the performance of your listing to those of your competition:

>> **Overachieving:** Your listing is leaving little money on the table. In other words, your listing is achieving more booking revenue compared to your competition by being able to charge higher nightly rates, have higher occupancy, or both. This is only achievable with a great listing profile and excellent execution. Your goal here is to maintain this high performance.

>> **Comparable:** Your listing is leaving some money on the table. Your listing here is performing near the middle of the pack for booking revenue versus similar listings in your market. Your average night rates and occupancy are average so you're doing some details right but may have opportunities to earn more. Your goal here is to look for opportunities to make incremental improvements to your listing or operation.

>> **Underachieving:** Your listing is leaving the most money on the table. In other words, similar listings in the market all outperform you on nightly rates and occupancy rates. Your total booking revenue is at the bottom of the pack — potential guests aren't willing to pay market rates for your listing or willing to even book in the first place. Your listing and operations have significant opportunities for improvement. Your goal here is to focus on the basics: have a great listing for your property (Chapter 6) and deliver great guest experience consistently (Chapters 12-14).

For a more detailed discussion on how to research your competition and create benchmarks for your listing, refer to Chapter 4.

Picking the Low Hanging Fruits First

Before you attempt any cost-cutting or revenue-increasing strategies for your Airbnb listing, you must address the low hanging fruits first (in other words, the basic, easy-to-implement changes that have immediate potential to improve your Airbnb performance). The following two sections are the prerequisites for optimizing your Airbnb to increase profits. Not doing so is a waste of time and effort because that would be like trying to fine-tune a race car that doesn't have a proper engine or wheels.

Having a great listing profile

A strong listing profile includes having great photos, a great title, great descriptions, proper amenities, guest friendly policies, and optimized pricing. Without a great Airbnb profile, you limit your profit potential before you even interact with any guests. Refer to Chapters 5 and 6 on how to create the perfect Airbnb listing.

Delivering five-star guest experiences consistently

If you are getting bookings but aren't getting 5-star guest reviews for most of your guests (such as 75 percent or greater) and averaging an overall guest rating of 4.5 or better, you're limiting your long-term profit potential by diminishing the listings appeal to future guests. Address any and all reasonable guest experience shortcomings. Part 4 (Chapters 12–15) explains how to deliver a 5-star guest experience consistently.

For every complaint you receive publicly in a review, many more guests likely felt the same way but never mentioned it to you directly. Instead, they gave you a lower guest rating after they checked out. Take every complaint as though it represents the complaint of five or ten other guests.

For example, if you're receiving poor guest feedback, getting more guests before you address your guest experience shortcomings will hurt your long-term profitability more than it would help. You'll continue to receive even more poor guest reviews that will lead to lower search rankings, fewer future bookings, and thus lower future profits.

Reducing Operating Costs

Every single dollar you save on operating your Airbnb is a dollar you get to keep in your pockets. Therefore, we recommend that you first look at cost-cutting efforts before looking to increase profits through increasing your revenue, where you get to keep only a fraction of every extra dollar you earn in revenue.

The key to cost cutting is to reduce or eliminate costs that are unnecessary or unnecessarily high without compromising guest safety or the quality of their stay. When approached haphazardly, cost cutting could hurt your performance in the long run. Sometimes, you may even choose to accept lower short-term profits by spending more on worthwhile amenities to maximize the long-term profits of your Airbnb listing.

In the sections that follow, you discover the many cost-cutting opportunities available to Airbnb hosts, including those where you may not want to cut costs at all.

Recognizing where to take special care when cutting cost

Not all cost-cutting opportunities are created equal. Cut costs in the wrong areas and you could have bigger and costlier headaches. Here are some categories you must take extra care before cutting costs:

>> **Safety related:** For any operating costs that have safety implications, only cut costs if you can find suitable alternatives that deliver the same results. For example, you can hire another company to service your HVAC system at a

lower cost, but you shouldn't stop the maintenance entirely just to save on costs. Poorly maintained HVAC equipment could lead to higher energy costs as it loses efficiency and worse lead to dangerous gas leaks or even fires.

» **Airbnb essentials:** With the basics, such as toilet paper, soap (for hands and body), shampoo, towels, linens, and pillows, you must always have enough for your guests for the length of their stay. They don't need to be expensive or come from recognized brands. When in doubt about quantity, leave more. Refer to the nearby sidebar for a host's cost cutting gone bad.

» **High-touch items:** For high-touch items, such as towels, pillows, and bedsheets, prioritize comfort over costs. A slightly higher replacement cost is well worth it if you end up receiving positive receives from guests. Guests often rave about "soft thick towels" or the "comfy beds" in their happy reviews. High-touch, comfort items are worth spending a little more for in the short term for consistently happy guests over the long run.

» **Wi-Fi speed:** With 5G mobile phones starting to become available with connection speeds faster than most broadband Internet speeds in homes, consumer expectations for Wi-Fi speeds will only increase. Slow Wi-Fi alone can turn an otherwise 5-star guest stay into a 1-star review. Wi-Fi is that important. Get the fastest internet connection available to your property and purchases the fastest, multiband Wi-Fi router you can afford.

PENNY-WISE, POUND-FOOLISH HOST

James booked a five-night stay at a seven-bedroom villa with four bathrooms in downtown Miami for 13 guests at a total booking cost of $2,444 ($489/night). At first, the property seemed properly stocked with all essentials along with some extras (it had an expresso machine!). But on the second evening, James and his family realized that all the bathroom toilets only had starter toilet rolls. When they couldn't find the extra toilet rolls anywhere, James reached out to the host for help. To his surprise and immediate irritation, the host told him that the house only stocked the toilets with starter rolls, and if James and his family needed more, they would have to get their own.

A few extra rolls of toilet paper would have been nominal cost for the host to provide, yet in trying to save a small amount, the host ended up losing far more from the public one-star guest rating that James and his understandably irritated family left for the host.

If saving a few dollars is a rounding error on the total booking cost and has the potential to annoy your guests, reconsider what you're about to do. Always prioritize long-term profits over short-term gains.

Strategizing your cuts

Examine your cost-cutting opportunities by categories and specific steps you can take with each group. To help you lower your operating costs and increase profits right away, we recommend that you reduce the following:

>> **Cleaning fees:** If you're hiring someone else to clean for you, be sure to shop around because the cleaning rates can vary. Expensive doesn't mean better. Do trials with at least three providers and then select the lowest cost cleaner that meets your high cleaning standards. Refer to Chapter 10 for a detailed discussion on all things cleaning, including how best to hire cleaners.

>> **Laundry costs:** If you reduce the frequency of loads, you can save money on utilities and make easier turnarounds for you, your co-host, or your property manager. You can reduce the frequency of laundry loads by

- Investing in large capacity washer and dryers

- Having enough extra sets of all linens, sheets, blankets, and towels for two average length guest stays

Doing so allows you to batch your laundry sessions into fewer runs and give you more flexibility to not have to run and wait for finished laundry to compete your turnaround.

>> **Entertainment fees:** Although guests expect you to have at least one HDTV in your unit, most guests today don't expect you to provide cable or satellite television options that often cost $50 to $100 per month. Lower that cost significantly by replacing with a streaming service, such as Netflix, Hulu, or Amazon Prime, all of which have basic plans that start under $10 per month. If you don't have a smart TV, you need to purchase a streaming device, such as an Amazon TV Stick or a Roku for each TV.

>> **Utility costs:** Airbnb guests on vacation don't think about their energy use, which can lead to high utility costs from always-on lights, heating, or air conditioning. Use friendly reminders, install water-saving toilets and shower heads, and when replacing appliances, do so with energy-efficient ones. Think long term.

>> **Consumable costs:** From essentials, namely toilet paper and soap to coffee, snacks, and drinks, always order in bulk. Guests want what works and care little about the brand or how expensive they are. For drinks and snacks, put enough out assuming each guest will have one drink and two tiny snacks per day and leave enough for only two to three days, nothing more. Store more out of view for longer guest stays. Leaving 20 granola bars for two guests staying two nights is unnecessary and an invitation for guests to take them. *Tip:* When buying the drinks and snacks, buy in bulk or buy items on sale.

- >> **Welcome gift costs:** Do overdo it. Match the value of your gift to the overall value the booking. Spend up to 3 percent of the total booking value, but almost never exceed $50 per stay on the total value of the welcome gift. To read more about welcome gifts, refer to Chapter 12.

- >> **Property management fees:** Shop around, get multiple bids, check references, and base the management fee on actual *collected* rents after accounting for vacancies. For larger, higher-priced Airbnb listings, placing an upper limit on fees on top of a lower percentage fee to begin with is not uncommon. Chapter 10 discusses best practices for hiring property managers for your Airbnb listing.

- >> **Repair and maintenance costs:** Figure out how to make basic repairs in and around your property (YouTube videos are a great start) and reserve the big repair items that you can't do on your own for the professionals. Doing it on your own can save hundreds of dollars a year.

- >> **Tax liability:** You may deduct part of or all your expenses to reduce your tax liability. If you make significant improvements to the property through renovations, new fixtures, or appliances, you may be able to depreciate these capital improvements to lower your overall tax liability further. In addition, you may be able to have your property reclassified from residential into a locally taxed advantaged classification.

WARNING

Taxes can get very complicated and differ from municipality, state, and even county, so you should consult with a local tax expert familiar with the local tax codes to see what is best for your situation. Check out Chapter 17 for more information about Airbnb taxes.

Spending Smart: Best Purchases That You Can Make Now for Profits Later

Even though you want to minimize unnecessary costs, consider these decisions over the entire life of your Airbnb listing, not just in the short haul. Sometimes to cut costs and increase profits in the long run you need to spend more in the short term.

These smart purchases might increase booking revenue, free up your time, reduce operating costs, minimize big unplanned expenses, or improve overall guest experience, all of which help to increase profits. We asked hosts from around the world what their best and most worthwhile Airbnb purchases were. Feel free to incorporate them into your Airbnb budget:

>> Purchases that directly increase revenue potential:

- Increasing your listings maximum occupancy by replacing a normal couch with a sleeper sofa bed could permanently increase earning potential. Refer to the later section, "Increasing Occupancy Capacity" for more information.

- Using automated dynamic pricing from providers, such as Wheelhouse (refer to Chapter 8 for pricing) can ensure optimal pricing throughout the calendar to maxing booking revenue.

>> Purchases that free up your time and minimize headaches:

- Utilizing smart locks, keypad locks, or lockboxes to enable remote check-ins and check-outs can save time for both you and your guests.

- Using messaging and calendar automation tools, such as SmartBNB to cut down as much as 90 percent of guest inquiries. Refer to Chapter 10 for a detailed discussion on Airbnb automation.

- Purchasing items to simplify cleaning and turnover can make your life easier. For example, placing a rug outside every entrance or a shoe rack inside every entrance reduces dirt getting into the property. Wrinkle-free bedsheets can eliminate ironing or steaming without sacrificing quality.

>> Purchases that win over guests:

- Spending a bit more for quality high-touch items (sheets, pillows, and towels), comfortable mattresses (mattress toppers can mask subpar mattresses), and even an outdoor storage locker can give you an edge over other listings.

- Buying items or amenities that create a unique guest experience for your listing can make your guests leave a glowing review — for example, providing access to an outdoor firepit to grill fresh oysters for an Airbnb listing near a popular fishing wharf known for oysters.

>> Purchases to reduce energy bills:

- Adding solar panels to your property allows you to be more environmentally friendly and save on your heating and cooling bills.

- Replacing old energy-hungry appliances with new energy-efficient ones can help you save on utility bills for years.

- Purchasing a large capacity washer and dryer can significantly reduce both water and electricity while also reducing the time it takes to do laundry by reducing the number wash and dry cycles needed.

- Similarly, a large capacity dishwasher can reduce the cycles needed to clean all dishes, making for a more efficient turnover.

- Using smart HVAC controls to automatically run the heating and air conditioning can help you save on energy costs. According to Nest, makers of a popular smart thermostat, their customers save on average 10 to 12 percent on heating and 15 percent on cooling. In hot or cold areas, this can equate to over $100 a year in savings.

>> **Purchases to prevent big unplanned costs:**

- Adding protective covers for mattresses and furniture protect against spills, accidents, and bedbugs that require costly replacements or downtime for decontamination.

- Removing and storing all expensive or irreplaceable art and personal items can prevent accidents from happening. Unless you're operating an ultra-luxury listing commanding the highest premiums on Airbnb, having extremely expensive items is a recipe for disaster. Store your $10,000 painting somewhere safe.

- Having luggage stands to help minimize and isolate bedbugs from spreading by preventing the bugs from hitching a ride onto guest luggage. Although this is only helpful for the guests and their next Airbnb host, consider this purchase to "pay it forward" with your fellow Airbnb hosts.

MATCHING A HOTEL'S AMENITIES

From the Airbnb's humble beginnings when founders Brian Chesky, Joe Gebbia, and Nathan Blecharczyk laid three cheap air mattresses on their living room floor to rent to strangers to help pay rent, to the many ultra-luxurious offerings on the platform today that would put many 5-star hotel offerings to shame, guest experiences have come a long way on Airbnb.

Back then, guests expected little more than something to sleep on. Over the years, as more hosts listed more properties, they collectively forced each other to raise the bar as they competed for the bookings. Now, guest expectations for an Airbnb listing often match their expectations for a comparable hotel room.

When you're unsure of what amenities you should invest in for your listing, just match the offerings of a comparable hotel room. If your Airbnb guests were to stay at a hotel instead, would they more likely stay at a 3-star, 4-star, or 5-star hotel? If your guests would likely stay at 3-star hotels, then match or exceed the amenities offered at the best 3-star hotel rooms.

Increasing Booking Revenue

After you start to optimize your costs, you can quickly discover a limit to how much you can cut. Your next best option to boost profits is to increase your booking revenue for your Airbnb listing. You can do that by increasing your occupancy rate, your average nightly rate, listing availability, or all the above. The following sections examine each in greater detail.

Boosting occupancy rate

You can boost revenue by increasing the number of days your listing is booked versus the number of days that your listing is available for booking. For example, if your listing is available 365 days a year, then increasing the number of days booked from say 182 days booked to 274 days booked would roughly increase your occupancy rate from about 50 to 75 percent. All things the same, boosting your occupancy rate increases your booking revenue.

Raising average nightly rate (ANR)

You can also boost revenue by increasing the average price of each night booked. For example, if your listing current books 200 days out of the year at an average nightly rate of $100 per night, then the gross booking revenue are 200 days booked times $100 per night equals $20,000. However, if you could increase your average nightly rate to $120 per night, even without increasing the number of days booked, your gross booking revenue would now become 200 days booked times $120 per night for $24,000. Raising your ANR will increase your booking revenue.

Expanding listing availability

You can increase revenue by having your listing available for booking for more days out of the year if it's only available for a fraction of the calendar year. For example, if your listing is only available for booking during the summer months from June to August, then making it available for booking from September through November would double the number of days available for booking. Doing so may not double revenues or profits, more than likely it'll mean more bookings. Expanding your listing availability increases your booking revenue.

Doing all three: Yes or no?

Couldn't you just maximize your revenue potential by maximizing all three factors (your occupancy rate, your average nightly rate, and listing availability)? Not so fast. Just because you want to increase each of these factors doesn't mean you can just magically make that happen.

You may find that your local city regulations limit the number of days you can make your listing available for rent on a short-term basis and thus choose to only host during the busiest parts of the year to maximize earnings. In addition, you often must make a tradeoff between increasing your occupancy rate or your average nightly rate the two metrics an inversely correlated — when one goes up, the other goes down.

That's because Airbnb travelers are price sensitive. All things equal, an increase in price for a listing reduces the demand for the listing because some potential guests can become priced out and look to cheaper alternatives.

Figure 9-1 illustrates the inverse relationship between the occupancy rate and the average nightly rate. As you can see, the point at which profits are maximized is when neither the occupancy rate nor the average nightly rate is at their maximum values. The implication here is that these two metrics are inversely correlated — go higher on one and the other will fall. For either metrics, going to too high may lead to lower profits.

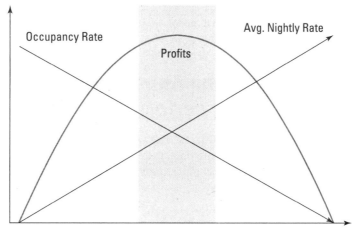

FIGURE 9-1:
The relationship between occupancy rate and average nightly rate.

© John Wiley & Sons, Inc.

The optimal point for your Airbnb listing depends on how it's positioned relative to its competition and the underlying Airbnb demand in the market. If local Airbnb demand is low and your listing is inferior to its competition, the optimal occupancy and average nightly rates will settle below the average rates in your market. If local Airbnb demand is high and your listing is superior to its competition, the optimal occupancy and average nightly rates will be higher.

To understand your listing's performance and how it compares to that of its competition, you must obtain the following information:

>> **The average occupancy rate for similar listings in your market:** Preferably over the prior 12-month period by month.

>> **The average nightly rate for similar listings in your market:** Preferably over the prior 12-month period by month.

>> **The stabilized occupancy rate and average nightly rate for your listing:** This calculation must be at least 3 months after your ramp-up pricing period. But for best results, having a full 12 months of stabilized data allows you to know with certainty how your listing is performing in your market versus competition.

We recommend getting that data from a third-party market data provider, such as MashVisor, AirDNA, or AllTheRooms rather than attempting to gather the numbers on your own. At best, the data is incomplete and quickly outdated. At worst, you have inaccurate information from which to base your decisions.

After you have that data, you can compare your listing's performance on occupancy rate and average nightly rate versus your market averages. If you don't have monthly data, you can just use the full year figures. Having monthly data lets you make this comparison on a month-to-month basis, allowing you to spot potential opportunities during different parts of the season.

Considering the four scenarios of Airbnb listing performance

What you can discover with the data is that your listing's performance versus its direct competition falls into one of these four scenarios (as shown in Figure 9-2) in terms of how your occupancy rate and average nightly rate compares to the market optimal point.

The following sections look at these four scenarios and how your listing's occupancy rate and average nightly rate compare to those of its competition in the market. In addition, you find out how to adjust your pricing accordingly if you find that your listing falls into either of the two of the sneaky scenarios.

Clearly underachieving listings

The clearly underachieving listings are in the lower-left corner that have both their occupancy rates and their average nightly rates lower than what their market suggests they should be able to achieve. When a listing is underachieving in its market versus competition, it almost always has low hanging fruit.

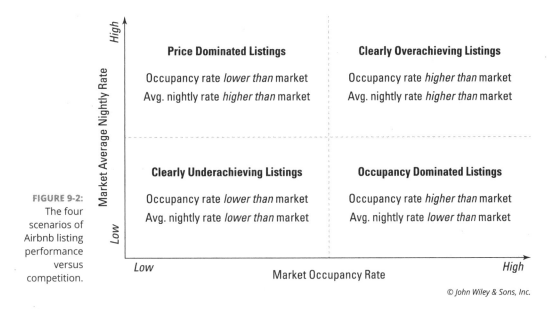

The diagram shows a four-quadrant chart with the y-axis labeled "Market Average Nightly Rate" (from Low to High) and the x-axis labeled "Market Occupancy Rate" (from Low to High).

Top-left quadrant: **Price Dominated Listings** — Occupancy rate *lower than* market; Avg. nightly rate *higher than* market

Top-right quadrant: **Clearly Overachieving Listings** — Occupancy rate *higher than* market; Avg. nightly rate *higher than* market

Bottom-left quadrant: **Clearly Underachieving Listings** — Occupancy rate *lower than* market; Avg. nightly rate *lower than* market

Bottom-right quadrant: **Occupancy Dominated Listings** — Occupancy rate *higher than* market; Avg. nightly rate *lower than* market

FIGURE 9-2: The four scenarios of Airbnb listing performance versus competition.

These listings often have poorly executed and incomplete listing profiles, with poor quality photos, inadequate or difficult-to-read descriptions, poor pricing, and subpar amenities. And their hosts aren't delivering consistently great guest experiences with one too many low star guest reviews on the profile. These hosts likely began hosting before they, their property, or their listing profile were ready for guests. These listings are leaving the most money on the table and have the most opportunity to increase profits.

TIP

If you've operated your listing for more than six months and your performance falls into this category, review all the essential recommendations from Chapters 4–7. Attempting any profit maximizing strategies when your listing is unable to charge a good rate or to attract enough guests to begin with is a waste of effort.

Clearly overachieving listings

The clearly overachieving listings in the opposite quadrant command both above-market occupancy rates and above-market average nightly rates. Not only are these listings booking more nights, their guests are willing to pay a premium to book those listings. These listings almost always have professionally executed listing profiles with perfect photos, catchy titles, detailed and easy-to-read descriptions, attractive amenities, and great guest reviews.

These listings have no opportunities for low hanging fruit. The hosts for these listings were ready from day one and have consistently delivered 5-star guest experiences and received 5-star guest reviews. These listings are leaving little to no money on the table.

TIP

To increase profits, hosts for these listings must think creatively outside of direct bookings to increase their revenue and profits.

Price-dominated listings

Inexperienced hosts often fixate on an arbitrary minimum nightly rate for their listing that is well above the market average nightly rates, leading them to over-price their listings. These hosts may say to themselves, "I'd rather have my listing sit empty than to list it for lower than [insert arbitrary daily rate not based in reality]."

The result is that they will enjoy an arbitrarily high average nightly rate but suffer a much lower occupancy rate as potential guests opt for more reasonably priced alternatives in the same market. Hosts with these listings could end up leaving thousands in profits on the table by having their listing sit empty when they could easily fill it with guests at lower rates.

Figure 9-3 looks at a hypothetical price-dominated one-bedroom listing in down-town Los Angeles and how much money it's leaving on the table by underachieving on occupancy due to its fixation on a high nightly rate.

	Market (Other 1-bedroom listings)	Price Dominated Listing	Vs. Market
Occupancy	85%	50%	35% Lower
Avg Nightly Rate	$125	$175	$50 Higher
Monthly Booking Revenue	$3,188	$2,625	17.7% Lower $563 Lower

FIGURE 9-3: The cost of a price-dominated listing.

By overpricing the listing and thus achieving a much lower occupancy rate, the host left more than $500 of money on the table each month.

TIP

If you find yourself in this quadrant, order a market report from a company, such as AirDNA (see Chapter 4) and reset your pricing expectations for your listing. Choose a price for your listing that the market demand will accept, not just what feels good to ask for.

Occupancy-dominated listings

The final quadrant is the other sneaky scenario where the Airbnb listings have much higher occupancy rates than their competitive listings in the market, often in the 90 to 100 percent range. These listings are booked almost every day. However, most can only do so by undercharging guests.

This scenario is arguably the most problematic and the most difficult to diagnose because the high occupancy rates of these listings can give the hosts a false sense of performance.

"I'm completely booked up. I must be doing great!"

And if the listings are also profitable, the hosts may never have the impetus to find out how much money they are leaving on the table. Hosts of profitable and fully occupied listings often never realize that they're leaving money on the table.

Figure 9-4 examines a hypothetical occupancy-dominated one-bedroom listing in downtown Los Angeles and how much money it's leaving on the table by listing at below-market nightly rates to achieve above-market occupancy rates.

	Market (Other 1-bedroom listings)	Occupancy Dominated Listing	Vs. Market
Occupancy	85%	100%	15% Higher
Avg Nightly Rate	$125	$90	$35 Lower
Monthly Booking Revenue	$3,188	$2,700	15.3% Lower $488 Lower

FIGURE 9-4: The cost of an occupancy-dominated listing.

Notice that the high occupancy rate comes at the expense of a lower average nightly rate. By undercharging the market to achieve a perfect occupancy rate, this host is leaving $488 on the table every month!

REMEMBER

Another incentive, besides increased profits, for raising prices when your occupancy rate is well-above market rates, is that you can achieve the same profits with fewer bookings.

If, for example, you can make the same profits but go down from eight bookings to six bookings per month, those two fewer bookings mean two fewer cleanings, check-ins, and check-outs. Especially if you're doing the turnovers, achieving the same revenue with fewer bookings can free up hours of your time without lowering your profits. Getting the same profit with less effort is always a good deal.

TIP

If you find yourself in this scenario, you need to adjust your pricing to increase your profits. Remember that the point at which you maximize your profits won't be at full occupancy. For high demand markets in or near urban cores, the ideal occupancy rate typically falls in the 70 to 90 percent range. In suburban or rural markets, it will be lower, and the range is wide.

But the only way to know for certain is to obtain a market report from a third-party data provider to compare your listing's performance to those of its most direct competition. Refer to Chapter 3 for more on market reports.

TIP

When you're ready to adjust your pricing, we recommend increasing your price up 5 percent every four weeks until you start to see your profits start to drop again. For example, if you're at 100 percent occupancy charging $100 per night when the market is at 80 percent charging $150 per night, raise your prices by $5 until your occupancy falls to 80 percent.

Charging a premium over competition

Unless your listing has a rare offering that can justify a market premium over its competition, start at similar rates to those of the most similar listings in your market. You can justify charging a premium with these following reasons:

>> Your listing is closer to desirable attractions (for instance, a minute walk to the beach).

>> Your listing has rare and appealing amenities (such as indoor movie theater or an arcade).

>> Your listing is a premium property with premium amenities catering to high-end travelers (such as a luxury condo in an exclusive luxury high rise).

TIP

If your listing is charging well above the average market rates and you're concerned about making a drastic price reduction, you can start slow. Adjust your pricing down 5 percent at a time every four weeks until your occupancy rate rises and you're happy with the improved profits.

For example, if you were charging $200 per night 50 percent occupancy when the market average is $150 per night at 80 percent occupancy, then start by reducing your price by $10 every four weeks until profits drop again.

During these price adjustments, your profit will go up as your occupancy rate moves toward the market rate. Stop the pricing adjustments or reverse the most recent change should you find that profits fell with the most recent price change. For example, if the change from $160 per night down to $150 per night didn't improve occupancy or profits, revert to $160 per night and then monitor going forward.

Using dynamic pricing to take out the guesswork

The previous pricing adjustment recommendations for the two sneaky scenarios assume you're setting your pricing manually. However, as we discuss in Chapter 8, we highly recommend that all hosts go with a third-party dynamic pricing provider to automatically set the proper pricing for their listing.

Only with a dynamic pricing tool that automatically adjusts the pricing of your listing in real time to account changes in the supply and demand of competitive spaces, including hotels, and their changing daily rates, can you truly maximize for your listing. It is impossible to do this manually.

Maximizing Overall Revenue Potential

After you optimize your pricing and occupancy for your listing in its current condition, you can do little to improve your direct booking revenue unless you change the offering for your listing or implement creative strategies to generate non-booking revenue for your listing. With both strategies, your aim is to maximize the overall revenue potential for your listing.

Improving your offering to increase revenue potential

If all you needed to do to get a higher nightly rate for your listing was to increase your pricing, then all hosts would do that and average nightly rates would soar on Airbnb. But just because you want to charge a higher rate doesn't mean the market will accept it.

To command a higher price than what the market will accept for your listing, you need to have good reasons to justify that premium you seek to charge. The following are common strategies used by hosts to improve their listing's offering:

>> **Increase maximum capacity.** If guests can squeeze an extra travel companion or two into your listing, they're willing to pay more.

- For per night listings less than $250, assume $5 to $10 more per night per extra person.

- For per night listings between $250 to $500, assume $10 to $25 more per night per extra person.

- For per night listings of $500 and more, assume $25 to $50 more per night per extra person.

>> **Make your listing kid and family friendly.** Guests who travel with young children pay a premium for listings that have extra amenities that cater to families with children.

>> **Create a pet-friendly listing.** Most listings prohibit pets outright, so the few listings that allow pets might see more bookings, and thus more profits, by appealing to pet-loving travelers who have a tough time finding accommodating listings for their furry travel companions.

>> **Make your listing business friendly.** Business travelers have very specific needs and are often traveling on an employer's tab so they're often willing to pay a premium for business-centric amenities that make their work travel less hectic.

>> **Cater to special traveler needs.** For example, consider adding accessible ramps, bathrooms, slip safeguards, rails, and so on to cater to mobility-challenged guests who come from afar to visit a nearby popular hospital. Guests pay a premium for the listings that cater to their specific needs best.

TIP

Not every market has the same mix of guest segments. Some markets draw only large family groups, whereas other markets draw a large segment of business travelers. Ask yourself this question: "What are the main reasons for travelers coming to my area?" The answers may provide insight into which guest segments you should target in your market. Refer to Chapter 12 on how to cater to the many types of travelers.

Increasing occupancy capacity

One of the easiest and most neglected ways to boost profits is to increase the occupancy capacity for your listing. A one-bedroom listing that can sleep four guests can charge more than a one-bedroom listing that sleeps only two guests, even if it means a cozier stay for guests.

Some price-conscious small groups traveling together would rather squeeze into a tighter space to save money than pay more for a larger listing or book multiple listings, creating a win-win where those travelers save money and the hosts make more money.

REMEMBER

Cozy works, but creating an unsafe situation with extra beds blocking fire exits won't. Follow these recommendations for increasing occupancy capacity without overdoing it:

» **Private room listings:** We recommend adding one to total additional occupancy by changing twin beds into full or queen beds.

» **Studio listings:** We recommend adding one to total additional occupancy. If you have room for a regular couch anywhere, you have room to increase your capacity by at least one by replacing it with a futon or sleeper sofa that sleeps two.

» **One-bedroom listings.** We recommend adding one to two to total additional occupancy. In addition to adding a couch upgrade, if additional open floor space (50 sq. feet or 4.6 sq. meters minimum) is available, you may provide a full-sized air mattress as extra option. Making all these changes might turn a one-bedroom's capacity from two to three.

» **Two-bedroom listings.** We recommend adding two to total additional occupancy. Couch to futon/pullout bed conversion, extra airbed, or bunk beds in one bedroom could each on their own add one to two additional occupancy.

» **Three-bedroom listings.** We recommend adding two to three to total additional occupancy. We offer the same recommendations as for the two-bedroom listing, but with an extra room you can increase bed size or replace a twin with a double bunk bed for the optional third extra occupancy.

WARNING

Although it may be physically possible and you may be tempted to squeeze as many beds as possible to maximize occupancy capacity, we don't recommend that. For instance, a one-bedroom unit that can sleep seven may not be able to charge a premium over similar one-bedroom unit that sleeps only three. At some point, fewer travelers are willing to squeeze in that tightly just to save a few dollars on travel costs. Crucially, you're most likely violating your local fire codes and putting your guests at risk.

According to the U.S. Fire Administration and the National Fire Protection Association (NFPA), one civilian fire-related death occurs every 144 minutes (a little over two hours'). House fires claim an average of 2,620 lives a year. By exceeding the maximum occupancy allowed by fire code, not only might you be putting your guests at risk in a fire, the city could also fine you and take away your license or permit for your Airbnb listing, if you're required to have one.

For most listings, fitting a futon or sleeper sofa instead of a regular sofa to add one more guest to your total occupancy won't push it past local fire code limits. For larger properties, adding additional capacity with bunk beds in some bedrooms might also be possible.

REMEMBER

You won't know for sure until you check and verify with your local fire codes, but you can estimate the maximum occupancy with the "2 + 1 Rule." Under this rule, assume two people per bedroom plus one additional occupant. So, a one-bedroom listing has a maximum occupancy of three.

WARNING

However, some municipalities, such as New York City, have extremely strict occupancy limits for Airbnb listings. Even if a one bedroom is large enough to add a futon, you may be breaking the law if you do so. Hence, we recommend that you consult your municipality's ordinances governing Airbnb.

Creating Additional Revenue Sources

Although most of your profits come from direct bookings, they aren't the only way to make money from your listing. Travelers staying at your listing are likely be interested in entertainment options and other travel-related services, which present extra opportunities for the savvy hosts to increase overall listing revenue.

Here are some additional creative sources of revenue you can use to increase your revenue:

>> **Add-on services for a fee:** Offer relevant and useful services your guests are willing to pay for.

- **Airport pickup/drop-off:** In markets with limited or non-existent ride-share coverage, guests appreciate having the option of being picked up and dropped off at the airport, even for an extra fee.

- **Additional cleanings for long stays:** When guests are staying a week or longer, you can provide them the option for extra cleanings during their stay.

- **Equipment rentals:** You can rent everything from bikes, water gear, sporting equipment, and so on. *Remember:* Be sure to have all guests sign a liability waiver before you release the equipment. Digital signing tools and a smart lock allow you to execute this remotely.

- **Luggage storage for the day of check-out:** Consider offering this for free.

- **An honor bar:** Like a hotel minibar with a larger selection, you can use a price list and a jar or ask for payment digitally through apps, such as Paypal, Square, and Venmo.

- **Almost anything for sale:** Include any add-on item or service you can think of by using the YourWelcome tablet and platform to turn your listing into a virtual storefront for your guests.

» **Airbnb of X offerings:** With the growth of the sharing economy, there are many Airbnb copycats that let you rent other assets besides your living space.

- **Rent your extra space for storage.** If you have an unused shed, garage, room, or land, you can use one of several apps to help you rent your space to local storage seekers. The space is nascent without a clear global winner yet so find one that has traction in your market. Here are some of the more popular options currently available:

  - CityLab.com

  - Neighbor.com

  - Roost.com

  - Spacer.com

  - Sparefoot.com

  - StoreAtMyHouse.com

- **Rent your unused vehicle on Turo.** Just like Airbnb but for cars.

- **Host a home-cooked meal through BonAppetour.** Like an Airbnb for hosted dinners.

- **Host campers on your property through Hipcamp.** An Airbnb for camping space.

- **Rent your RV through Outdoorsy.** Airbnb for RVs.

- **Rent your boat with Antlos.** Airbnb for boats.

- **Rent your home office space on Pivot Desk.** Airbnb for home offices.

- **Rent your recording studio to musicians through Studio Time.** Airbnb for recording studios.

- **Rent your camera gear on KitSplit.** Airbnb for professional photography gear.

- **Rent your outdoor equipment on Spinlister.** Airbnb for outdoor equipment.

- **Rent your extra parking on Carmanation.** Airbnb for parking spaces.

If you have any space or commodity that is valuable and unused, some Airbnb-inspired platform is likely available for you to rent them out.

>> **Host an Airbnb Experience.** By creating an appealing Airbnb Experience, you can make money without even having a property to host. Some only offer Experiences whereas other hosts do it in addition to hosting their property. We explore Experiences more in Chapter 16.

REMEMBER

Not all properties in all markets can implement the same strategies. Review them all and determine which is most likely to work for your property in your market. If you're unsure, look at the top performing listings in your market and read through their descriptions and guest reviews. Top Airbnb hosts use creative amenities or offerings to draw potential guests, and happy guests will often mention these amenities in their raving reviews.

However, you may not want to charge for some added amenities to deliver exceptional guest experience and earn more five-star reviews. Charging extra for every little additional amenity could come off as nickel and diming and turn off guests.

TIP

To decide whether to charge for an extra service, ask yourself these two questions:

>> Does adding the amenity cost me, the host, a nontrivial amount of extra cost?

>> Would most Airbnb guests expect to pay extra for this?

Unless you answer yes to both questions, consider offering the extra service as a surprise complimentary bonus for the guests.

Chapter **10**

Going on Cruise Control and Still Making Money

Your goal as a host is putting all the systems at your disposal in place so that your Airbnb largely runs on its own. In fact, you can automate a lot with your listing. After you automate, your involvement as a host can be whatever extent you want. In fact, hosting will require only minimal input. Rather than being fully involved in every aspect, you can intervene every once in a while, when automations or outsourcing may fall short, or when you desire to do so.

This chapter details how to use different tools to make your job easier as a host and discusses what you can eliminate, automate, and outsource so that you aren't spending so much time on the daily operations and you're maximizing dollars while minimizing the hours.

One of the biggest challenges for hosts is that they don't automate at all or don't know what software and opportunities are available. They don't know what to eliminate or what can be outsourced. By trying to take on every aspect of the business that is Airbnb hosting, you can get burnt out and frustrated, which can lead to fewer bookings or stopping hosting completely. We include three sidebars to illustrate examples of different hosts and their level of automation and host burnout.

Choosing Sanity over Profits: Steer Clear of Burning Out

When hosting on Airbnb, one of your main choices is prioritizing your sanity over profits to avoid burnout. In other words, you want to make sure that your profit is worthwhile *and* sustainable. Nearly all people have a burnout point, and you can reach that point much quicker if you aren't properly managing your own sanity. Over the lifetime of your hosting you can actually make less profit if you don't manage your own sanity because you won't be able to sustain yourself as a host for long enough to reap all your rewards.

The following sections help you to determine how much you can handle as a host. From there, we assist you to view your hosting as a business so that you can make the right decisions, avoid burnout, and have long-term success.

Figuring out what you can handle

The fine line of burn-out differs from person to person. What may cause one person to burn out may not affect you. It's important to know your line so you don't cross your own personal burnout line. To do so, differentiate what you actually want to do from what you feel you need to do as a host, which is unique to each Airbnb host.

REMEMBER

Look at the effort you're putting in to hosting and make sure that effort is adding value or taking away stress. As long as you're doing something that's adding value or enjoyment to your life and you're drawing a profit, then you should keep doing it. The flip side is you're making money but it's taking away from you and your family and friends and causing stress, anxiety, and frustration. You're spending that time on hosting when you want to be doing something else. That's when you'll experience burnout and stop hosting.

For example, refer to "The fully automated host" sidebar in this chapter to see how one host used automation to avoid burnout. He hired a virtual assistant to handle his guest communication and a cleaner to clean the unit. If he had been heavily involved in managing all his properties, he would probably have gone insane and stopped hosting or switched to long-term rent, which would have meant a significant loss in profit. For him to keep his sanity while maximizing profits, he needed to completely remove himself from the equation.

You don't need to hire outside help for everything like he did. You could decide to hire out certain tasks like the retired couple in the "Keeping what you love and outsourcing what you don't: The hosts who loved to host" sidebar did. To stay sane, they stopped cleaning and hired a cleaner to handle those responsibilities. If they hadn't hired a cleaner, more than likely they would have stopped hosting on Airbnb altogether. Hosting just wouldn't have been worth their while.

However, because both sets of hosts put the automations in place that worked for them, they can now host indefinitely. They've made it to a place where there isn't a mental or physical cost on them, and they can truly enjoy the act of hosting while generating profit at the same time.

Automating day-to-day operations is about giving you the freedom to do the parts of hosting you want to do when you want to do them rather than completely removing yourself as a host. If you want to step back, you can, but most hosts enjoy some involvement. What's key is you're involved because you choose to be involved rather than because you have to be involved.

REMEMBER

When figuring out what you can handle, you want to find the right balance. Ideally, you want your hosting to be set up in such a way that it requires little to no sacrifice on your part. Rather than being something that you don't enjoy but that earns you money, hosting should be something that you both enjoy and earn money from.

KEEPING WHAT YOU LOVE AND OUTSOURCING WHAT YOU DON'T: THE HOSTS WHO LOVED TO HOST

James stayed with hosts in Florida who were great hosts and who absolutely loved hosting. They were recently retired and had put all the systems in place to automate the process. They had cleaners who helped with the room turnovers, although they managed all of the guest communication. During my stay they came over to check on me and even brought a gift. The hosts were friendly and enjoyed meeting new people. They offered tips about the area and made me feel welcomed. Overall, they were nothing but huge value adds to my stay. I loved having them around even if it was just for the little bit of free time they had in their day.

When they had first started, they were cleaning on their own, but it had gotten to be too much. Although they had a lot of free time, they started looking at the cleaning as a chore and not something they wanted to continue doing. They enjoyed the extra income from Airbnb but didn't necessarily need it, so overall continuing to do the cleaning themselves wasn't worth it to them. However, they loved hosting and realized they could do the rest of the responsibilities through their cellphones. They became the perfect example of hosts who were able to outsource that aspect of their business that they didn't enjoy and still remain active and involved as hosts, which allowed them to continue to host and create awesome experiences for their guests.

Minimizing your time and stress is just as important as maximizing profits

For you to continue hosting long-term, you need to actually enjoy hosting. If hosting causes you a great deal of stress and you view it as a time-suck rather than something that you actually enjoy doing, inevitably you'll quit hosting at some point. If you quit hosting, your income will dry up, so naturally in order to maximize your profits you want to host for as long as possible. To do so means reducing or eliminating any part of hosting that you find overly stressful.

Think of it this way: When hosting, you're paying yourself a certain amount of dollars to perform each task rather than earning an income from hosting. For example, if cleaning would cost $60 per turnover, then by choosing to do it on your own, you're paying yourself $60 to clean the property. When choosing profits over your sanity, you have to ask whether it's worth your time to clean your property for $60? Maybe you enjoy cleaning and it's relaxing to you and adds value. Otherwise the answer is no. If so, you should be paying someone else to do it. If you hear yourself thinking or saying, "I don't want to keep cleaning, so I have to stop hosting," instead say, "If I don't want to clean, then I have to outsource the cleaning."

Thinking about your hosting like a business

Hosting is just like running a business where you can outsource different components to be more profitable or to move away from doing tasks you don't enjoy. Say you owned a window cleaning business but didn't like going to the store each week to buy soap. Rather than closing your business because you dislike the chore of getting cleaning supplies, you'd simply outsource that task. By hiring a delivery service to drop off the soap each week, you can still enjoy the act of cleaning windows and successfully run your business. Closing your business simply because you don't like going to buy soap each week would be ridiculous. Think about hosting in the same way.

REMEMBER

Some hosts are stuck seeing their revenue as profit. When you look at all your hosting income as profit, then you see costs such as paying for a cleaning service, using software, or hiring a virtual assistant for guest communications as out-of-pocket fees. In reality, they're just costs to running your hosting business. Every business has costs and revenue and having costs is simply a necessary aspect of operating your business.

SHE TRIED TO DO IT ALL: THE BURNT-OUT HOST

I (James) stayed with a host at a quaint property on Vancouver Island. The host lived on the property and had a guesthouse where she hosted Airbnb guests. She and her daughter did everything to upkeep the property. When her daughter went away for school, she was left managing everything on her own.

She was a very involved host. She went above and beyond what's expected from a host by doing extras such as bringing over fresh fruit every morning. I discovered by talking with her that she really did everything on her own: the cleaning, the turnovers, the guest communication, and everything else the property required.

I asked if I could have leave my bags for an hour and have a slightly later check-out. She was flustered and said there was no way because another guest was checking in soon. She had to do the cleaning, so everything needed to be turned over right away.

During our conversation, she told me how much she loved hosting, but she was going to start dialing back. She couldn't handle having these many turnovers along with the stress of only a four-hour window between guests. In addition to the time she spent messaging guests, she felt she always had to be on. She was doing all of this in addition to working a full-time job. It was just too much.

Automating some of these duties could have reduced the stress she was feeling and the time she spent managing the listing. She was a great host, but because hosting was draining her time and stressing her out, she had to pull back.

Identifying What You Can Eliminate

The best way to identify what you can eliminate in hosting is by shifting your mind-set. You must get critical about everything you provide and identify any assumptions you're making about what is absolutely necessary to the success of your listing. If you don't have conclusive evidence to show that something is entirely necessary, then you can consider eliminating it.

REMEMBER

Develop a critical mind-set concerning what you can eliminate regarding the cost to you, the benefit to your guests, and what's most ideal for your situation. Depending on the type of property you list on Airbnb, guests are going to have different expectations. For example, if you have a 5-star villa with a personal chef, more than likely your guests will want to be welcomed by someone in person. If you have a beautiful property that's perfect for a romantic getaway, then it's likely your guests will want that bottle of champagne or another kind of gift. Unfortunately figuring out what you can eliminate is on a case-by-case basis. There isn't a definitive list of things you can eliminate.

For example, many hosts believe they can't eliminate in-person check-ins. They assume that every guest must be welcomed in person and then led into the property. However, in most cases that's not true. Most guests actually prefer to check themselves into the property because it's more convenient and they can arrive whenever they want. If you believe this may be true for your listing, you can test your theory and ask for guest feedback. You can reach out to your guests to see if they prefer an in-person check-in or that you leave a lockbox at the property with keys inside so they can check themselves in. You may find that guests overwhelmingly want to check themselves into the property. You may discover that you can provide instructions to use a lockbox and eliminate the entire guest welcoming process. Chapter 13 discusses more on how you can make the check-in process seamless.

Try looking at what you can't eliminate. Consider if you chose never to clean your property. You don't need to test this theory because you can pretty clearly conclude that if you stopped cleaning your property, you'd have unhappy guests. You can easily see the impact if you were to eliminate cleaning. For something more ambiguous such as a check-in gift, test it out. Ask your guests or actually eliminate it and see what happens. Just be sure that any time you eliminate something you update your listing accordingly. If you promise a welcome gift in your listing description, be sure to remove it from your listing before actually eliminating the gift.

THE FULLY AUTOMATED HOST

Consider the host whose property I (James) stayed at in San Diego. Although I stayed at this property for months, I never met the host who owns this large complex. His profile said he lived in New York. This host is an example of fully automating the Airbnb hosting experience. I communicated with a virtual assistant, and a cleaning company maintained the property. The virtual assistant knew everything about the property and answered all my questions. I checked in on my own and was provided a guest manual and instructions to the property. Anything I needed was clearly and properly outlined or answered by the virtual assistant.

Automating to Make Your Life Easier

Ultimately, automating gives you more flexibility and in turn makes your life easier. You do tasks because you want to do them, not because you have to do them. Automating has two advantages:

>> **It gives you a contingency plan.** You may not mind messaging guests or doing check-ins yourself, but what happens about messaging guests when you have a family emergency or checking guests in when your car breaks down?

>> **It gives you options and ultimately provides a better service.** You can achieve the same results with more ease, efficiency, and consistency. Machines are typically a lot more consistent and effective than human beings.

For example, with guest messaging you can set up software that automatically reads an incoming message, analyzes it, and responds accordingly. If your guest is asking for the Wi-Fi password, the software automatically sends it. Compare this to you needing to pull out your phone, see the notification, and then respond to it, which may take 5 minutes, 10 minutes, or maybe an hour before you can respond and the guest is frustrated waiting to connect to the Internet.

The result of proper automation is that your guests are more satisfied, and you have more time and flexibility. Automating is not about completely removing yourself and creating a ghost host or robotic, impersonal experience for the guests. Automating is about focusing your time and energy to where it provides the most value to both you and your guests.

The following sections identify a couple ways you can automate your listing to make your life less hectic and your guest's experience more relaxing.

Automating check-ins

Although you have choices if you decide to automate your check-in process, what's most important is that whatever process you choose works all the time. You don't want to have to worry about it not working part of the time where guests can't get into your property. Here are the available options for automating your check-ins, each with different levels of security and reliability, from highest to lowest.

Smart lock

A smart lock is a lock that can be operated remotely and in most cases can be unlocked by guests via a mobile app or custom numeric code. Some smart locks such as the August lock even integrate with your Airbnb account so that when a guest books your property it automatically creates and registers them as a guest. Locks that have this functionality are incredibly secure because guests can only get into your property from their check-in time until their check-out time. Furthermore, you don't need to interface with it at all. However, these types of locks on their own tend to be on the lower end in terms of reliability. Sometimes guests won't have a smartphone or download the app before they get there, and upon arrival they may not have Wi-Fi or Internet access. Also, it's possible your smart lock's signal won't work.

With most smart locks you'll want to buy a compatible keypad, which will increase reliability for your guests. In case they aren't able to access your property using the app alone you'll have the keypad as a backup. You can typically add a code to the keypad that's only usable for a short period of time and is easy to change. As for security, smart locks are the best because the guests are only able to access your property for the duration of the stay and you never need to visit the property to change codes, because you can do everything remotely.

Door code

This option allows you to use an electronic lock on your door rather than a standard keyed lock. You can provide your guests with the code so they're able to check in on their own. You'll want to change the code as often as you need to feel comfortable and secure. Changing the code will often need to be done at the property, which lowers the convenience of this option because it can't be done remotely. Just be aware that if you don't choose to regularly change the code, guests may be able to access your property before and after their reservation.

Lockbox

A lockbox is the lowest tech option but the highest in terms of reliability. You attach a lockbox to a doorknob or railing, and guests can unlock it with a code to access the physical key. Because lockboxes are mechanical and not electronic, the only time a lockbox can be unreliable is when it can get jammed or frozen during cold weather. Another disadvantage: Some lockboxes don't allow you to change the code, and it's unlikely that you'll want to frequently rekey your locks, so providing a guest with the key creates a higher security risk for your property. Guests could copy the key or return and open the lockbox in the future.

Which one is right for you

The best option for you depends on your specific operation and needs. We recommend a smart lock as the best option with our favorite being the August Lock (https://august.com). It offers the best balance in terms of reliability, security, and ease of use. It enables you to optimize for 100 percent reliability. Having a contingency plan in place is important in case something does go wrong. If you're going to use a smart lock or electronic coded lock on your door, we recommend having a lockbox somewhere else on the property as a backup option.

Automating pricing

Automating pricing means using software so that you don't need to constantly update your pricing for different seasons or events that come to your area. The software completely automates that process and conducts calculations behind the scenes to ensure your listing is optimally priced — so you don't miss out on making more money. Our favorite is Wheelhouse (`www.usewheelhouse.com`).

Optimizing your pricing doesn't simply mean updating your numbers every once in a while. You have to research the events and seasons while keeping your calendars updated at least six months into the future. Updating your calendar is quite time consuming, which is why automating that process makes sense.

Another benefit to using this type of software is that your pricing will be updated consistently. If you're updating your prices manually, then you're more than likely going to make mistakes over time that end up costing you revenue because life gets in the way. The software leaves less room for error than if you were performing the task yourself. Refer to Chapter 8 for more details about setting your listing price.

Outsourcing Different Tasks

Outsourcing means hiring someone to perform those tasks that you can't do or don't want to do. Sometimes having someone else to perform a task makes more sense. When determining whether outsourcing makes more sense to you, consider the same point that we mention in the earlier section, "Minimizing your time and stress is just as important as maximizing profits." If you're not paying someone else to do this task, then you're paying yourself to do it. If you aren't paying yourself enough for your time, then you shouldn't be doing it.

You can outsource an array of tasks, including guest communication, guest reviews, cleaning services, and property management, which we discuss in greater detail in these sections.

When you do choose to outsource, consider these three factors:

>> You must find the right person or people.

>> You must train them to deliver services that meet your expectations.

>> You must give them the tools and systems that they need in order to meet your expectations consistently.

Outsourcing guest communication

Guest communication, which entails responding to all guest messages before, during, and after their stay, is one task you can automate. Because this responsibility can be outsourced for roughly $5 to $7 per hour, that's what you're paying yourself to do it yourself. Ask yourself if it's worth your time to handle the guest communication or if you should be outsourcing it.

Hiring a virtual assistant (VA) can be a lifesaver to handle your guest communications. With most VAs, you only pay for the time they spend actually responding to guest messages so the overall cost is quite minimal. Our favorite place to find virtual assistants for guest communication on Airbnb is UpWork (www.upwork. com), a digital platform for freelancers where you can ease the burden at a reasonable cost.

You want to use a combination of both software and virtual assistants to take guest communication off your plate because using software alone has its shortcomings. For example, your guest may ask a question such as "How do I adjust the thermostat? It's not working right now." Most software won't be able to effectively answer that question. For more basic questions such as "What's the Wi-Fi?" software such as SmartBNB (www.smartbnb.io) will do a great job. For more unique or more complex questions however, you need a virtual assistant. Hiring a virtual assistant typically costs anywhere from $5–$7 per hour.

However, you won't be able to assume your VA can perform the job as you would. Using a VA has a learning curve. You must give your VA the tools and system to operate consistently and efficiently. By creating an overview document of exactly how to communicate with your guests, your VA can handle all commonly asked questions and concerns. Your VA needs to know all about your property so they can refer to that information when needed. Then, if there is information that they need but isn't provided, you have to instruct them on how best to research to find the answers.

For example, a guest may ask where the nearest public pool is located. Your VA needs to know what instructions to give and how to effectively communicate that knowledge. This may require going on Google to look up the address or instructing the guests how to do so. Walk your VA through anything that may cause questions, so she has a solid set of systems to rely on to do her job effectively. After you have your completed systems in place, you won't have to intervene. If you don't have the right systems in place, then you're going to have to intervene more often.

The better you do at training people you outsource to in the beginning, the less you have to intervene and be involved in the long run.

REMEMBER

Outsourcing guest reviews

Similar to how guests are asked to rate their hosts after their stay, you also review your guests. This is another task that can be outsourced to VAs. When reviewing guests, have your VA communicate with your cleaners to make sure there were no issues with the guests that would impact whether or not a future host should accept them at their property. From there, your VA can draft and submit a positive review for great guests or a negative review for any guests who caused issues or damages.

Your guests can receive a poor review if they caused issues with the guest communication team or didn't respect your property by leaving your space dirty or damaged. When the guest communication team opens a line of communication with the cleaners, they can pool their joint knowledge to write an accurate review.

Hiring a pro for cleaning

Cleaning and handling turnovers is one of the most common ways Airbnb hosts outsource. Cleaners come to your property after each guest checks out and complete a full, top-to-bottom turnover of your listing. In most cases cleaners do everything from tidying up the space to washing linens to restocking sundries such as toilet paper, paper towel, and soap. Hiring cleaners to take care of these tasks eliminates several hours of work from your plate for each guest. Another benefit to outsourcing your cleaning is that it's one of the few tasks that requires you to physically be present at the property. Handing this task over to someone else means that you can take care of your remaining hosting duties remotely from wherever in the world you may be.

Before hiring cleaners, ask yourself some of these questions to help you solidify your needs and expectations:

>> Do you want to notify or schedule your cleaners for every cleaning? More likely you'd prefer to integrate them with your calendar so they can schedule themselves every time a guest checks out. This reduces constant communication and allows them to work autonomously.

>> What time do you want them to come by? What expectations are you setting? By outlining your check-out and check-in time for each guest, you're clear on exactly what you want.

>> What tasks do you want them to take care of? Most likely you want them to handle everything from cleaning to laundry to replenishing supplies. Be clear about this up front and find cleaners that can meet your needs.

After you outline these specific responsibilities and expectations, you can create a comprehensive listing on online classified platforms such as Craigslist (worldwide), Kijiji (Canada), or GumTree (Europe). You can also perform a Google search for Airbnb cleaners in your area.

REMEMBER

During your interview, clearly communicate your needs and expectations. Many hosts assume cleaners know what they expect. However, the job entails much more than simply going to the property and mopping some floors. Because each property and each host is unique, only you know how to clean or fix certain aspects of your property. The cleaners won't have your knowledge or experience with the space.

For example, your cleaners may leave the towels on the bed versus leaving them in the bathroom. If you want something done a specific way, you must share that information. You have to be clear on all those intricacies and identify which ones are nonnegotiable and which ones aren't a concern. You may not mind if the towels end up in the bathroom or in the bedroom as long as they're clean and neatly folded.

Different cleaners may or may not fit your needs and expectations. Some areas have Airbnb-specific cleaning teams such as MaidThis (www.maidthis.com) or a large cleaning company that provides what you need and is a great fit. Those two options may not be available in some areas, so you may find working with an independent cleaner is the best option. Thoroughly ask them about their experience and ask for references. Depending on your individual situation you can find what best fits your needs.

After you hire your cleaners, the next step is to train them. Figure out anything that is nonnegotiable and determine your expectations. Outline those nonnegotiable items and then express them to your cleaning team. Give them instructions for how to do anything that may be more technical or particular. Create a checklist so they won't miss anything every time they come to clean.

TIP

We recommend doing a couple cleanings with them so you can go over everything and make sure they understand exactly what you want. If you try to tell cleaners to just go and clean, then they're going to do it in their own way. You may have miscommunication, or something will be forgotten from your list. By going there in person and remaining with them for the duration of the clean, you can set clear expectations.

After you join the cleaners a couple of times you can leave them on their own and perform your own quality control inspection afterward. This way you can make sure they're still performing the same quality work when you're not there.

Your guests will also give you feedback. Try to personally check in or have your guest communications team check in with guests on their satisfaction with your property. Make note of any issues so you can provide your cleaners with feedback and then remedy the situation immediately so you avoid any bad reviews.

Hiring a professional property manager

Another option for outsourcing is using a property manager or property management company, based on your unique situation. A property manager or property management company typically handles every aspect of hosting for you, leaving you to just sit back and relax. This option is ideal for those hosts who want absolutely no involvement in hosting but want the premium returns that short-term rentals can offer.

REMEMBER

Determining whether to hire someone to take over this role requires having a better understanding of what managing the property yourself means. Managing your property takes the most work in the early stages when you're manually pricing your listing, finding and training your cleaning and guest communication teams, and then creating systems so they can perform to your expectations. If your only listing is a spare bedroom in your home or a guesthouse behind your house, then a property manager doesn't make sense. However, if you have one or several investment or vacation properties, then hiring a property manager may be a wise choice.

Ask yourself these questions when considering hiring a property manager:

>> **Do you want to be completely removed from hosting?** If you truly enjoy being involved and acting as a host to your guests, then hiring a property management company may not make sense. The management company wants the autonomy to operate properly.

>> **Do you want to avoid going through the setup process yourself?** The greatest difference in time input is during that initial setup process. Getting all the processes and systems in place so that your hosting is relatively hands-off may take a couple months.

If the answer is yes to both of those questions, then hiring a property management company is ideal. Although you're equipped to perform those tasks yourself, if you don't have the time or energy to do so or you want to be removed from your guests, then look into hiring a property management company. A property management company can handle all those tasks, and your inputs will no longer be needed after just a few days.

The specific property management company you hire depends on your unique needs. Most hosts are going to lean toward a small property management company that manages between 5 and 70 properties. This type of company is probably a good fit for anyone who has less than 20 properties that need managed. If you have more than 20 properties, you'll want to give them all to one large company that can service thousands of properties. The challenge with larger property management companies is that they don't offer the customized services most hosts desire.

For example, if you're a real estate investor, you probably care mainly about the dollars and cents. You never want to hear from your property management company. You want accurate monthly reporting, and you expect your property management company to maximize your profits. On the flip side, if you're a vacation homeowner, you may also care about those details, but they aren't your main priorities. More importantly, you want to make sure you have thorough cleaners and that the property is well maintained. You want to be kept in the loop on your second home, so ultimately you have more communication with your property management company to make sure it's effectively screening the guests and managing your property well.

TIP

When looking for a property management company, check out company websites. Determine whether each company can ensure that it will actually meet your needs and offer solutions to your problems. If you don't do your due diligence during the selection process and end up with the wrong property management company, working together more than likely will be challenging and time consuming because that company may not be able to deliver on your expectations or meet your specific needs.

THE FUTURE OF AIRBNB AUTOMATION

With automation software and artificial intelligence constantly improving at an exponential rate, it's likely that much of what you do day-to-day as a host will be easily automated very soon. Currently, many of the daily tasks that take up a great deal of a host's time can be easily automated with a high degree of reliability. As technologies improve, more than likely new hardware and software will become available that will do an even better job of helping to make hosting easier for everyone.

An additional benefit to the automation is that it often provides a better experience for guests. Human error is drastically reduced when hosts equip themselves with the right tools, meaning that fewer mistakes are made that negatively impact the guest experience.

Chapter **11**

It's a Bird, It's a Plane... No... It's a Superhost!

Airbnb has created a number of different designations within its platform to recognize hosts for meeting certain criteria with the most prestigious being the Superhost status.

The different statuses, including Business Travel Ready and Family Friendly, are how Airbnb has categorized different listings and different hosts based on amenities and performance metrics they've hit. These categories help prospective guests to identify which properties and which hosts they want to stay with and provide more consistency on the platform. Guests can trust that these hosts and listings fit their specific needs when searching for a place to stay.

Achieving Superhost status is an ultimate goal for all hosts who seek to be as successful as possible. Superhost status offers a variety of benefits including more traffic to your listing, and in most cases, more bookings. Achieving Superhost status is contingent on your success as a host in several areas. Throughout this chapter we examine what the Superhost status means and what you can do to achieve it and get it back if you lose it. We also explore the two additional statuses: Business Travel Ready and Family Friendly.

What Makes a Superhost: Putting the Guest First and Foremost

The greatest difference in Superhosts versus those hosts who aren't Superhosts is that they focus on providing an exceptional stay for their guests. The guest is always first. Rather than focusing on themselves and how they can benefit from hosting and make more money, Superhosts prioritize their guests. They ask themselves questions such as "How can I make the guest's stay better? More incredible? More special?"

Being a Superhost comes down to taking that extra step to bring the experience above and beyond. Doing so shows through in all of the Superhost metrics that we discuss in the next section. If your main goal is to provide your guests with the best experience possible, then you're likely going to be a world-class host and achieve Superhost status.

UNDERSTANDING HOW SUPERHOST STATUS CAN HELP YOU MAKE MORE MONEY

An AirDNA study showed that hosts who had Superhosts status versus hosts who didn't have Superhost status experienced up to a 53 percent increase in their overall revenue (refer to the following figure).

Superhost	Revenue	ADR	Occupancy Rate	RevPAR
No	$19,936	$170	26%	$45
Yes	$30,457	$153	47%	$72
Δ	53%	−10%	81%	60%

Source: https://www.airdna.co/blog/airbnb_superhost_status

This increase in revenue is partly because the Airbnb algorithm favors Superhosts. A Superhost performs better overall and offers a higher value experience to guests. As a result, the process of achieving Superhost status also helps to improve your search ranking on Airbnb, even before you get the status itself. The better you're performing as a host, such as replying to guest messages and getting great reviews, the more the search rankings will promote you. It's essentially a snowball effect.

Meeting Superhost Requirements

Superhost status has certain criteria you as a host must hit, and these requirements get updated or changed from time to time. Being a Superhost isn't as easy as having a nice property, establishing it, and forgetting about it. Airbnb distinguishes and differentiates hosts who are doing a truly exceptional job.

The first step to taking advantage of all the benefits of being a Superhost is to actually become a Superhost. The following sections explain the requirements and suggest how to reach the status.

Becoming a Superhost

In order to achieve Superhost standing, your account must meet certain requirements. Airbnb measures your last 12 months hosting, although you don't necessarily need to have been a host for a full year to qualify for Superhost status.

According to www.airbnb.com, here are the specific requirements you must have met if you want to be a Superhost:

>> Completed at least ten trips or completed three reservations that total at least 100 nights

>> Maintained a 90 percent response rate or higher

>> Maintained a 1 percent cancellation rate (1 cancellation per 100 reservations) or lower, with exceptions made for extenuating circumstances

>> Maintained a 4.8 overall rating (this rating looks at the past 365 days of reviews, based on the date the guest left a review, not the date the guest checked out)

Airbnb assesses your profile quarterly on January 1, April 1, July 1, and October 1 every year. By measuring your past performance, Airbnb notifies you following each of these assessment periods whether or not you've achieved Superhost status.

For example, if during your first quarter hosting, you meet the necessary requirements, you can still achieve Superhost status although you've only hosted for the past three months. However, just because you achieve Superhost status in your first quarter doesn't necessarily mean you'll keep it in the second quarter. Even if you maintain Superhost status for the past six quarters, you can lose that status over poor performance. You must constantly meet the requirements and maintain your performance in order to remain a Superhost.

What you can do to reach Superhost status

When attempting to improve your performance and reach Superhost status, we suggest you do the following:

Stay at your own property

Review the overall experience of staying at your own property. How is your check-in? Try finding the key and using the lock. Make sure your listing isn't missing anything such as frying pans or extra rolls of toilet paper. Spend a few days as a guest at your own property. What do you wish you had? Make a note of anything you feel is missing that would make your own experience better so you can later add it.

Have a close friend stay at your property

Ask a friend stay at your property as a guest and review his overall experience. Ask him to take diligent and honest notes about everything that could be improved from check-in to check-out. Having an objective third party's opinions can be a great way to avoid the potential bias of reviewing the experience yourself.

Stay with a regular host and stay with a Superhost

You can quickly realize the differences when you stay with a Superhost compared to a non-Superhost. We suggest you choose a longtime Superhost who has hundreds of reviews. What you oftentimes realize is that the Superhost cares tremendously about you as a guest. Keep notes about anything you find nice to have as part of your visit. Don't keep track of expectations but rather focus on elements the Superhost did exceptionally well that elevated your experience.

For example, the Superhost may be super responsive and quick to answer your messages. Perhaps they left you a small gift upon arrival or a charger by your bed along with different adapters for different cellphones so the space is accessible to any guest. Maybe the have complimentary water bottles in the fridge or a carton of eggs so you don't have to go out and buy groceries or breakfast after you arrive.

You'll notice all these matters that aren't grandiose acts but rather an accumulation of small details that end up making a big difference to you as a guest. Then, stay with a regular host, see what they do, and compare the two experiences. Doing so is the best way to understand what it means to care immensely for your guests and to experience firsthand being a guest who is put first by the host. Rather than research what makes a Superhost a Superhost, go experience it for yourself.

Maintaining Superhost Status

Keeping your Superhost status requires keeping your goal in mind and knowing the criteria you're operating under. After you have it, it's yours to lose. If you're able to do what it takes to become a Superhost, then it should be relatively easy to maintain.

The good news is after a host has maintained Superhost status for a period of time, it's less likely the host will lose it for two reasons:

>> Hosts likely have in place the systems and processes necessary to maintain their Superhost status. They know what it takes to become a Superhost and are able to continually perform that way.

>> The more data points hosts have, the harder it becomes to sway that overall ranking. The more reviews a host gets, the less impact a poor review will have on that host's overall star rating. For example, if you only have ten bookings and ten 5-star reviews, then one poor review can bring your overall rating down to an average of 4.9 (or lower). On the other hand, if you have 100 5-star reviews, then you'd need substantially more poor reviews to lower your average to 4.9. The better your track record, the harder it becomes to sway and the more likely it is that you're going to retain your Superhost status.

To maintain your Superhost status, you want to monitor the following three main aspects of your hosting and ensure that you stay within the acceptable limits for Superhosts.

Your response rate

The *response rate* means how quickly you respond to booking inquiries and to your guests when they message you through the Airbnb platform. Doing so isn't rocket science. Just make sure you never leave a message unanswered. Even a simple "thank you" is still considered a response. You may not be interested in an inquiry and don't want to take their booking, but rather than leave their request without a response, you need to respond as to why you aren't accepting the booking.

REMEMBER

When you leave that message unanswered, you're hurting your overall response rate, which can affect your eligibility for Superhost status. Keeping your response rate above 90 percent is just part of being a responsible host. You can use automation software to make sure your guests are answered promptly, which takes the burden off you, especially if you have a lot of obligations. Using this type of software means you don't need to constantly be plugged into your phone or computer monitoring and responding to guest messages. Chapter 10 discusses automation in greater detail.

Your cancellation rate

The act that causes most hosts to lose Superhost status is their *cancellation rate*, which is calculated by dividing the number of bookings you cancelled by your total number of bookings. In order to maintain Superhost status, you have to maintain a 1 percent cancellation rate or lower. Even if you complete 100 reservations without a single cancellation, you'll lose Superhost status if you cancel just two of those bookings. Even with a high number of successful bookings, a few missteps can throw you off and you can lose your status, which understandably can frustrate many hosts.

A high cancellation rate creates a huge negative impact for guests. Airbnb is holding you to a high standard due to the impact it has on your guests and therefore on Airbnb as a company when you cancel a reservation. As a result, Airbnb's policies provide the necessary amount of leeway. Overall, Airbnb wants to ensure it balances that grace to hosts with the impact on guests and avoids unnecessarily large inconveniences to guests who book through the platform.

Avoiding cancellations

The best way to keep a low cancellation rate is to make sure you're planning ahead. Be mindful and make sure whenever you open up dates on your calendar that they're absolutely, 100 percent available. You may not want to open up your calendar six months in advance if it means there's potential for you to cancel. For instance, figure out whether you have family or friends who may be coming and need a place to stay. Are you listing a vacation home or guest suite that you'll potentially need to use?

TIP

If so, your best course of action is to look at your calendar and block off any questionable dates. You can always open them up later. Deciding later that you want a date back after a guest has booked will require you to cancel that guest's booking, so plan ahead now to have peace in the future.

Understanding Airbnb's extenuating circumstances policy

The good news is that this 1 percent policy doesn't apply to cancellations made through Airbnb's extenuating circumstances policy. You can read about the policy at www.airbnb.com/help/article/1320. This policy covers scenarios such as death, illness or injury, government mandates, severe damage to the property, airport and road closures, travel cancellations, and other circumstances that require special review.

If your situation falls into one of these extenuating circumstances, then you're not going to get a mark against you for cancelling on your guests. Those situations in the policy are the only times cancelling doesn't negatively affect your hosting profile. If possible, you want to avoid cancelling on your guests for any reason. However, Airbnb allows for cancelling under these circumstances because in these scenarios, guests likely wouldn't enjoy an optimal experience at your property had they been allowed to stay.

For example, say your listing had a pipe burst that caused a flood, resulting in severe damage to your property. Although a cancellation is inconvenient for your guests, staying in a flooded property would be more inconvenient. Generally, if you're cancelling because of something completely outside your control that prevents you from delivering a quality experience to guests, more than likely it will be covered by Airbnb's extenuating circumstances policy, and you won't be penalized for it.

However, if your cancellation doesn't meet this policy and your guests will be inconvenienced, then Airbnb will penalize you. For example, if you have family unexpectedly coming to town, then you're better getting a hotel or Airbnb for your family members versus cancelling last minute on your previously booked guests.

Your overall guest reviews

Maintaining a 4.8-star rating is the last obstacle to manage to maintain your Superhost status. Everything comes down to your rating. In order to maintain a strong rating, you need to continuously deliver a high-quality guest experience. How do you do that? Check out these tips (although this list is far from being all encompassing):

>> **You offer a clean and well-maintained space.** No one feels comfortable in a dirty or poorly maintained space. If guests are uncomfortable, it will show up in your reviews. Chapter 15 covers everything you need to know for cleaning and maintenance.

>> **You're friendly and communicative in responding to all guest questions or concerns.** Guests like hosts who are friendly and responsive, so be mindful of the tone you use when sending messages and always get back to guests promptly. Check out Chapter 12 for more on this.

>> **Your property has essentials.** Make sure you have the essential amenities that guests expect and add a few nice-to-have amenities that guests will appreciate. We discuss which amenities will do the trick in Chapter 5.

>> **You and your listing are honest.** Always be honest with guests and be sure to set the right expectations in your listing so that your guests don't end up frustrated or disappointed. Take a look at Chapter 6 for guidelines on how to set up your listing the right way.

>> **You ask your guests for a 5-star review.** We know doing so may feel uncomfortable at first. Even when you're doing a great job, your guests may not think to review you unless prompted. Perhaps some guests may not naturally give 5-star reviews, and in that case you want to express the importance of the Airbnb ratings system and why a 4-star review can negatively impact you.

>> **You're making sure to monitor all your guest reviews.** Look at what you're doing well and what guests have mentioned in their reviews are issues. Send a friendly message in the app about any review that is less than 5 stars and ask what you could have done better. Thank them for their response and try to take the comments and implement them to improve your hosting. Chapter 14 provides more advice about how to handle guest reviews.

Basically you're doing a great job as a host.

REMEMBER

When striving for 5-star reviews, mistakes or issues oftentimes don't cost you. Typically, the way you deal with those concerns is what can affect your rating. Most guests understand that issues can arise and will care substantially more about how you handle those potential issues. Dealing with the issues is a lot more important or just as important as trying to eliminate or minimize the issues themselves.

For example, if your air conditioner breaks down during the summertime, your guests are likely going to understand that such a problem can arise and that it's out of your control. That alone likely isn't going to cause a negative review. If you're communicative and quickly get the problem resolved, your guests will be appreciative and most likely not respond negatively to that situation. We suggest you also offer a sincere apology and in some situations a small gift. Negative reviews happen when you don't resolve the issue right away, take hours to respond, and let your guests to fend for themselves.

Fortunately, Airbnb takes the time to monitor the validity of your guest reviews. If ever there is a review that is questionable or a review that was made for the wrong reasons, you can contact Airbnb and request that they evaluate it. If it's deemed unreasonable or unmerited, then Airbnb will either remove it from your listing or take that mark off so it no longer counts against you on your Superhost status eligibility.

Losing Superhost Status and Bouncing Back

If you ever do lose your Superhost status, getting it back is of the most importance. We suggest you do the following to help you earn back your Superhost status if you lost yours:

REMEMBER

>> **Remain objective.** We know hosts can become emotional and frustrated with the Superhost process and the platform. Consider that the Airbnb platform is data-driven and based on measurable, quantifiable statistics.

Staying calm is easier said than done, but don't worry too much. You may not have the results you had before, but you'll likely see only a small decrease in your overall revenue if any, assuming that you keep doing the work that got you to Superhost status in the first place. You can see a decline in your overall revenue when you let your emotions impact your hosting. If you go on a downward spiral, you become a worse host and provide less value for your guests, which leads to less overall revenue for you.

>> **Identify and isolate the issue.** Look at whatever metric — your cancellation rate, your guest rating, or your response rate — caused you to lose Superhost status. If it was multiple issues, focus on each one and look introspectively on what you can do to improve those metrics. Critically ask yourself if you were doing all you could to maintain that Superhost status. Were you being a great host? Were you actually responding to guests? How can you make sure you're continuing to improve in order to get it back? How can you ensure you aren't cancelling on guests in the future?

If you're not consistently getting 5-star reviews, what can you do to make sure that changes? How can you improve the overall guest experience? Find out how to make sure all your guests are having great stays and leaving 5-star reviews. Rather than a moment to get frustrated and emotional, look at it as an opportunity to improve.

>> **Resolve the issue.** Whatever caused you to lose your Superhost status, take the necessary steps to undo the damage. Unfortunately you probably won't be able to accomplish this overnight. By properly identifying the issue, you can put together a plan and determine what you need to do differently moving forward to make sure that you regain and maintain the status in the future.

KEEP YOUR SUPERHOST STATUS: AVOID HOST BURNOUT

Oftentimes hosts who are burnt out from hosting are pushed over the edge when they lose Superhost status. They've been putting in so much work and pouring in energy by doing everything by themselves. When they lose their Superhost status, they throw in the towel.

Being a great host is more difficult when you're doing it all yourself and you don't have automations in place. If you're on the edge of burnout, it's simply a matter of time before a trigger pushes you over the edge — whether it's losing Superhost status or having to clean up after a terrible guest. If you're teetering on the edge for too long, you're eventually going to hit a tipping point.

Examine how you can eliminate the stress by putting in place better systems, getting outside help, or using automation software (refer to Chapter 10). Then you'll only be doing the work that you want to be doing as a host. Long term, you'll be able to enjoy hosting and do a great job with it.

REMEMBER

Ultimately whether or not you have the Superhost status, working toward getting it back is going to drastically improve your results as a host. Consider training for a marathon. Whether you win that marathon or not, you're going to be fitter, healthier, and able to run a lot farther and faster than when you started. After you reach the finish line, you're gaining much more than just the title or accolade. You also have better health, better fitness, and be farther along the path of becoming the best runner you can be.

Similarly, reaching Superhost status isn't one moment but rather the months and months of effort it required to get there. Then one day you may be rewarded with Superhost status. Even if you don't reach the status, you're still going to be a much better host and offer an overall better guest experience for anyone who stays at your property.

Eyeing Superhost Alternatives: Business Travel Ready and Family Friendly

In addition to Superhost status, there are two other main designations on the Airbnb platform — Family Friendly and Business Travel Ready. You can achieve either or both of these qualifications for your listing, and you can achieve both of them alongside also achieving Superhost status. Prospective guests can search for listings by either requirement, so adapting your space to accommodate for families and business travelers is in your best interest. The following list examines in greater detail these two alternatives to Superhost:

>> **Family Friendly:** This means that the space is well suited for families. To make your listing Family Friendly, it must be well suited for family groups and children. Make sure you have child locks, cribs, gates, and no large staircases. With this designation families will know they can stay at your property without any issue and have their needs met. Airbnb assesses listings for the Family Friendly status automatically so you don't need to apply after you've met the requirements. Many vacation destinations will see as many as 60 percent of guests return year over year. If you make families happy, they'll often come back to your listing for years to come.

>> **Business Travel Ready:** This means that the space is well equipped for business travelers. Your property should include a workstation and ironing board and any other additional items your business travelers may require.

Consider that many businessmen and businesswomen travel to the same locations on multiple occasions. After they find a place they like, they'll likely want to book there for every visit. Rather than a cool location or unique space that a vacationing guest may desire, business travelers often want consistency and the peace of mind knowing that they'll have everything they need.

It's important to note that unlike SuperHost status, Airbnb doesn't determine which listings are "family friendly" or "business travel ready" based on a specific list of criteria. Instead, Airbnb's algorithm determines which lisitings to show family and business travelers based on reviews. In order to consistently have your listing show up when travelers search with the "Work Trip" toggle enabled, you need to first host business travelers in your space and receive great reviews. The best way to attract more business and/or family travelers is therefore to do everything that you can to make your space more accommodating to those types of people.

REMEMBER

With both designations, Airbnb automatically assesses listings so you don't need to apply after you meet the requirements.

In a practical sense the benefit to having either one of these statuses is that you can get more bookings. Guests can filter specifically for these types of listings, so your listing shows up in more search results. Additionally, Airbnb's search algorithm favors your listing because it's suitable for more guests. Adding these amenities and meeting those criteria also means you're improving your guest experience and offering more value. Achieving one or both of these variations is quite simple: The requirements are similar to those of Superhost status. You have to be a good host, but if you're already a Superhost, then you can easily add these other titles by including certain amenities.

Depending on your market and property, appealing to business travelers or families may make more sense for you. In general, large cities such as Toronto or New York draw mostly business travelers or both business travelers and families, whereas the Caribbean Islands or Florida may have more family travelers than business travelers.

The same is true for your property type. If you have a five-bedroom property in Downtown Toronto, then you'll have more people with families attempting to book. If you have a single bedroom condo in the same location, you'll probably get more business travelers than families because few families stay in a one-bedroom condo while traveling. Generally, you want to be mindful of the area and your property.

Obtaining both statuses is beneficial if possible, but which status is ultimately more valuable depends on your specific location and property.

4

Mastering Your Guests' Experience

Understand the fundamentals of guest satisfaction to deliver five-star guest experiences consistently.

Put yourself in your guests' shoes to identify opportunities to become a better and more thoughtful host.

Create a seamless guest stay that minimizes stress and friction for your guests.

Ensure your space is ready to receive guests by designing a first impression that appeals to all senses.

Create a seamless check-in and check-out process that is preferred by your guests and easy on you as a host.

Automate the check-in and check-out process by going remote with the use of smart locks and automation tools.

Manage and respond to guest reviews gracefully to earn more 5-star reviews and minimize the impact of negative reviews.

Master the cleaning process to minimize your headaches, whether you do it yourself or hire outside help.

Chapter **12**

Comprehending What Being a Good Host Means

Whether your guests ultimately enjoy their stay in your Airbnb depends on how their actual guest experience compares to their initial expectations. Fall short on even a simple but crucial guest expectation, and you could say good-bye to that five-star guest rating. On the other hand, exceed your guests' expectations consistently and you'll set your Airbnb listing up for long-term success.

In this chapter, we explore the simple formula for delivering a great guest experience, how to put yourself in your guests' shoes, and how you can design your own guest-centric game plan for hosting on Airbnb. In the post-pandemic travel environment, with more competition and higher guest expectations, consistency is more crucial than ever.

Understanding the Guest Search Experience

When guests book their next vacation on Airbnb, they don't just magically land on your listing profile when they open their browser and click the "Reserve" button. As much as you'd like it to be that easy, guests often take many more steps before they get there. Comprehending these steps can help you better grasp what guests experience during their Airbnb search experience.

Looking at the steps to reach booking

How many steps does a typical guest have to take to get to confirming a booking with your listing? Much more than you may realize. The following examines how a search experience for a guest can play out on the platform to reach the point of booking. The guest's steps include:

1. **Go to** www.airbnb.com. **Select "Stays."**

2. **Input a destination into the left part of the search bar labeled "Where."**

   This search leaves out Experiences and Restaurants in the search results. For example, a user wanting to stay in Tokyo, Japan, types that destination into the search bar section labeled "Where."

3. **Click the "Check in" option under the search bar to select the check-in date for their intended trip.**

   Doing so limits search results to those listings available on the desired check-in date. For example, if a guest sets June 5, 2023 as the check-in date, only listings that are available for a check in on that date show up in the search results.

4. **Click the "Check out" option under the search bar to select the check-out date for their intended trip**

   Doing so limits search results to those listings available on the desired check-out date. For example, if a guest sets June 12, 2023 as the check-out date, only listings that are available for that check-out date, and the prior designated check-in date of June 5, 2023, remain in the search results.

5. **Click the "Who" portion under the search bar to input the number of adults, children, and infants for the trip.**

   This part limits search results to listings that can accommodate the requested number of guests, children, infant, and/or pets. For example, if a guest inputs for an infant and a pet, then only listings that both accommodate infants and pets show up in the search results.

6. **Click the red search icon under the search bar.**

Doing so reveals a set of additional travel category icons to easily filter the type of stays by categories, such as: Desert, Beach, Cabins, Campers, Golfing, OMG!, Amazing Pools, Islands, Artic, Tiny Homes, Design, Surfing, A-Frames, and dozens more. Clicking any of these icon options further filters search results that match that desired travel category.

7. **Click the "Filters" icon under the secondary set of search options to reveal a filters window that enables the user to further filter results.**

The filters window enables the user to use any combination of the additional filters of price range, type of space, rooms and beds, property type, amenities, booking options, accessibility features, top tier stays, and host language.

8. **Set a minimum and a maximum price to limit search results to listings that fit a certain price range.**

Even though users can set both low and high limits, most adjust only the high limit to the maximum price they're willing to pay per night for this trip.

9. **Click the "Instant Book" option to limit search results listings that enable the guest to book instantly without having to wait for approval from the host.**

In the digital age of instant gratification, few guests want to wait 24 hours if immediate options are available.

10. **Click the "Show Maps" option and adjust the map of the search results to a narrower geographic radius to further restrict search results.**

For guests who know exactly where they want to stay on a map, they can search by adjusting the Airbnb map rather than changing the search filters. By default, the "Search as I move the map" option is selected and search results change automatically as the guest adjusts the map.

11. **Scroll through and compare the search results by looking at the photos, titles, nightly rates, trip totals, and ratings for each listing.**

At this stage, the guest may spend less than one second on each search result; each potential guest emphasizes one factor over another.

12. **Right-click the listings and open the listing profiles on new tabs on their browser.**

Clicking directly on a search result automatically opens the listing profile in a new tab, but it also takes the user to that tab rather than keeping them on the search tab. Guests here may open a few or more than a dozen listings to further examine.

13. For the new tabs, the guest likely clicks through the photos for each listing selected, quickly rejecting and closing the browser tabs of those that don't make the cut for whatever reason.

Personal preferences become split-second closes on browser tabs.

14. With only a handful of listings making the previous cut, the guest then digs deeper into the remaining listings by scanning the descriptions, reading a few recent guest reviews, and scanning the breakdown of the guest ratings.

The guests may compare house rules or cancellation policies. What any guest cares about most differs here. They may send the listing to their travel companions for feedback to help with decision making.

15. If the guest has questions that they can't find answers to immediately, they can message and query the hosts.

Some guests may try to get discounts from the hosts, especially if they're booking long stays that are a week or more.

16. The guest moves forward to complete their booking and confirm their reservation.

Not all guests go through all 16 steps when making a booking, but many go through most of these steps. Yet even with so many potential steps in the process leading to a booking, there are few places for hosts to influence the guests' decision process besides building a great listing for their property that minimizes barriers to booking.

Eliminating friction from the booking process

During the search process, guests only give a few seconds to evaluate each potential listing. Besides standing out from the sea of competition with a great listing, you must get rid of other points of friction that could potentially prevent guests from booking your listing.

Here are the most common barriers hosts can either eliminate or minimize:

>> **Making the guest work:** If your listing makes it harder for potential guests to glean the information they're looking for compared to competing listings, more than likely you'll lose the booking. That's why having well-executed photos, a concise title, and an informative and appealing description is so important. This concept is especially crucial for newer listings that haven't

already earned hundreds of five-star guest ratings to fall back on. Refer to Chapters 6 and 7 for details on building the perfect listing and taking great photos.

» **Overpricing the listing:** Pricing matters. Charging more than competitors or adding excessive fees that significantly increases the booking total without a compelling reason for guests can lead to early eliminations in the search process. Head to Chapter 8 for setting the optimal pricing strategy for your listing.

» **Being slow with communications:** In the early days of Airbnb, the site published both the response rate and average response time of the hosts — for example, "95 percent" and "within an hour." Even though the company doesn't publish that information now, it's likely still tracking these metrics because guests are more likely to book with and receive great service from the most responsive hosts. The goal back then was to respond to 100 percent of all inquiries within 60 minutes, and they're still good targets to aim for today.

REMEMBER

You may wonder: "How is it possible to have an average response time of less than 60 minutes?" In the early days, your only viable option was to hire a virtual assistant on the opposite side of the world to manage and respond to guest inquiries when you're sleeping. Today, many Airbnb automation tools are available for hosts at reasonable prices that can help to automate up to 90 percent of the messages. Chapter 13 discusses what messages to auto-mate and what it takes to get the most out of messaging automation tools.

» **Responding poorly to bad reviews:** Receiving a poor guest review about your listing and your hosting hurts. You feel it in your gut and it dings your bookings for some time. And while you may feel tempted to leave an angry rebuttal in your response, doing so only scares away future potential guests — no guests want to deal with an aggressive or angry host. Refer to Chapter 14 on strategies to minimize both the occurrence of and damage from poor guest reviews.

Identifying the Fundamentals of Guest Satisfaction

The secret to receiving consistent five-star guest ratings from happy guests on Airbnb is simple. Set proper guest expectations and then exceed them during their actual stay. Yes, we realize the concept may be simple to understand but it's sometimes challenging to execute with consistency.

Recognizing the factors that can affect guest satisfaction

Many factors can help guests form their expectations of your property and you as the host — from the moment when your listing catches their eye in the search results all the way to when they confirm and pay to secure the booking with you.

The following factors help set guest expectations:

» **Listing photos:** By far the photos are the most important factor in setting guest expectations. Many guests often make a reservation based purely on what they see in your photos. Show what you can deliver consistently. See Chapter 7 on how to take the best photos for your listing that are honest and accurately showcase your property.

» **Listing description:** Even though not all guests will read your entire description, let alone remember the details, guests will refer to it if they feel anything isn't meeting their expectations. "Well, you mentioned air conditioning in your description when you only have a large fan" or "You didn't disclose the fact that your building had no elevators to get to your unit on the 20th floor." Upset guests will look for ammunition in your listing description to support refund requests or scathing reviews.

» **Initial guest communications:** Although more and more guests are booking their reservations by sending no inquiries to hosts as listings increasingly turn on Instant Book, any early interactions will set the tone in how guests expect to communicate with you. Being courteous and responsive encourages guests to be the same.

Being realistic

There is a fine line between showcasing your listing in the best light and exaggerating — you want your photos, description, and communication to encourage bookings but not set you up for failure by setting unrealistic guest expectations. Your listing and your initial communications with guests set expectations that can be too low, too high, or just right.

After the guest makes a reservation, meeting or exceeding their expectations requires you to

» **Provide a painless check-in process:** Nothing gets a stay off to a bad start more quickly than a frustrating check-in process. Making the guests wait on you for in-person check-ins, sending confusing or incomplete information, or sending them check-in details too late can all add additional stress to what is typically already a stressful part of traveling — just getting to and settling into their booked property.

>> **Create a seamless guest stay:** From well before their painless check-in to well after their painless check-out, everything you provide and do in between determines the quality of the stay for your guests and whether you meet or exceed their expectations.

We explore in greater detail in Chapter 13 and 14 on how to create a painless check-in and check-out process and a seamless and stress-free guest stay from start to finish.

You can set guest expectations too low, just right, or too high and then the actual guest stay can fall short, meet, or exceed those expectations. Figure 12-1 shows the different scenarios between how you can set and meet guest expectations.

Guest Experience Delivered

		Misses	Meets	Exceeds
Guest Expectations	**Too High**	Overworked and punished	Overworked and underappreciated	Burnt out but appreciated
	Just Right	Property and/or host not ready	Average host average results	Appreciated and rewarded
	Too Low	Why are you even hosting?	Subpar host subpar results	Underselling host leaves money on table

FIGURE 12-1: The guest expectation matrix.

© John Wiley & Sons, Inc.

Here we look at the combinations and why there's only one place you should aim to be — setting just right guest expectations and exceeding them.

Sandbagging guest expectations — setting them too low

"Underpromise and overdeliver!" This common advice given as a sure-fire way to obtain happy customers misses on one very important point — underpromising your offer also undersells your offer.

Taking this approach on Airbnb means not showcasing your listing in its best light. And with more listings coming online daily, your listing needs every advantage to shine among the ever more intense competition. Underselling to sandbag guest expectations can result in fewer bookings for your listing than you deserve.

Overpromising guest expectations — setting them too high

The opposite of underselling is to overpromise, which can be just as bad but for a different reason. Taking this strategy can cause more initial bookings, but it raises guest expectations to levels that are unreasonable and unsustainable.

The outcome is that you either underdeliver against these unrealistically high expectations, leading to poor guest ratings and thus poor long-term performance for your listing, or you must keep going above and beyond just trying to meet these expectations. Feeling overworked and underappreciated is a great way to achieve hosting burnout.

Getting into the Goldilocks zone — setting them just right

To neither handicap your listings ability to win bookings nor set yourself up for burnout, you must set realistic guest expectations by only promising what you can deliver for all guests for all bookings.

Meeting guest expectations is easy, but exceeding them is possible and your efforts appreciated. Here you get the best outcome — receive glowing reviews from happy guests and all without unsustainable overworking on your part. Although setting unreasonably low or high guest expectations each has enticing incentives, both come with costs regardless of the actual guest stay you deliver. The best place to be is to set just right guest expectations and then exceed them.

Creating Your Guest-Centric Plan

Being a guest-centric host means anticipating and proactively addressing stress points that could occur when guests stay at your Airbnb property. One of the biggest stressors for guests is not knowing — either not knowing how to do something or where to find something.

By adding all the relevant details into your guidebook and looking for opportunities to create small positive interactions with your guests, you can minimize potential stress for your guests while improving your odds of receiving five-star guest reviews.

Minimizing guest stress with a guidebook

Creating an accessible, easy-to-read, and detailed guest guidebook with all the relevant information for guests is the best way to address frequently asked questions and minimize guest stress during their stay.

Here are essentials to include in your guest guidebook:

- **»** **Contact information:** Include your phone number and your email.
- **»** **Wi-Fi information:** We recommend putting little stickers with your network name and password on every floor and every room right by the main light switches.

REMEMBER

Easy, painless access to fast Wi-Fi is more important than water for most guests. If they can't sign in instantly or if they can notice any lag in speed during normal usage, guests can report that the sign-in process is too complicated and the speed is too slow.

- **»** **Extra essentials information:** Specify where to find extra toiletries, towels, linens, bedsheets, pillows, or any other consumables with extra supply.
- **»** **Emergency information:** Add a local emergency number, locations of first aid kit and fire extinguisher, and addresses and phone numbers of nearest hospital with an emergency room, fire department, and police station.
- **»** **House rules:** These rules include items, such as quiet hours, maximum occupancy, pet rules, no parties allowed, smoking rules, any fines for violating local noise ordinances, or additional cleaning fees. Check out Chapter 6 for more tips on house rules.
- **»** **Local transit information:** Provide directions and basic information (address, phone numbers, and operating hours) to the nearest subway, metro, and bus stations, including any maps. Offer any relevant information or tips on rideshare apps in the area.
- **»** **Special instructions:** This includes remotes for any entertainment systems, appliances in the kitchen, washer and dryer, fire pits, outdoor kitchens, heating and air conditioning, and everything else that isn't as obvious as an on/off switch. Add any property specific instructions, such as how to access the rooftop.
- **»** **Free or for purchase information:** Be clear on what is complimentary and what costs extra and how much. Tell guests everything in the welcome gift basket is complimentary but let them know that the wine selection in the wine

bar is available for purchase and at what price. You need to clearly mark anything that is for purchase as so to avoid unhappy guests and poor reviews.

>> **Check-out instructions:** Specify when check-out time is, what to do with the keys, what to do with the trash, and how to leave the linens. Explicitly include what you want guests to do and what you don't want them to do.

>> **Local attractions and events:** Provide a list of attractions (tourist favorites, local favorites, and hidden gems) and a full calendar of local events that may interest guests. Include any insider tips and tricks and discount codes or coupons for these recommendations.

As you host more guests, you'll spot new opportunities to include more useful information. Think of your guidebook as a "work in progress" that you'll update often.

ON THE WEB

Have both a physical copy of the guidebook in a neat binder or folder placed in a conspicuous location where guests will spot immediately upon entering the property and a digital version guests can access from their mobile phones. For the digital version, we find it to be easiest to share a view-only Google Doc link — that way you can update and change details on the fly without having to change the link you shared to the guests. To download a guest guidebook template that we created for our readers, go to www.learnbnb.com/airbnbfordummies.

Creating pleasant little surprises

To exceed guest expectations, create opportunities that pleasantly surprise your guests during their stay, giving them something that they weren't expecting and appreciate.

Here are three effective ways to do just that:

>> **A welcome gift:** Although most hosts provide some form of welcome packages, you can still pleasantly surprise your guests when they aren't expecting much at check-in. You don't have to go overboard and offer expensive items. Keep it consistent with your listing. For most listings, hosts should spend at most $50 or 5 percent of the total booking value, whichever is less. Popular items include snacks, drinks, a bottle of wine, chocolates, fruits, and local mementos.

>> **A parting gift:** The parting gift should differ from the contents you provided in the welcome gift basket. Store it in a drawer somewhere and give it the guests to open the morning of their check-out. Think small and easy to carry — local postcards, bookmarks, or any small souvenir item that is cost effective for you and convenient for your guests.

>> **A personal touch:** Leaving a personal touch is harder but much more impactful. It requires you to discover something about your guests, such as who they're traveling with, what the purpose of their stay is, or what their interests are and then leaving a personal note with specific recommendations just for them. For example, a couple may be staying to celebrate their anniversary, so you gather a list of the top romantic restaurants and destinations and maybe even a cancelable reservation at the frequently overbooked ones.

TIP

The secret to making the gestures work is in the surprise. Don't show photos of the gift basket, parting gifts, or personal touches. When guests know about them in advance, they lose their utility to help you exceed guest expectations. So, keep them as surprises and let your guests enjoy as they would a surprise gift.

Catering to Your Ideal Guest Type

Your guidebook answers questions that your guests may have. What makes your listing stand out from your competition to win more bookings and earn more raving five-star guest ratings is by understanding who your guests are and catering to their specific needs beyond the pages of the guest guidebook.

Every market attracts a different mix of types of guests that travel to their area. The better you understand which travelers are most likely to stay with you, the better you can cater to their travel needs.

TIP

Although it may not be immediately obvious exactly which types of travelers your market predominantly attracts, it becomes clearer as you host more guests. Keep a private guest log and don't rely on memory alone. The results may or may not surprise you. After a trend emerges, look for ways to improve your amenities and add extra touches to cater to their specific needs.

The following sections explore the biggest Airbnb guest segments and how to cater to each type more effectively as a host.

Business travelers

As more businesses encourage their associates to use Airbnb instead of pricier hotel options, it's not surprising that more hosts are adding business travel–friendly amenities to attract this traveler segment. According to AirDNA, the leading Airbnb and short-term rental analytics provider, business travel–ready Airbnb listings make an average of $10,000 more in top markets. Blazing fast Internet speeds is a must. Some hosts offer parking passes to local parking garages in parking-deprived markets.

Listings catering to business travelers should aim to mirror the experience, amenities, and cleanliness of hotels. For the most competitive business travel markets, some hosts even add a dedicated work area equipped with a second monitor, laptop docking station, wireless keyboard and mouse combo, and a networked printer scanner just to stand out.

Senior travelers

Late adopters as both guests and hosts on Airbnb in the early days, senior travelers are now one of the fastest growing segments on both sides of the platform. Often retired and affluent with high disposable time and income, the segment sees Airbnb as a fresh new way to travel compared to the more traditional senior favorites in cruises and resorts. First-time senior Airbnb users sometimes come in expecting a traditional bed-and-breakfast experience, complete with breakfast, requiring clarification to set proper expectations.

Take care when automating because some senior travelers require a bit of hand-holding with new technologies, such as the latest smart locks. Senior travelers often expect and appreciate more frequent and in-person conversations, making remote hosting less ideal when serving primarily this segment. Having additional safety features, such as support rails in the bathroom, anti-slip mats in the showers and tubs, and anti-slip house socks or portable bedside toilets can also come in handy. Although a few hosts may say some of their most challenging guests have been seniors, most senior guests are a joy to host.

International travelers

Airbnb is often the most economical and most locally authentic way for international travelers to experience a new city. This segment is easy to please if you put yourself in their shoes. Often jet-lagged from a long flight, international guests want to find your property and check-in painlessly. Provide options to professionally translated instructions and guidebook in different languages (along with international units where relevant) that cover most of the regions your international guests are coming from.

Send your check-in instructions before their departure because they may not have Internet access on their cellphone. Some hosts even provide Wi-Fi details before check-in so that guests can access it near the property in case they don't have cellular access. Expect potential language barriers and cultural differences and exercise patience with guests who arrive without a full understanding of local etiquette and norms of your city. Provide universal plug adapters. Also, make local recommendations for food, places, and entertainment.

Families with young children

Parents traveling with young children often struggle with how much they must pack for their trips. Sometimes, just knowing that some items they need are already available at the Airbnb can be all it takes to secure a booking from this audience. This segment prefers the added privacy and kitchens of entire homes that also meet the Safe Kids Worldwide safety standards (www.safekids.org/safetytips), which include having smoke and carbon monoxide detectors on every floor and all sleeping areas, a fully stocked first aid kit, a portable crib with firm fitting crib sheet, cordless window blinds, safety gates for stairs and pools, secured storage of household chemicals, furniture and appliances secured to prevent tip overs, and hot water set to only 120 degrees Fahrenheit (about 48.9 degrees Celsius). In addition, family travelers appreciate family-friendly books, toys, and board games. Stock some often forgotten travel items, such as kid-version toiletries and sunscreen.

Young travelers

Young tech-savvy travelers were the early adopters of Airbnb and continue to be a staple of the platform. This segment prefers convenience and use of smart technologies. Even though they may be more budget conscious than their older counterparts on accommodations, they're also most willing to spend on experiences. These guests appreciate recommendations for unique experiences.

Pet owners

Whereas some travelers must bring their furry service companions on their trips, other pet owners prefer to travel with their furry pals. With limited pet-friendly options, you can easily appeal to this target audience. However, doing so can come with greater liability risk and likely longer turnaround times (pet hair and fur can hide in crevices and are difficult to clean). In addition, you could risk higher refund requests from future guests who are allergic to pets. Hosts must set limits to the kinds and sizes of pets allowed as suitable for their listing.

Sanctuary seekers

Some travelers seek quiet and relaxation instead of fun and excitement. For example, city folk could be seeking a relaxing weekend getaway. Or maybe a patient of a local hospital is seeking a sanctuary to accompany his recovery. Quiet and remote locations away from city and street noises are preferred. They appreciate mindfulness rooms ideal for yoga or meditation. Other items include blackout curtains, white noise machines, and essential oil diffusers.

Chapter 13

Creating a Seamless Check-In Process

You were expecting your guest to arrive at 4 p.m. to check in and it's now 5 p.m. You send a message to her through the Airbnb app asking her to notify you 30 minutes prior to her arrival so you can meet her to check her in. You leave, awaiting her message 30 minutes away.

Meanwhile, your guest's delayed international flight arrives four hours late. She grabs her luggage late, gets in the taxi late, and arrives at your property late. In the mad rush to get out of the airport, she forgets to purchase a SIM card to have data plan in the new country. And it's raining.

As she drags her now rain-soaked luggage to the porch, she realizes she doesn't have a way to reach you. Cold, wet, and desperate, she knocks on the neighbor's door. After some awkward conversation, she finally has access to Wi-Fi and messages you. Then she waits a little more before you finally arrive to let her in.

Could you have done better as a host in this situation? Yes. With the right strategies in place, you could have wowed your guest right from the start. Instead, they started cold and drenched in the dark. A horrible start to your guest stay, even through no fault of your own, will hurt your chances of getting that 5-star guest rating.

Even when circumstances are out of your control, you can still create a seamless and painless check-in experience for your guests. In this chapter we share some strategies you need to use to anticipate and thus eliminate potential headaches during check-in in order to make a great first impression.

Communicating Check-In Information with Guests

To create a smooth and seamless check-in for your guests, you must first understand what guests want and don't want to experience during their check-ins. Only then can you make the necessary preparations for a smooth and painless check-in for all your guests.

Just as you were responsive and timely in your communications with prospective guests before they made their bookings, you must communicate with your guests after they book and before they check in. In this section, we discuss the ins and outs of communicating check-in details with your guests.

Sending messages to your guests prior to check-in

A common mistake we see early hosts make often is sending too much information too soon. No guests want to read a whole essay in your booking confirmation message, especially if they're weeks or months from their trip. Keep it on a need-to-know basis in the booking confirmation message.

Aside from responding to questions from guests before their arrival, here are the two messages that you must send to all guests and what to include in each.

Welcome message

Send a warm welcoming message to all your guests after they complete a booking with you to thank them and confirm their reservation with you. Because guests are often booking their trips weeks in advance, you don't need to share too much information at this point.

Here's the formula for a solid welcome message:

>> **Keep it casual.** Start with a "Hi" or "Hey" instead of a cold and informal greeting as in "To Whom It May Concern." Guests choosing to book their stays

on Airbnb instead of hotels are seeking a more relaxed and casual stay experience.

>> **Thank them for choosing you.** Show a little appreciation to your guests. They didn't have to book with you. They could have chosen any of the other alternatives in your area.

>> **Tell them what you plan to tell them:** Even though Airbnb has many more repeat travelers, the platform is still adding many new travelers who are booking their first Airbnb stay and don't know what to expect. With your welcome message, you can tell them. Let them know you send important check-in instructions and other details when it's closer to their arrival.

>> **Welcome questions:** By letting them know that they can reach out to you in the meantime if they have questions, you help reduce potential anxiety, particularly if they're new to Airbnb.

Figure 13-1 is a simple template for the welcome message you can send to all your guests. Note that you don't need to follow it verbatim. Adjust as necessary to fit your personality and tone. Just keep it short and simple.

Hey *Jane,*

Thanks for choosing to stay at our place for your trip to *Los Angeles*!

There's nothing you need to do now. We'll be in touch with detailed check-in instructions closer to the check-in date.

But if you do have any questions in the meantime, reach out anytime!

Cheers,

James

FIGURE 13-1:
Welcome message template.

Check-in instructions message

The message you send with the check-in instructions is the most important message you send to your guests. Done correctly, it can prevent many headaches for you and your guests. Done poorly, it can create unnecessary stress for you and your guests.

Share check-in information prior to your guests departing for their travels, which is typically the day before check-in. Some hosts choose to send check-in information to guests the morning of check-in to avoid the rare scenario of having unwanted early arrivals while another guest is still in the unit. But sending check-in information the day of just causes unnecessary stress and anxiety for their guests. For example, international travelers may not have data access until arrival and thus will worry about checking in during their travels. Eliminate their stress by getting the information to them before their departures.

However, for hosts remotely resetting access codes for each guest using smart locks or those who change their lockbox combinations between each guest, they can and should send check-in information 48 hours before check-in. Doing so gives guests, especially international travelers, ample time to process the information and plan accordingly before their hectic travels.

Here are the minimum details to include in your check-in instructions message:

>> **Confirmation of booking details:** Your guests may have multiple future Airbnb reservations so reminding them of the date and address of their reservation is useful.

>> **Check-in time:** Include the time and a short message on why you can't accommodate early check-ins if they've requested one. We discuss strategies for handling early guest arrivals later in the "Handling the Check-in Process" section in this chapter.

>> **Directions to your property:** Include detailed instructions to your property from airports, train stations, or other transit stops. Include any special instructions for parts of the commute that could confuse most guests or their drivers.

>> **Parking instructions:** Even if you have obvious parking options on premises, lay out the instructions in your message. For anything else, be as specific as possible with location, payment, and restrictions if any.

>> **Check-in instructions:** Here, include all relevant details and steps guests needed to gain access to your property. Start from where they'll park their car or get dropped off.

>> **Wi-Fi details:** Include them here and let your guests know they can access it outside if needed. Include network name and password that matches your listing title. For example, instead of using generic network names that come with the router, such as "LinkSys1283," you can have "Jane's Downtown City Loft."

>> **Your contact information:** Include both an email address that you check frequently and a direct phone number that your guests can text.

>> **Additional questions:** We recommend asking guests for their flight number and their intended check-in time, especially for hosts doing in person check-ins; this info allows you to check if their flight is delayed and to avoid finding yourself waiting for your guests to arrive while they're stuck on a delayed flight unable to notify you.

Figure 13-2 is a check-in instructions message template you can use and adapt as a starting point for yours. Replace sample information with yours and adjust as necessary.

Hey *Jane,*

We are looking forward to hosting you and just want to welcome you to *Los Angeles* in advance! A few quick things before your check-in on *January 13, 2021.*

Cozy Main Street Loft
123 Main Street #33
Los Angeles, CA 91108

CHECK-IN TIME: 3:00 PM
Our professional cleaners need the time from 11:00 AM - 3:00 PM to ensure the unit is in the best condition when you check-in.

HOW TO ACCESS THE UNIT:
The entrance to the apartment building is on the corner of *Broadway Road and Main Street.* Take the elevators to your right and head up to the third floor. Upon exit, head left to find unit #33.

Access code: **Last four digits of your phone number**

PARKING:
There is plenty of free street parking on Broadway. Note: There is street sweeping on Friday with sweeps on the eastside from 9AM-12PM and on the westside from 12PM-3PM.

WIFI:
Network: *Cozy Main Street Loft*
Password: *#9Cozy_Loft%7*

Please feel free to reach out if you have other questions/concerns at *cozymainstloft@gmail.com* or text/call us at *+1 (323) 555 - 1234.*

Cheers,

James

FIGURE 13-2: Check-in instructions message template.

© John Wiley & Sons, Inc.

As an added resource for our readers, we provide additional templates for other common messages you should prepare in advance. Go to our online resources page at www.learnbnb.com/airbnbfordummies to locate the message templates you can download and adjust to your needs.

Preventing potential issues before check-in

To best identify potential issues that may arise before your guests check in, ask yourself, "What hurdles can I eliminate or minimize to help my guest get from the airport (or from wherever they're coming) to my door and into my unit?"

Thinking of everything possible can help you anticipate and mitigate potential issues for your guests. Here are some common issues that frequently frustrate Airbnb travelers before their check-in and what you can do as their host to help:

>> **Using the wrong address:** Although rare, but it does happen. For hosts who manage multiple listings in the same area with similar addresses, they can easily mix properties up in their communications with guests. Double-check the full address before sending it in any guest messages.

>> **Navigation maps to wrong location:** A bad way to start off with your guests is for them to arrive at the location on the map using the address you provided, only to discover they're not at the right location. Many navigation tools rely on Google Maps, so ensuring that Google has correctly marked your property on its maps can prevent this problem for practically all guests. Search your address on Google Maps and check that the red map marker is in the right location. If the red marker is marking your property at a different location instead, find the "Report a problem on *[YOUR ADDRESS]*" option on the screen and report the issue to have it fixed.

>> **Difficulty in finding the property:** Guests can be frustrated thinking they can finally check in and relax after their long day of travel to find themselves lugging heavy bags around unable to find their Airbnb instead. If your property isn't immediately visible upon parking or a taxi drop-off, provide detailed instructions for your guests.

>> **Unclear building instructions:** If your property is in a multi-floor building, provide specific details to avoid any confusion due to different floor conventions used around the world. For example, in North America, the ground floor is the first floor whereas in Europe, the ground floor is floor level zero. Provide information such as, "After entering the main door, go up two flights of stairs and then turn left."

>> **Unexpected road closures:** Whether because of weather, construction, or even a parade, road or public transit closures near the property or anywhere

that affects their commute to the property can cause stressful delays. If you know of any closures or delays in advance, be sure to notify your guests and recommend alternative routes or solutions in the check-in instructions message so they can plan accordingly.

» **Access code or keys not working:** Even though we recommend that you use smart locks to simplify the check-in process, technology can malfunction. Having a backup solution is crucial in preventing an angry guest during check-in. Keep a spare manual key with a trusted neighbor or in a nearby lockbox that you can have the guest access. Along with the spare key, include a small token of apology for their inconvenience, such as a $10 Starbucks card.

» **Unable to reach the host:** Having trouble checking in is frustrating enough. Not being able to reach the host on top of having trouble checking in is a recipe for an angry guest and a low rating. Be sure you don't accidentally set your phone on silent that day, but especially in the three hours before and after their scheduled check-in when issues are most likely to arise.

Putting in the extra effort to help your guests from the moment they arrive in your city or town until they get inside your property can help them avoid unnecessary headaches before they check-in. Frequent travelers will notice and appreciate your effort.

Preparing for Your Guest Check-In

Just helping to get your guests to your door without issue is not enough for a seamless check-in; both you and your space must also be ready to receive the guest. Here we discuss the often small and overlooked preparation that can make or break your check-in process.

Getting your property ready for check-in

First impressions matter. When your guests first step inside your property, those first few seconds in your property determine whether they think your property meets the expectations set by your listing's profile.

For example, does your listing look like what they saw in the photos? Does it seem to have everything they were expecting? Getting your property ready for guest check-ins means making sure your property meets or exceeds guest expectations.

In order to make sure you make a perfect first impression at check-in, do the following:

>> **Keep your listing updated and accurate:** First impressions start with setting the right expectations, specifically your listing profile. Ensure that photos and descriptions are accurate. If you've changed decor or have replaced furniture or amenities, update your listing. Most guests prefer to walk into something they're expecting than something different. Review the elements of a great listing profile in Chapter 6.

>> **Have a warm welcome:** Make sure your welcome gift and house manual are immediately visible upon entering the property. If you must set it out somewhere out of view, hang a photo frame with an arrow and the phrase "Start Here" to let guests know where to go first.

>> **Pass final cleaning spot checks:** All it takes is one missed cleaning opportunity to ruin an otherwise 99.9 percent clean property. Have your cleaners dust the surfaces by and behind night stands, check for hair on linens, look for any grime or hair around sinks or toilets, and examine coffee machines for old coffee grounds or filters.

>> **Make Wi-Fi information available everywhere:** Have the Wi-Fi information in a frame by the house manual and posted on every floor of the property. Also include Wi-Fi details in your check-in instructions. Occasionally, check to make sure Wi-Fi router works properly and Internet speeds are at expected levels.

>> **Check for and neutralize strong or offending odors:** Looking clean isn't enough. Your property must smell clean. Air out the unit and use an odor neutralizer as needed. Avoid highly fragrant candles, essential oils, or incense products because some guests may be sensitive to olfactory overload.

>> **Replenish and fully stock supplies:** From snacks and drinks to toilet paper and towels, replenish all items and ensure extras are available.

Refer to our online resources page at www.learnbnb.com/airbnbfordummies for a list of recommended amenities and quantities.

ON THE
WEB

Getting yourself ready for the check-in

You must also prepare yourself for your guest check-ins, especially if you plan on doing them in person. Being unprepared as a host can negate all the preparation you did elsewhere.

Do the following to ensure you're ready to make a perfect first impression at check-in:

>> **Be presentable.** If you're doing in-person check-ins, you're representing your listing. Looking disheveled as if you haven't showered in a week can make your guests wonder just how clean your property is. You don't need formal business attire; put yourself in your guests' shoes and dress accordingly. If you're a remote host, communicate in an appropriate and respectful manner in all messages to guests.

>> **Clear your calendar to avoid conflict.** If you're doing in-person check-ins, don't schedule important appointments the hour before or after the scheduled check-in time. You don't want to risk being late and having your guests wait or having to rush through the check-in should they arrive late. Also notify family and friends that you'll be unavailable during that time.

>> **Keep your phone on and accessible.** Ensure that your phone isn't on silent and keep it near you the day of a check-in so you can be responsive. Guests may have questions early in the day before they get on their flight or hours after they check in.

>> **Have the Airbnb app on your phone.** Some guests only use the app to communicate with their hosts. Unless you'll be frequently checking your computer, you need to have the app installed on your mobile device with notifications turned on so you can respond to guests as needed.

>> **Have a backup plan.** Emergencies can happen. If something were to prevent you from getting to your property to welcome your guest, you can let your backup check in your guest and take over being host until you're back.

>> **Save frequently used messages.** Prepare and save your messages to frequently asked questions from guests. Save them both in your Airbnb account with Saved Messages and save a copy on your phone so you can quickly respond from anywhere without having to type out a cogent response each time. Check out Chapter 10 on how you can outsource guest communications entirely.

Although these preparations apply more to the hosts doing in-person check-ins, they're also useful for remote hosts. Ultimately, you as a host will interact with guests in some capacity, and how you present yourself to guests during your interactions can enhance or detract from a great check-in process.

Handling the Check-In Process

For designing the check-in process, you need to decide whether you want to do them in person or remotely. Each option has its pros and cons and considerations for executing without a hitch, which we discuss in the following sections.

Doing in-person check-ins

Travel can be fun and exciting, but getting to your desired destination can be hectic and stressful. After a long car ride or flight, more waiting for luggage, and more waiting and riding in a taxi or rideshare, guests just want to check in to their Airbnb to relax.

In-person check-ins are becoming rarer among Airbnb hosts today than in the early days of Airbnb when remote management technology, such as smart locks, was less reliable. Plus, in the post-pandemic world, more and more guests prefer contactless check-ins. However, under certain situations described here, in-person check-ins can still be a consideration:

» **Very large properties:** For very large properties hosting large groups, having in-person check-ins can help guests relax and get acquainted with the ins and outs of the property. A friendly guided tour can help a large group of guests get settled in more smoothly.

» **Complicated access:** If your listing has a complicated route from the street to the property and ultimately to get inside where clear written instructions would take pages, then do an in-person check-in.

» **Complicated features or amenities:** Do you have a fancy new hot tub that takes 20 steps to set up, turn on, and heat up? If you have such an amenity, then walking your guests through the process with detailed instructions is probably necessary. Include photos or graphics as needed to help your guests feel comfortable using the amenity. For very complicated steps, some hosts even create instructional videos, host them on YouTube as private videos, and share them with guests.

» **Potential catastrophic risks:** If you have something, such as a propane-powered pizza oven or a gas-powered fire pit that requires lighting a big match in a particular way and in a specific location, then you can demonstrate it to your guests in person with clear instructions. If you're unsure, consult with your legal advisor to determine the best ways to limit your liability risk, including whether to require a signed waiver from guests before permitting use of the amenity. Certain high-risk amenities and activities may not be covered by Airbnb's Host Protection Insurance. Check the latest information on conditions, limitations, and exclusions on the company's website at `www.airbnb.com/host-protection-insurance`.

>> **Frequent first-time Airbnb guests:** If your property attracts first-time Airbnb users, where your property is the guests very first stay using the Airbnb platform, more common with senior or less tech-savvy travelers, in-person check-ins may be worthwhile.

>> **Your appeal:** If your personality as a host is a big part of the appeal for guests to stay on your property, then do an in-person check-in. Although if you're not sure and have to ask, then it's safe to assume you don't have "it" like the rest of us.

Doing in-person check-ins can be time consuming because they require you to be on location when your guests arrive. You also must plan on spending approximately 10 to 20 minutes to show your guest around, make any demonstrations, and answer questions.

TIP

Don't attempt to do in-person check-ins if you don't live near your Airbnb property. The extra back-and-forth commute for each check-in can add many hours to your hosting and additional costs, such as gas and wear and tear to your car, while adding very little value. If you're more than a 15-minute trip to your Airbnb, we highly recommend setting your Airbnb property up for remote self-check-ins instead.

Doing a remote self-check-in

With the proliferation of smart locks in recent years, setting your listing up for self-check-ins for guests is easier than ever. And for most hosts, the advantages of going remote outweigh doing it in person. Reasons for setting up remote self-check-ins are as follows:

>> **They provide flexibility.** Guests can check in on time or after the designated check-in time. If guests show up after their intended check-in time, which happens often due to unforeseen delays, you won't find yourself on standby waiting for them to arrive.

>> **They free up your time.** Going from in-person to remote self-check-ins can help you save up to a hundred hours a year — hours that you could put to better use and more fun for yourself.

>> **Most guests prefer it.** For the experienced Airbnb travelers, most prefer the flexible self-check-in option over meeting a host at check-in in person. Guests prefer not having to coordinate their arrival times with their host or breathe the same air in close vicinity.

>> **They enable you, the host, to travel more.** Besides freeing up your time, doing remote self-check-ins also frees you from being tethered to your property. With the proper automation in place, you can even be halfway around the world and still host.

When deciding to go the remote self-check-in route, you have two options: low-tech or high-tech lock options. Consider the following advantages and disadvantages for each.

Using low-tech locks

A low-technology approach for executing remote self-check-ins is to use purely mechanical devices that don't require batteries, Wi-Fi, or Bluetooth connection for operation.

The simple option without having to change the locks on your door is to use portable combination lockboxes to house the keys securely just outside the front entrance. Hosts often secure these lockboxes around a metal pole or screw them to a surface. They often have a four-digit combination or have a 10-digit keypad. Figure 13-3 shows examples of both popular pole-mounted and surface-mounted lockboxes.

FIGURE 13-3: Combination portable lock box.

Pole Mounted

Surface Mounted

© John Wiley & Sons, Inc.

Simple and reliable, these portable lockboxes are favorites among hosts around the world for an easy, no frills remote check-in process.

The big advantage to going low tech is their reliability. These lockboxes have fewer moving parts and thus fewer places for things to go wrong unlike the high-technology options where batteries require changing, Wi-Fi can go down, and Bluetooth can malfunction, all leading to a frustrated guest experience.

If you're not keen on replacing batteries every 6 to 12 months and don't have reliable Internet and cell signals in the area, consider the low-tech option.

TIP

Because lockouts can occur and you don't want your guest waiting out in the cold while they wait for a locksmith or you to arrive to the property, keep a second lockbox with a backup set of keys on the premise. You can secure this second lockbox in a more inconspicuous location set with a different combination code that you only reveal to the guest if needed in an emergency.

Using high-tech locks

Smart locks have come a long way in recent years. What started as fancy futuristic locks that did everything else but work reliably as a lock now is entering its fourth generation with many more options and many previous kinks worked out.

Here are the major advantages to using a high-tech smart lock:

>> **You can manage access remotely on your phone.** Because you can manage it all on an app, you can manage access from practically anywhere in the world. And you always know whether you, your cleaner, or your guests locked the door to your property or not.

>> **You can create multiple access for multiple people.** Because the smart locks are programmable, most allow authorized access to multiple people at the same time. You can grant access to your guests, family, friends, and cleaners, all with different access codes easy for you to track.

>> **You're notified of unauthorized access.** Unlike traditional locks, smart locks notify you immediately when you have unauthorized access to your property.

>> **They eliminate re-keying for lost keys.** House keys are among the most frequently misplaced items. Guest are human, too. With smart locks, you no longer need to worry about misplaced keys and having to create replacements.

TIP

Smart locks come in all shapes, sizes, and combinations of working with Wi-Fi or Bluetooth and all come with accompanying apps for smartphones. However, we recommend you get a smart lock that doesn't require guests to download the app to get in. We recommend getting a smart lock with a keypad or an interface that only requires the guest to enter their access code to get in. Requiring a download is an extra step that can lead to confusion and errors, especially with less tech-savvy travelers.

Before deciding to use a smart lock, make sure you consider these potential disadvantages as well:

>> **They require additional steps from guests.** Some smart locks require guests to download an app on their phone, thus requiring an extra step that can lead to confusion.

>> **They require batteries.** Smart locks need power to operate so you'll need to replace batteries regularly depending on usage. The latest models can last more than 12 months, much longer than the early models from a few years ago.

>> **They're hackable.** Although improving, smart locks are hackable. Some brands and models have proven to be easy targets in the past so be sure to do your research and find the latest models on the market.

>> **They're more expensive.** Unlike traditional locks, smart locks are more complex and thus cost much more to purchase. The latest models can cost between $200 to $400 dollars.

Although smart locks aren't without some disadvantages, they're still the best option for most hosts in most locations. They provide the flexibility for hosts to manage their listings remotely while creating a seamless check-in process for guests. Figure 13-4 shows four popular smart lock brands, each offering multiple models for hosts. Note the different interface with some requiring a phone to access while others have a keypad.

Handling early arrivals

As a host, eventually you deal with early arrival requests or even worse, the rare unannounced guest who shows hours before the property is ready and before the previous guest has even checked out! Often, due to no fault of their own, Airbnb guests may find themselves in these situations.

Maybe they were expecting to meet with friends before checking in but found themselves stood up. Instead of wandering around town lugging their suitcases, they call you to check in early. But you're not done cleaning the place yet. What do you do?

FIGURE 13-4:
Examples of six
popular smart
locks.

As you can see, early arrivals can be stressful for both the guest and host. Follow these tips to prepare and minimize the impact of early arrivals:

Minimize the potential for early arrivals

The best way to avoid the early arrivals is to prevent them from happening. Having to deal with early arrivals is stressful so make sure you're not volunteering to accept them.

REMEMBER

Making it clear in your listing that you can't accommodate early arrivals is a great first step in discouraging early arrival requests. Write something to the effect, "Check-in time is 4 p.m. or later only. To ensure my cleaner has enough time to properly clean between guests, I regrettably am unable to check guests in before 4 p.m."

Prepare recommendations for your guests

Even with a clearly stated check-in time on your listing, you may still get early arrival requests. When that happens, gently remind your guests that they can't check in early because you need the time to properly clean the space and restock supplies for them.

However, you can prepare a list of recommended places they can go to or activities they can do while they wait:

» **Restaurants:** Guests love food recommendations. Have a list of local restaurants to recommend to guests where they can have a nice meal while they wait. Be specific by recommending specific dishes at the restaurants.

» **Entertainment:** Look for three to five nearby interesting activities that can provide a fun distraction to your guests while they wait.

» **Popular photo spots:** With the growth of social media, more and more travelers are looking for that perfect travel photo from their trips. Find and recommend a few of the most "Instagram worthy" spots near your listing. Be sure to include some examples of the photos.

Handle the luggage for your guests

If your guests end up arriving early anyway, offer to help them with their luggage. No one likes having to lug their heavy suitcases all about town until check-in time.

If your property has the space, installing a large outdoor storage box along with a combination lock can help you accommodate the early arrival and take a load off them. This storage allows the early guests to head out without having to bring their luggage and gives you time to clean your property.

Assume one large suitcase and one small carry-on size backpack for each guest. So, if you typically have four guests, make sure the box is large enough to store four large suitcases and four small backpacks. Use a four-digit combination lock that you can reprogram occasionally.

If you reside in or near the property and have the space for guests, you can hold their luggage in your room or property. For remote hosts, if your property doesn't have the space necessary for an outdoor storage box or you have concerns about potential theft in your area, then see if you can recommend any luggage storage services in your market. These services offer cost-effective ways to store luggage and are becoming widely available in most urban and downtown locations; look for the most established provider in your area to recommend to guests.

IN THIS CHAPTER

» **Making a great first impression**

» **Ensuring an enjoyable guest stay**

» **Creating a smooth check-out**

» **Handling the post check-out**

» **Managing guest reviews**

Chapter **14**

Continuing a Stress-Free Guest Stay Through Check-Out

Although you do everything you can to help your guests arrive at your property without a hitch, the work to ensure a stress-free stay is only just beginning after they successfully check into your property.

From creating the best first impression when guests walk in the door all the way to what you need to do to manage and respond to guest reviews after they check out, small seemingly insignificant decisions can affect your long-term success as a host.

This chapter discusses strategies for how you can capitalize on both the opportunities and avoid the pitfalls during the time when your guests first walk check into your property to well after they check out.

Setting the Tone for Your Guests' Arrival

Just as people form first impressions of others in the first minutes upon meeting, so too will guests form first impressions of your Airbnb listing in the first minutes upon entering the property. During these crucial early minutes, guests subconsciously decide how the property stacks up against their expectations. That's why your property needs to knock off their socks.

Here are some suggestions you can take to form a great first impression and set a positive tone for the rest of your guests' stay:

>> **Creating a pleasant first impression:** What guests see right after they walk in mostly determines how they feel the property measures up to the listing profile. Besides the recommendations that we outline in Chapter 13 on how to prepare your property for check-in and ensure that it looks the way you present it in the listing profile, we also recommend that you keep the entrance area well-lit by leaving on the lights. Use a high efficiency and warm (between 1800 and 2700K temperature rating) LED light bulb to both minimize energy usage and to create a cozy and welcoming glow. Ensure the welcome kit is visible or the path to it is well-lit and obvious.

>> **Being mindful of the noise:** Distracting loud noises can pollute an otherwise serene and welcoming space. Is your property near a loud and busy street during typical check-in times? If so, close the windows near the entrance and have a small digital radio or portable speaker playing some relaxing instrumental or coffeehouse playlist. Music should only be audible upon entering and not from the outside. Be sure to include instructions for guests to play their own music or to turn it off.

>> **Creating a pleasant aroma:** Foul orders can ruin a great first impression for your property. No sight can be beautiful enough to mask a bad smell. You can air out your listing with open windows and use odor neutralizer as needed. Avoid using strong fragrances as a mask because doing so can irritate guests with olfactory sensitivities. Most guests welcome fresh-baked cookies or fresh fruit. If using fresh flowers, opt for hypoallergenic varietals with little to no pollen to avoid setting off allergies for guests. When in doubt, choosing clean and sterile always beats musty and stuffy.

Whether or not you planned for it, your property gives a mood based on how it looks, sounds, and smells to guests right after they walk in the door.

Ensuring Your Guests Enjoy Their Stay

Although the ideal scenario is when guests have no questions or concerns during their stay, the typical guest stay almost always involves some opportunities to address guest questions or concerns.

The question isn't whether you'll have something to answer or address for your guests, but how you go about doing that while ensuring an enjoyable overall stay for your guests.

Providing a clear way to make guests feel comfortable communicating with you and finding ways to add value during their stay can help earn more 5-star guest reviews.

Understanding why guests won't voice complaints directly

In the world of business, marketing experts estimate that for every customer complaint there another dozen or more silently unhappy customers. Even though loud and vocal complainers may represent most unhappy customers, they're only a small fraction.

The same is true with Airbnb guests: Most guests won't message their hosts directly even if they find something amiss with the property after checking in.

Here are common reasons why most guests do not voice their complaints directly to you:

>> **It requires effort.** However little, reaching out to hosts requires effort by the guests. Unless they're really annoyed by something, many guests stay silent and mentally note the shortcoming of the property and the host to post later in their review.

>> **They don't want to bother you.** No one likes a complainer and no one wants to be perceived as one either. Unless the host creates a friendly opening during communications for guests to voice their concerns, guests won't take the initiative themselves.

>> **They already made up their minds.** Many guests have already decided by the first night regarding whether your property met their expectations. Barring something notably good or bad, their opinion will stay the same.

To overcome these barriers and create an open, inviting line of communication between you and your guests, you must make it easy and natural for your guests to communicate with you.

Opening communications with guests

The best way to get guests to notify you what they're thinking is to ask them directly. However, you have a fine line between inviting and annoying messages. Keep them short, friendly, and infrequent.

Here are some suggestions to help you keep the lines of communication open with your guests:

>> **Send a post check-in message the first night:** Two to three hours after the guests check in, which should be plenty of time for them to get settled into the space, send them a short text message as in, "Hey Joe! Just wanted to make sure you're properly settled into the space. Here if you need anything at all. Just text/call me on this number. Thanks, Sam."

>> **Touching base every two to three days for long stays:** For long guest stays, you should aim to touch base with your guests every two to three days with a short message. Ideally, try to find some useful information to share with guests to make a more natural follow-up message. For example, "Hi Joe, just a heads-up that there are road closures tomorrow on Main St. Take Broadway instead. Everything good? Here if you need anything. Just shout!"

When your guests feel comfortable communicating directly with you, they won't keep their complaints to themselves or worse, put their complaints in their online review of your listing.

Keeping a guest book for guests to sign

Different from the house manual that provides all the relevant information house information and instructions to your guests, a guest book is more for fun. However, a guest book can also encourage your guests to focus on the positives of their stay.

TIP

Include a guest book in your Airbnb listing to reap the following benefits:

>> **It shows that you value them.** By memorializing their stay in a well-designed guest book, you're indirectly showing your guests that you value them. By capturing their names, the date of their visit, and their comment, it shows them that you want to remember them — that they're not just another set of strangers that you'll soon forget.

>> **It conditions guests to see the positives.** Almost no guests leave negative comments in a guest book during their stay so your guest book essentially will be filled with the positive messages left from your previous guests. Even for guests who ultimately don't sign the guest book, many will read it, more likely to see their stay in a similar positive light.

>> **It's something you can keep and be proud of.** Even though being an Airbnb host presents many rewards, it's not without its fair share of headaches. Being able to look through a guest book full of happy and appreciative guests can help you remember and focus on the positives.

TIP

Find a guest book with pages you can easily tear out or use a binding that allows you to remove pages. For the very rare occasion where you get inappropriate or negative entries, you can easily remove that page without having to start all over with a brand-new guest book.

Going the extra mile for your guests

A sure-fire way to win guests over is to give them more than they were expecting. Besides having the basic information in the house manual and welcome package, here are strategies hosts use to go the extra mile for their guests:

>> **Help guests save money.** "I hate saving money!" said no guest ever. Guests love a good deal. If popular shopping destinations or activities are near your listing, try to score some coupons, discounts, or freebies for your guests.

>> **Help guests get special access.** Getting access to a sold-out or a difficult-to-get-into event or venue makes most guests happy. Do you have a personal relationship with a popular restaurant, bar, comedy club, or the like? Scoring tickets or getting reservations for something guests want but wouldn't be able to get on their own can be a huge win.

>> **Include something seasonally appropriate.** Are you hosting guests during the winter holidays? If so, add holiday specific offerings when possible, such as adding a pumpkin-spiced latte to the coffee options.

>> **Include something regionally.** Is your town or region famous for something? Jerky? Corn bread? Ice cream? Identify what a tourist is eager to try and, if economical, include a sample in your welcome package, or if too costly to provide, recommend to guests the best place to get the treat.

TIP

More than likely guests will notice your efforts on most occasions, but don't leave it to chance! If you're offering anything beyond guests typically expect, such as having water and basic snacks, make sure you get the credit you deserve by drawing their attention to your extra effort. For example, if you're offering a bottle of wine, include a friendly note like, "Hey Natalie and Josh, here's a complimentary bottle of wine to help you both relax and unwind. Enjoy!"

Ultimately, having guests feel as though they got more than they were expecting is a great way to keep them happy during their stay. And the efforts you make after their check-in can create an outlet for guests to voice their wants or concerns and thus create an opportunity for you to intercept any issues before they balloon into something bigger.

Ensuring a Smooth Check-Out

According to psychologists, people remember beginnings and endings better than they do the middle of experiences, even if the middle were technically stronger parts of the whole experience. So, what are you to do as a host? Create strong beginnings and strong endings.

All the effort you've put in so far with your listing culminates to the end of your guests' stay when they finally check out of your property. A big slipup here can negate all that hard work by leaving your guests with a bad aftertaste — like finding a bug at the bottom of an otherwise tasty salad.

Here we discuss how you can plan a great check-out process as well as weigh the tradeoffs between doing in-person and remote check-outs.

Planning your check-out

Your aim in creating a check-out process, as is with your check-in process that we outline in Chapter 13, is to minimize the hassle for your guests. Don't make your guests work more than necessary.

Follow these strategies to put together your check-out and finish strong:

>> **Be specific with your check-out time.** If you don't specify a specific check-out time, Airbnb defaults it to 12 p.m. local time. However, 12 p.m. may not give you or your cleaner enough time to clean, sanitize, and turn the property over before the next guest checks in, typically by 3 or 4 p.m. We recommend most hosts start with an 11 a.m. check-out time. Any earlier and you'll make your listing unappealing to potential guests. Make sure you clearly state your check-out time in your listing, in your house manual, and in your check-out communications.

>> **Be specific with detailed instructions.** Before you finalize your check-out instructions, run it by some friends and family and have them go through the process to see if there are any points of confusion or lack of clarity. For any steps that would be easier to explain with an illustration, include them in your house manual.

For a check-out instruction template you can build on, go to our online resources webpage at www.learnbnb.com/airbnbfordummies.

ON THE
WEB

>> **Discourage late check-outs.** Ensuring a smooth check-out is as much for your guests' benefit as yours. A sure way to have a stressful check-out is when guests leave late and cause a delay in your turnover of the space for the next guest. One way to avoid late check-outs is to deter it by stating a fine in both the listing profile and in the house manual for every hour that a guest is late in checking out. A fine of the full daily rate for each hour is more than enough to motivate guests to leave on time.

>> **Provide a small parting gift.** End on a good note by having a prepared parting gift inside a drawer near the exit. It can be a small local souvenir with some light snacks for the road trip back. Include a tiny note as in, "It's been great having you! Here's a little something for your safe travels!"

>> **Send friendly reminder messages.** The day before check-out, send a friendly reminder message in the early evening before 8 p.m. as in, "Hey Jane, hope you're enjoying a wonderful evening! Let me know if you need anything or have questions before your check-out tomorrow morning by 11 a.m. Thanks!" The morning of check-out, send a final message about two hours prior (9 a.m. for an 11 a.m. check-out time), "Good morning Jane, it's been wonderful hosting you and your group. If you have questions about checking out, please let me know. Also, check the top-right drawer by the exit on your way out! :)"

WARNING

Having your guests return the keys to the lockbox and lock the doors behind them on their way is reasonable. Expecting and requesting guests to run the dishwasher, collect and take all the trash out, strip all the linens and put them into the washer, run the washer, and text you when they leave is asking for too much. Guests don't like feeling as though they're doing most of the cleaning after having already paid the additional cleaning fee on top of their reservation. Yes, knowing if your guests check out early would be nice, but pestering them to message you creates a burden on them.

Doing remote check-outs

For most Airbnb situations, we recommend a remote check-out process for the benefit of both guests and hosts. For many guests, having a host hover at the end can create an awkward finish to an otherwise great stay.

Here are reasons for setting up a remote check-out process:

>> **Flexible check-out:** Not all guests check out at the very end. Many guests often leave early for many reasons, perhaps to catch a flight. By having the check-out remote, your guests don't have to wait for or coordinate with you to leave.

>> **Frees up your time:** Having a remote check-out process can help you save dozens of hours a year — hours that you can put to better use.

>> **Preferred by guests:** As more travelers become familiar with using Airbnb, more of them prefer flexible check-in and check-out options to in-person check-ins and check-outs. A remote check-out is less stressful and requires less coordination and communication.

>> **Frees you to travel:** Along with more time, remote check-outs free you from being tethered to your property. By creating a remote check-in and check-out process, you can host from anywhere.

Like opting for remote check-ins, you as a host have the option of using either low-tech locks or high-tech smart locks for remote check-outs. See Chapter 13 for the pros and cons of each and why we recommend smart locks for most hosts.

Doing in-person check-outs

Even though we recommend a remote check-out process for most hosts, doing an in-person check-out makes sense in some limited situations. If any of the following situations apply to you, then consider doing your check-outs in person:

>> **You had repeat issues with theft or damage.** If you experienced repeat incidents of theft or damage in the past, then announcing and doing check-outs in person can serve as a deterrent against guest shenanigans because they know that you'll notice any damage or missing items right away.

>> **Your guests would welcome the help.** If you have guests who have disabilities or are elderly with lots of luggage, offer to help with their check-out. Even though most won't accept your offer, the few who do will appreciate your helpful gesture.

>> **You have a complicated lockup process.** When guests are ready to leave with their luggage, the check-out process shouldn't take them more than three minutes. If the process is much longer, such as having multiple steps with multiple locks and gates to getting out of the building and off the property, then consider being present to lessen that burden for your guests.

TIP

Doing in-person check-outs is fine, but just make sure you notify your guests of your procedures the day before if you plan to be present during the check-out. State it in your house manual that you could be around to help when they check out, leaving you the option but not the obligation to be present.

Knowing What to Do After Guests Leave

After your guest checks out, your work as their host still isn't complete. The hours and days afterward are an opportunity for you to put the finishing touches to a successful reservation.

After check-out is a great time to follow up with your guests and provide some incentives to encourage potential future bookings. You should also check the condition of your property, especially if you suspect any potential for damage or theft.

Assessing the state of your property

Whether you're doing the turnover yourself or hiring a cleaner to do it for you, make sure you or the cleaner accesses the state of your property after your guest checks out. A simple checklist to account for both the presence and condition of all major appliances and furniture will do.

ON THE WEB

As an added resource for our readers, we provide a "Turnover Checklist" on our online resources page at www.learnbnb.com/airbnbfordummies.

Filing a claim with Airbnb

If you find damage or missing items, take good photos for documentation and file a claim with Airbnb against the security deposit and/or Airbnb Host Guarantee right away. Include any written communications between you and the guest that corroborates or supports your claim, especially for any retaliatory damages.

REMEMBER

You have until your next guest check-in or up to 14 days to file a claim, whichever occurs sooner. In most cases, your window for filing a claim is just the few hours from the prior guest's check-out to the next guest's check-in, typically between 11 a.m. and 4 p.m., making it a smart move for you to assess your property during each turnover. After your next guest checks in, you can't make a successful claim because the damage or theft could now be due to the next guest.

For minor claims that can be made on the security deposit, you can follow these steps:

1. **Go to** www.airbnb.com/resolutions.
2. **Click Request money.**
3. **Choose the appropriate reservation to make your claim.**
4. **From the Select a reason options, choose Request compensation for damages.**
5. **Click Continue.**
6. **Type in details of specific damages or reasons for the claim and requested compensation amount.**
7. **Submit to complete your request.**

Your guest has 72 hours to accept your request, which would then be paid out to you in approximately five to seven business days. However, if your guest doesn't respond or refuses to accept within 72 hours, you can log back into your Airbnb account, go to the Resolution Center, and choose the "Involve Airbnb" option to bring Airbnb in to help resolve the claim. Airbnb may ask for additional information, such as receipts or proof of the condition of the damaged item prior to the reservation in question, which you must provide within 72 hours. According to Airbnb, most claims on security deposits are resolved within a week.

Following up with your guests

With guests receiving so many notifications from just about everywhere, many hosts are hesitant to add one more message to their guests' inboxes. But sending a follow-up thank you note can make the all the difference for your performance.

TIP

Send a thank you note within 12 to 24 hours after their check-out and include these three important items.

Expressing sincere appreciation

Share your sincere appreciation with your guests for choosing to stay with you. They could have chosen any other listing in your area, but they chose to stay with you.

TIP

Thank them for being great guests if they left your property in good condition and were otherwise pleasant for you to host. Not only does this prime your guests to be in a better mood after reading your note, it may also encourage them to look back at their stay through a more positive lens.

Asking your guests for a review

From our own survey of hosts, the percentage of their guests that leave reviews can range from as low as 30 percent to as high as 100 percent. Even though Airbnb now automatically sends emails to remind guests to leave reviews after check-out, these messages can get lost in their inboxes or guests may simply ignore them. Asking your guests to consider leaving you a review can drastically increase the percentage of your guests who end up leaving reviews.

REMEMBER

Asking is especially crucial if your listing is new with little to no reviews. Notify your guests that you're quite new to hosting and that every review helps tremendously. Guests who otherwise enjoyed their stay with you are typically eager to oblige.

In addition, Airbnb has many requirements when evaluating a host for Superhost status. One requirement is that at least 50 percent of the guests who stay with the host ends up leaving a review. By not asking your guests to leave a review, you risk falling below on this metric right from the start. (Refer to Chapter 11 for more information about being a Superhost.)

Providing incentives for future stays

A good way to end your thank you note to your guests is to offer them an incentive to book a future stay with you (as Figure 14-1 shows). Many hosts offer a discount of 5 to 15 percent to former guests and their family and friends.

> Hello!
>
> Just wanted to say a big THANK YOU for choosing to stay at my place. It was such a pleasure hosting you--I wish all my guests could be like you! I will be letting future hosts know by writing a positive review for you soon. :)
>
> If you also enjoyed your stay, would you mind leaving a review through Airbnb? It only takes 2 minutes and it'll really make all the difference for a new host like me.
>
> If you're ever visiting the area again in the future, I'd be honored to host you again. As a small token of appreciation, I'd like to offer a 10% discount (15% if you stay more than a week!) to you, your family, or your friends. Just message me first before booking and I'll respond with a special offer.
>
> Thank you again for being an awesome guest.
>
> Best,

FIGURE 14-1: Sample follow-up thank you note to guests.

© John Wiley & Sons, Inc.

This sample thank you note hits on all three points: expressing sincere appreciation, asking for reviews, and offering value. Use the template to create your own.

For guests traveling to visit family for on an annual trip, they may well take you up on the offer. During low season periods, getting referrals can help you fill up some nights that otherwise would stay vacant.

Blocking out a day or two before and after reservations for preparation time

In rare situations, you may need to block a day or two in between reservations to have enough time to turn around and prepare the property for the next guests.

TIP

Consider blocking off a day or two before and after each reservation if your property needs extra time for a proper turnaround. For example, if you list a listing with a large building and many amenities on a vast property where you and your cleaners require more than four to five hours to properly clean and turn, add the extra day or two in between reservations.

If you're not seeking to maximize your profits and would prefer a more relaxed hosting experience, adding the extra day or two between reservations reduces the hectic chaos that can ensue for same-day turnarounds.

WARNING

However, adding this extra buffer means giving up those days of potential revenue because you'd be blocking those days off with each reservation that comes through. If your typical reservation lengths are short, say on average three days, then blocking off one day before and after takes your available days for booking down by 25 percent. The impact is less severe if your guests typically book long stays, such as losing a day or two for a three-week average stay length.

To block off one of two days between reservations, follow these steps:

1. **Log into your Airbnb account.**

2. **Click Availability settings from your Calendar.**

3. **Click the drop-down menu under the Preparation time label with the coffee cup icon.**

4. **Choose either Block 1 night before and after each reservation or Block 2 nights before and after each reservation.**

5. **Click Save.**

TIP

Choose the one-day option first to see if that's enough time for you. You don't need to block off more days than necessary unless you prefer the extra break between guests.

Managing and Responding to Guest Reviews

By following and adapting the best practices we present in this chapter and book, you can expect at least one out of every two guests to leave you a review for their stay.

Whether you're looking to build momentum for your new listing or to maintain strong performance for your established listing, properly managing and responding to guest reviews is crucial for long-term performance. Although most guest ratings on Airbnb are positive, all hosts eventually get their share of negative reviews whether they're deserved.

In these sections we discuss why reviews tend to skew positive on Airbnb as well as how to respond to both positive and negative reviews. Even though most hosts can expect to receive mostly positive reviews when they follow hosting best practices, they inevitably receive their share of the occasional negative review. Although you may not be able to prevent negative reviews, you can minimize their chances of occurring and their damage when they do occur.

Understanding the nature of Airbnb's positive leaning reviews

One of the unique aspects of Airbnb is the two-way aspect of reviews where guests and hosts can rate each other after a reservation, unlike many other travel platforms where only guests rate the places and hosts.

This tiny feature creates for more mutual respect and explains why the same properties that appear on multiple platforms often are rated more charitably on Airbnb than elsewhere. When hosts can evaluate them back, guests are more thoughtful and often more forgiving in the reviews they leave on Airbnb than elsewhere. The rating process is blind: You only get to see the other person's review after you've left your review.

Here are some of the other reasons for the positively leaning ratings:

>> **People are nicer to people.** If you browse the reviews on Yelp.com, a website that collects customer reviews for businesses of all sizes, you may notice that the reviews for small local businesses are often more positive than those of the big chain brands. Why? People understand that small businesses are the livelihood of real individuals, often whose business name is their namesake. Similarly, Airbnb guests understand that they're not just rating a property but another person.

>> **Hosts are selective.** Some self-selection occurs on the platform because hosts may reject guest requests for stays from guests with a questionable identity or prior negative reviews from hosts. Hosts accepting more bookings from guests who are less likely to cause trouble and more eager to earn their own high ratings creates a mutual and positive feedback loop between hosts and guests.

>> **Hosts put in more work.** As the platform itself became more popular and thus more competitive for hosting, hosts make ever increasing efforts to earn every advantage they can. Getting great reviews helps with searching rankings and thus booking revenue.

With reviews on Airbnb leaning positive, it means hosts who implement the best practices outlined in this book can get mostly positive reviews from their guests. However, it also means that your fellow hosts in your market probably have mostly positive reviews, raising the bar for everyone involved.

Responding to positive guest reviews

Even though most of your guest reviews will probably be positive, you still need to respond to each review. Even positive reviews give hosts an opportunity to appeal to future potential guests who are reading these reviews.

Here are some reasons to respond to all positive guest reviews:

>> **Address veiled concerns.** Five-star guest reviews are great, but many can include a complaint buried between compliments. Responding graciously lets you show appreciation to the guests and respond to the complaint. For example, if a guest raves about her stay but also mentioned that she could have used a more comfortable pillow, you should thank her for being a great guest and include a note that you upgraded all the pillows. Other potential guests who read the review will know that they need not worry about uncomfortable pillows.

>> **Help former guests feel appreciated.** Seeing confirmation that you not only read but taken the time to respond to a guest's review helps your former guest feel heard and appreciated, which can help you secure future bookings and recommendations from former guests.

>> **Show a consistent pattern of engagement.** Potential guests seeing that the host took the time to respond to each guest review shows you're an attentive host who truly cares about your guests.

>> **Push down negative reviews.** Guest reviews show up on the bottom of the listing profiles and are paginated with only 6 to 12 reviews on each page depending on the lengths of the reviews and the hosts' responses. By responding to all positive reviews, especially if they're already on the first page, you can push the negative reviews onto later pages. Reviews that appear on the front pages are usually the more recent reviews, but some older reviews do occasionally appear.

>> **Show more sides of the hosts.** If you only respond to negative reviews, which almost always requires an apology, then potential guests only see you apologizing for mistakes in your responses. By responding to all the many more positive reviews, you can show potential guests your gracious and fun side far more often.

TIP

Responding to positive reviews doesn't require much effort. Mostly, a simple response, such as the following will do, "Thank you, Nicole! It was such a pleasure hosting you and your family. If you plan to visit the area in the future, I'd be honored to host you again!" If the guests had a complaint or concern, don't make excuses but address them directly. For example, "Sorry about my new AC breaking down in the middle of the night. I already replaced it with a new, more powerful model and a backup portable one in storage."

Minimizing the occurrence of negative reviews

Eventually, you receive your first negative guest review. Even though you can take certain measures to minimize the damage after receiving one, the best way is to prevent getting one in the first place.

To minimize their occurrence, you need to understand the different reasons guests leave them, which we discuss in the following list:

>> **They didn't get what they paid for.** The biggest reasons for guests to leave negative reviews is if their stay grossly underdelivered on their expectations.

- » **They feel unheard.** Guests want hosts to hear and validate their experiences, especially if they had a negative experience. And as much as some hosts think the guests leave a negative review only to hurt them, these guests mostly want to help other potential guests avoid their bad experience.

- » **They're unappeasable.** Although very rare, some guests have such unreasonable and unrealistic expectations that they can't be satisfied no matter what you do as a host.

- » **They're retaliating.** Certain guests may rarely retaliate with a negative review that often includes exaggerations or outright lies after hosts refuse to comply with their outrageous requests. By responding to the many more positive reviews, you can show potential guests your fun and friendly side as well.

Delivering on guest expectations

Meeting or exceeding guest expectations during their stay is the best way to prevent negative guest reviews. That means delivering on the promises you made in your listing profile. Refer to Chapter 12 to better understand the fundamentals of guest satisfaction.

However, sometimes even with the best preparation, you may fall short of guest expectations through no fault of your own. For example, your brand-new air conditioner may break down in the middle of the night or an unexpected construction nearby may create significant noise for your guests.

REMEMBER

Although you can't predict or prevent many issues that may arise, you can show your guests that you'll make every reasonable effort to help them improve their stay given the unforeseen circumstances. While waiting for a new air conditioner to arrive, get them fans and offer a discount on their stay. To mitigate the construction noise, provide ear plugs or a white noise machine. It doesn't have to be grand or expensive gestures; just be proactive and show your guests that you took their comfort into serious consideration. The best way to avoid a complaint is to address the issue before it can become a complaint.

Helping your guests feel heard

Providing a welcoming outlet for the guests to message you and tell you what is missing or for you to fix issues can help you intercept many potentially negative guest reviews.

TIP

For the guests who are shy about directly communicating with their hosts, you can provide a suggestion box for them to anonymously submit their feedback and recommendations. A locked envelope box, a simple form, and pen is all you need. Be sure the box already has other submitted forms in it. A digital suggestion box in the form of an anonymous online survey can also work. Provide printed instructions with a shortened URL that guests can go to.

For guests with minor complaints or concerns, having an outlet to voice them can satisfy their need to be heard. And by intercepting the feedback through your own suggestion box, you can keep many of the complaints from reaching your Airbnb profile because many will have no desire to write it again.

Addressing the unappeasable guests

The most problematic guests come with unreasonable expectations for their Airbnb stay. And they're often first-time Airbnb guests with no prior Airbnb experience. They may come from previously having only stayed in hotels or other full-service hospitality offerings.

TIP

To avoid these first-time Airbnb guests, you can set your Instant Book option to require that your guests have traveled at least once on Airbnb and have never received a negative review from previous hosts. And unless you have had repeat bad experiences with Instant Book guests, we recommend keeping that feature on because your booking revenue will probably suffer if you turn it off. Airbnb prioritizes listings with Instant Book turned on over those that have it turned off. Refer to Chapter 6 for the ins and outs of Instant Book.

Protecting against retaliatory reviews

For retaliatory negative reviews, a shakedown along the lines of "Give me something or I'll give you a bad review!" almost always precedes them.

These guests from hell arrive at their Airbnb reservations intending to bully their hosts into giving them undeserved concessions, such as a significant cash refunds for insignificant or seemly made-up grievances.

Take the following precautions to protect yourself should you be unfortunate enough to cross paths with these guests:

>> **Direct all communication to text.** Default to communicating either directly through the Airbnb app, text messages, email, or other forms of text messaging so you have written records. Should you have a need for dispute, you have proof to support your case.

>> **Avoid or minimize in-person interaction.** If you have any reason to suspect guests may set you up for an in-person shakedown, avoiding or minimizing in-person opportunities to interact forces them to message you. If they call you, reject the call and message them back, "Sorry, I'm not able to talk, but I can check text or email. What's up?"

- >> **Stay calm and collected.** If they catch you off guard and attempt to solicit a concession in person, it's understandable for you to be upset; no one enjoys feeling cornered. But we suggest you initially play dumb and respond with, "I've haven't had this kind of request before. Let me think about ways to make this work and get back to you later today."

  What you can then do is to message them via text with a clarifying question, such as "Hey, I just want to make sure I understood you earlier. You want 50 percent refund in cash from me for your stay, and you'll promise not to leave me a negative review? I need to know you'll keep your promise if I agree." Although sending this type of response won't always work, the allure of being so close to seeing their cash may get some to respond to you, giving you all the proof you need to contact Airbnb's Resolution Center.

Minimizing the impact of negative reviews

Even if you do all the right things, you can only minimize rather than prevent the occurrence of negative guest reviews. When you get your first negative guest review, it will sting. Yet how you respond can either minimize or amplify the damage.

If you receive a negative review, take the following steps to minimize their damage:

- >> **Wait before replying.** Don't respond under heightened emotions. Wait. Cool off. If you must, write a response on paper. Then toss it in the trash bin. Only when you feel calm and collected should you start to craft a thought-ful response.

- >> **Respond with grace.** Although you may be tempted to attack the guest for his unfairly negative rating, hurling an aggressive response only hurts your cause. Appearing as a combative or aggressive host only scares away prospective guests. Instead, respond in a neutral tone, don't make excuses, and show what you've done to help the guest and to mitigate the issue for future guests.

- >> **Offer a genuine apology.** Be honest with yourself. If your property or your hosting fell short, offer a genuine apology. Apologize even for something outside of your control. Prospective guests will see how accommodating you are and how unreasonable the guest was.

- >> **Contest the negative review.** If the guest rated you negatively for not being able to meet their impossible and unreasonable expectations, such as expecting full concierge services from you, then you should attempt to contest the negative review through Airbnb. Although Airbnb can remove negative reviews with clearly unreasonable guest expectations, you gathering proof in writing is crucial.

>> **Move past them.** After you do everything you can, you must move past it and let it go. Even though negative Airbnb reviews can affect your short-term performance on Airbnb, positive reviews will outnumber the negative ones in the long run. Also, most potential guests can tell when negative reviews are unreasonable.

Reviewing your guests in return

Just as you want guests to be charitable in their reviews of you as a host, opt to be charitable with your Airbnb guests in your reviews of them. Unless your guest violated common decency, caused damage above and beyond the coverage of the security deposit, committed theft, or something of a similar magnitude, try to find something you appreciate about the guest and write your review based on that.

Regardless, we recommend that you always write a review of your guests to contribute to the overall community. Most guests will be great, and it's helpful for other hosts to know how great they are. As for the few who are bad, it's even more important for you to let other hosts know that as well.

When we poll our students and readers, hosts leave positive reviews for their guests for more than 90 percent of their guests, closely reflecting the overall positive experience that they receive from guests as Airbnb hosts.

Here are a few simple templates for good guest experience reviews that you can utilize:

>> "Jason and his family were wonderful guests; it was a pleasure hosting them. They communicate well and took great care of my property. Would welcome them back anytime!"

>> "Had a nice experience hosting Jane and Michael. From start to finish, they were a pleasure to communicate and interact with. Perfect guests!"

>> *"Considerate, clean, and respectful, Jack and Liz were ideal guests. Any host will be lucky to have them as guests in the future!"*

Always use the guest's first name in the review to make it more personal.

For the rare guests who require negative feedback, stay professional and be specific.

>> "Although Jason was great to communicate with, I'm disappointed that he tried to sneak two additional guests and a large dog into my property when we've communicated about house rules on multiple occasions. I wouldn't recommend him to other hosts."

>> "Jane and Michael booked my property under the pretense of a quiet visit with family, but instead they threw a party that led to more than $2,500 in property damage. Hosts beware."

>> "After refusing to give Jack a full cash refund upon arrival because he 'changed his mind,' Jack proceeded to leave a negative review with lies. Hosts beware and avoid at all costs!"

Chapter **15**

Upkeeping Your Space to Keep the Reservations Coming

One of the most important aspects to hosting on Airbnb is cleaning and maintaining your property. By focusing all your attention on the marketing and the pricing automation, hosts can sometimes can get caught up in all these peripheral aspects to hosting and forget the importance of cleaning and upkeep. However, the act of hosting is to create great experiences when inviting guests into your space, and having a well-maintained, clean property is imperative.

Making sure that your space is exactly what your guests are expecting is vital. If you meet or exceed those expectations, your guests will leave satisfied. However, not meeting or exceeding them can leave guests underwhelmed and disappointed with your space, which can drastically affect their overall experience (and your ratings). A huge part of hosting is preparing and cleaning your space. This chapter dives into how you can make sure your space immaculately clean and well maintained so that you're always ready to welcome guests and have them enjoy their stay.

Maintaining Your Space to Ensure Long-Term Success on Airbnb

In order to ensure long-term success on Airbnb, you need to make sure your space is well cared for so your guests are ultimately happy staying there. It doesn't matter how great your pricing strategy is if your place isn't maintained.

For example, consider it's the peak of the summer and your air conditioner is broken. How well you optimize your pricing and how quickly you respond to guest inquiries are irrelevant. Your guests are still going to have a terrible time and leave terrible reviews if you don't tend to the broken AC. In other words, maintaining the following aspects of your listing can ensure your guests leave happy. If you don't upkeep these areas, you can expect guests to leave negative reviews, which hurt you in the long run.

Smoke and carbon monoxide detectors

Ensuring your space is safe for all your guests is your top priority, and that starts with your smoke and carbon monoxide detectors. Check them on a regular basis to verify they're working.

TIP

The easiest solution is to direct your cleaners to regularly check that the detectors are in good condition and the batteries aren't dead.

In addition, you want to have fire extinguishers throughout the property. Make sure to check your local laws for the requirements for fire prevention and detection devices in your space. The total number can differ from place to place so you want to make sure you're compliant with your jurisdiction's requirements.

Doors and windows

Maintaining your doors and windows is easy to do, but if you aren't mindful of any potential issues, they can cause a negative impact on the guest experience. Concerning your doors and windows, make sure they're all in good working order. All the windows should lock properly and fully close with no drafts. Your doors should also easily shut and have proper working locks. Make sure you don't have any doors or windows that are difficult to open or close. Because both get used quite often, you want to prioritize that they remain in working order.

For example, if a door jams all the time or a sliding door doesn't slide on the track very well, it not only can pose potential safety hazards, but it's also energy inefficient. It's also a massive hindrance on your guests' experience when something they use so often is out of order.

Heating ventilation and air conditioning (HVAC)

This component involves all the heating and air conditioning in your home and is probably the most important area you want to maintain because it contributes massively to your guests' overall experience and can make or break their stay. No matter how beautiful, clean, or unique a property is, the experience will be miserable for your guests if the heat doesn't work properly in the winter or the AC doesn't work during the summer.

In either scenario, your guests aren't going to be happy. Nothing can make up for the fact that they're shivering or sweating through the night. They won't want to spend any time in your space if the HVAC isn't working, and aren't they paying you to stay there?

REMEMBER

If the HVAC does break during a reservation, your top priority is to get it fixed and at the same time ensure your guests are cared for in the meantime. First and foremost, verify your guests are safe and then check that they're comfortable. The best way to think about this situation is, "What would you want as a guest staying in your property with no working HVAC?" If it's springtime and you wouldn't use the AC that much anyway because it's not overwhelmingly hot or cold, then sending a nice apology or small gift or comping one night may be sufficient.

On the other hand, if it's the dead of winter and the heating is nonexistent or it's a hot day and you can't get the AC fixed, then you want to put your guests in a hotel for that night. Having the night comped doesn't really fix the issue at all, so put yourself in their shoes. Even if you comp them for that night, they're still going to be miserable when they're trying to sleep.

You may think putting guests up for a night at a hotel sounds like a crazy thing to do. However, in most situations it's only reasonable. What you promised them when they booked was a comfortable stay, and it's your responsibility to deliver that to them. If you were in their situation, you would probably want the same consideration. The specifics vary slightly depending on the particular issue. If you're at all unsure, your guests will tell you how they want it handled. If there's ever an issue that you're unsure how to handle, propose different solutions to your guests and ask them which one they prefer. For example, if the air conditioning breaks during the summer and it's not an exceptionally hot day, your guests may be perfectly happy if you simply provide them with a fan. They may, however, prefer to stay in a hotel for the night. The only way to ensure that your guests get what they actually want is to communicate and ask.

Oftentimes guests aren't quite as conscious of energy consumption as you'd like them to be, given that they aren't the ones paying the electricity bill! Additionally, when hosting on Airbnb, your property can often sit empty for days at a time, and heating or cooling it substantially during those times can be a pretty big waste of energy and money.

Consider installing a smart thermostat, such as a Nest Thermostat. That way, you can manage how your guests use your HVAC from afar, and also ensure that your home isn't being heated or cooled when no ones there.

Water heating

Another component to your guests' comfort is verifying that all your water heating and cooling is working properly. Although some people may prefer a cold shower first thing in the morning, a cold shower may be the worst way for some people to start their day. Your job is to ensure that doesn't happen. Similarly, if your shower is notorious for scalding hot or freezing cold water when turned just one millimeter too far, then you want to get it fixed.

Do anything you can so that these types of uncomfortable situations aren't happening to your guests. The showers and sinks are similar to the doors and windows in that your guests use them frequently and they can cause a big impact on the quality of your guests' stay. Most people have a baseline expectation that these things will work when they pay to stay somewhere. Your guests may not notice them when they're working correctly, but they definitely will when they aren't working.

Other aspects to consider

Overall, ensure your listing is presentable and doesn't show any damage. Here are some other details you need to do to ensure your guests have a pleasant stay:

>> **Checking and preventing water leaks:** Leaking water can be an uncomfortable sight. Your guests may worry about the risk of mold.

>> **Managing foliage:** Although there isn't anything wrong with some extra leaves or foliage, you want to showcase that your space — from the inside and out — is well maintained. You want your guests to get an overall sense that someone actively cares for this property. You don't want them thinking no one has visited in three weeks because of all the uncut grass and overgrown weeds.

>> **Protecting against insects and rodents:** Few conditions make a place feel less sanitary than insects or rodents. The last thing you want guests to feel in your place is disgust, so make sure you stay on top of this.

>> **Maintaining the common areas and appliances:** Guests are constantly going to be using your common areas and appliances, so keep everything in good, working order. If you list a spare bedroom in your home, doing so is especially important — even though your guests are primarily spending their time in the bedroom, they still expect all shared spaces to be well maintained.

>> **Tending to trash:** Make sure no trash is left around the property and keep a properly sealed trash bin that doesn't allow smell to leak out.

Generally, not maintaining these items shows a lack of care for the property and can lead guests to subconsciously or consciously think about what else isn't being taken care of there. If you keep your space clean and maintained, your guests will feel much more comfortable. You may have experienced walking into a space that's dirty and untended. You don't feel comfortable there and you don't want to sit down or go to sleep in the space. You just want to leave. When dealing with the upkeep of your listing, make sure your guests never feel this way.

Cleaning Your Space — The No. 1 Biggest Headache

Often what takes the most time and causes the biggest inconvenience for hosts is handling the turnovers and cleaning. If you don't live at your listing, these are the only times you need to physically be at the property. When done properly, cleaning takes a substantial amount of time compared to everything else that hosting entails.

Although cleaning and handling the turnover for the next guest is time consuming, they're necessary after guests check out and before the next guests arrive. Oftentimes you don't want to do these jobs. They aren't glamorous and probably not what you expected when you first considered hosting. But you can't skimp and cheat on these tasks.

In the following sections, we discuss how to properly do the turnover — whether you're doing it yourself or you're hiring a pro. Regardless of who is cleaning or doing the turnover, these tasks have to be done exceptionally well. After maintaining your space, cleaning your space is next in importance. However, the cleaning and maintenance of the property are tied together. If your property isn't sufficiently cleaned, your guests will be uncomfortable.

Mastering the turnover

When guests walk into your property, you want it to evoke a feeling. You want to control their reaction so that they experience certain emotions when staying with you. The best way you do this is during the turnover.

A turnover cleaning is so much more than a typical private home cleaning. Because your guests expect a hotel-like presentation, everything — and we do mean *everything* — must be immaculate. For example, MaidThis, an Airbnb cleaning company, has helped with more than 50,000 turnover cleanings and has put together a list on the main tasks you need to give attention to when turning over a unit to get a 5-star review. Figure 15-1 shows this checklist.

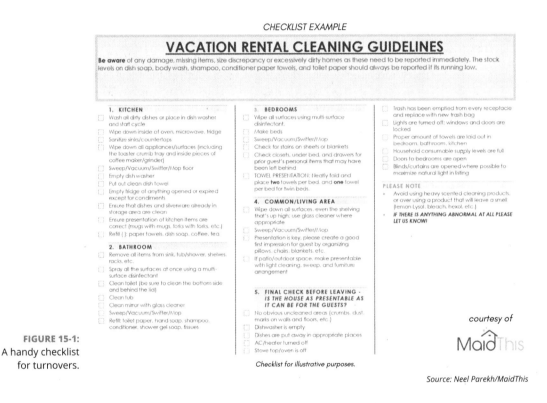

FIGURE 15-1:
A handy checklist
for turnovers.

Source: Neel Parekh/MaidThis

Checking for damages

The first step of turning over your unit between guests is checking for damages. People are sometimes hard on effects they don't own, so it's not uncommon for items to get broken or typical everyday items to experience higher-than-average wear and tear.

If you own some high-ticket items, you may choose to include a security deposit with your listing and let your guests know they'll be paying for any damages. If you do this, keeping track of when damages occur is imperative so you're not blaming the wrong guest. Chapter 6 discusses in greater detail about how you can use a security deposit.

REMEMBER

If a guest causes less than $20 worth of damages, we suggest you just let it slide. A stained towel or broken glass can be considered a cost of doing business. Nickle and diming your guests over these types of items can create a negative guest experience and require more of your time than they're worth.

TIP

One of the most common damages is stains on the sheets. We recommend to not always use pure white sheets because stains are more difficult to remove and you need to replace sheets more frequently. When you remove the sheets to launder them, if you find any stains, take the stained sheet out of your rotation and replace it with a new set.

Restocking consumables

Some consumables are essential, such as toilet paper and hand soap, and you should always keep them stocked with backups easily accessible. On the other hand, items such as facial tissues, paper towels, and travel-size toiletries aren't totally necessary, although your guests do appreciate them. Guests don't necessarily notice these types of items until they're not available when they need them.

Restaging rooms

Every time a turnover cleaning is completed, be sure to walk through every room and make sure it looks as presentable as possible. Your place should look completely unlived in for new guests.

Identifying what needs to be cleaned in a turnover: Your handy checklist

Determining the areas that you should clean in your Airbnb listing is a no-brainer. That being said, the cleaning process in these areas needs more scrutiny and attention to detail.

To be most efficient, focus on these two tasks that take the longest amount of time first as soon as you enter:

1. **Remove all the linens and towels from the rooms and start the laundry.**
2. **Load and start the dishwasher.**

   You can then focus on a room at a time and clean. The following can help you figure out what needs to be cleaned:

Kitchen

Do the following in this order:

1. **If you're using oven cleaner, spray it in the oven because it needs time to set.**
2. **Wipe down *all* surfaces — countertops, the exterior of all appliances and cabinets, and inside the sink — with disinfectant.**
3. **Wipe inside all your appliances and clean the oven, on average, every three months.**
4. **Check all the dishes and wash any that have even a hint of being dirty.**
5. **Sweep and mop the floor.**

Bathroom

When you move to the bathroom, do these tasks:

1. **Ensure there are no hairs on the toilet, on the floor, or in the shower.**

   Loose hairs are the biggest complaint!
2. **Disinfect all surfaces — sink, shower, tub walls, and shower door — as well as scrub the toilet (bowl, seat, cover, and exterior).**
3. **Clean the mirror.**
4. **Sweep and mop the floor.**

Bedroom(s)

In the bedroom(s), do the following tasks:

1. **Start by wiping down all surfaces.**
2. **Sweep and mop if you don't have carpet.**

   Vacuum if you do have carpet.
3. **Remake the beds with clean linens.**

Common area(s)

Focus next on the common areas and do the following:

1. **Wipe down all surfaces.**
2. **Sweep and mop or vacuum if you have carpet.**
3. **Fold and neatly place all blankets and throw pillows.**

Systemizing the cleaning process

A lot goes into a well-executed turnover. Here are three tips for how to stay organized and master your own process.

>> **Embrace a checklist.** If you're not a checklist person, now is the time to become one. Having a cleaning checklist isn't enough though. From check-out to your next check-in, write out a step-by-step process of what needs to happen to give your guests the best possible experience.

>> **Prepare ahead for hiccups.** Things happen. Be prepared. Seek out and develop relationships with reliable vendors for needs such as last-minute plumbing issues or guest lockouts.

>> **Stay well-stocked.** Consumables that run out quickly, such as toilet paper and tissues, are easy to store in a closet. Buy in bulk or when there's a sale. In addition, purchase linens when they're on sale so you're ready to replace them at a moment's notice if needed.

If you're stressed out with the idea of cleaning your listing after every turnover, consider hiring a professional cleaner. Specialized Airbnb cleaners handle everything and help ensure you exceed your guests' expectations every time. Refer to the next section for advice about hiring a professional cleaner.

If you're going to be doing your own cleaning, make sure you understand the reality that it does require work. Keep the following in mind:

>> **The amount of time it really takes:** Cleaning is something that needs to be done to a certain level of quality. You can't cut corners or shave off time without diminishing the quality. Depending on the size of your space, plan to spend at least a couple hours each turnover.

>> **The level of detail orientation required:** You have to be prepared to do the work to the quality it needs done.

>> **Any possible time constraints:** Cleaning can't be done whenever it suits your schedule. You have the time between when a guest checks out and the next guest checks in, and this window may be only a few hours.

TIP

Develop a system and a process to ensure a certain level of consistency. Every guest who checks in should receive the same quality of space. If you don't have a system and perform your turnovers differently each time, then maintaining that quality control is difficult. Whenever a guest has an issue with how something is done, you want to know exactly what it is so you can correct it and make sure it never happens again.

Using Professional Cleaners

In most cases we recommend using a pro for cleaning. Having this cleaning pro frees up much of your time and gives you the space and flexibility to focus on higher leverage areas of hosting. Hiring a professional cleaner also offers you freedom and flexibility so that you don't have to be cleaning at your property at a certain time. Not many other factors to hosting besides cleaning require you to work at specific times or impose a sense of urgency and time constraint on your life. When hiring a pro, consider these four important factors:

>> **Make sure you know what type of pro you need.** Even if you don't plan on performing turnovers in the long term, perform a few turnovers yourself when you're first starting as a host so you know exactly what you want and how you want those tasks performed. Doing it yourself a few times also gives you an idea of what the scope of the work is and how long it should take for the cleaning to be properly completed.

>> **Have a system for finding the right person to clean your space.** This factor comes down to knowing exactly what you're looking for and making a list of criteria. Take your time doing the research to find cleaners that are the best fit for your needs. One of the easiest ways to find a great cleaner in your area is to ask your friends or fellow hosts for a referral.

>> **Create a system for training your cleaners and make sure they're set up to deliver on your expectations and clean to your satisfaction.** Communicate what you want (and don't want) up front. The more specific you are, the better. Take the time initially to go into the space and make sure your cleaners are doing the tasks the right way. Don't expect them to perform perfectly out of the gate, and it's also fine if they aren't doing the unimportant details a specific way.

>> **Have a system for conducting quality control.** Devise your own system by conducting quality control and checking on the quality of your property's cleaning. However, don't micromanage your cleaners. Don't be at every cleaning looking over their shoulders and making notes on whatever they missed.

AIRBNB-SPECIFIC CLEANING COMPANIES

Nowadays many cleaning companies offer Airbnb cleanings as part of their services and some companies even specialize exclusively in Airbnb cleanings. Neel Parekh's company MaidThis is a great example of the latter. MaidThis, which put together the cleaning checklist in Figure 15-1, focuses solely on turning over Airbnb properties for hosts all over the United States.

Airbnb cleaning is quite different than other cleanings because it usually needs to be completed between 11 a.m. and 3 p.m. Furthermore, it needs to be performed in a specific way. Cleaners must go in quickly and finish up before new guests arrive.

In addition, Airbnb cleaning has a major element of staging so the listing is ready for the incoming guests. Due to the unique needs of Airbnb hosting, having a traditional cleaning company come in to clean can present certain challenges. Using a company that specifically focuses on Airbnb turnovers enables you to be confident that the cleaners know exactly what they're doing and can meet your specific needs.

TIP

Request the cleaning team take photos of the space and submit those photos to you after they're finished so you can ensure that they did everything properly. The photos also provide a record of the cleaning. You can also do sporadic check-ins after cleanings and before guest arrivals to double-check everything is done to the right quality.

Even though you hired pros, you can't neglect the cleaning as a host. You can't set up your cleaners and forget about them. Pay attention to guest feedback and reviews. After touching base with your guests, if you receive any negative feedback about how clean your property is, take care of it immediately by asking your cleaners to pay special attention to whatever the issue is and follow up to make sure they dealt with it.

Having a Cleaning Backup Plan in Place

No matter who is doing the cleaning, the bottom line is ensuring the turnover happens before your new guests arrive. Guests expect a clean space upon check-in. No exceptions. Sometimes emergencies happen that can wreak havoc on the cleaning schedule, which is why you need to have a cleaning backup plan in place, just in case.

You can break down your cleaning backup into two scenarios with different reasons, depending on how you're handling cleaning for your property. They include the following:

>> If you're doing your own cleaning

>> If you've hired professional cleaners to clean

The following sections examine when you may need to rely on your backup plan and what you need to include in your backup plan.

When you may need a backup

If you're doing your own cleaning, you need a backup plan in place for anytime your schedule doesn't permit you to turn over your property in time for an incoming guest. Even better, having a backup plan in place means you're no longer a slave to your hosting. If one day you just don't feel like cleaning, having a backup gives you the freedom to simply not do it.

If you've hired professional cleaners to clean your space, you also need a backup plan for any time that the cleaners you've hired are unable to come. This can be as simple as hiring a cleaning company with enough cleaners to guarantee your turnover gets completed every time. However, if you hire one individual to clean your space, you want to have at least one other individual cleaner who you can turn to in the event that your primary cleaner gets overbooked, is sick, or is otherwise unable to complete a turnover.

What to include in your backup

The most important matter to remember is that Airbnb cleanings are unique and time sensitive. Whatever cleaner you have in place as a backup needs to understand that and also be familiar with your space.

Regardless of who completes a turnover, it needs to be done properly. Make sure your backup cleaner understands exactly what you're looking for and exactly what your space requires. Having a backup cleaner in place who requires you to be there during the cleaning to explain how tasks are done isn't going to be of much use.

5
Tackling Important Money Matters

Understand the essentials to Airbnb taxes, file properly, and minimize your tax exposure.

Obtain and understand your Airbnb earnings reports to calculate your gross earnings from hosting.

Track and calculate your Airbnb expenses to maximize your deductible expenses for hosting.

Understand recent tax law changes and how they may impact your reporting and filing come tax season.

Identify profit boosting opportunities in your Airbnb operations to increase your earnings and reduce your expenses.

Maximize return on time spent hosting by focusing on freeing your time commitment towards hosting.

Scale your income by managing other people's properties as a co-host so that you can grow your Airbnb operation without having to buy or rent new properties yourself.

Chapter **16**

Hosting without a Property through Airbnb Experiences

As regulatory headwinds continue to reduce the number of existing listings, limit the addition of new ones, and allow fewer available days that homes can rent on a short-term basis, Airbnb has sought to achieve continued growth by expanding its business model.

Most notably, Airbnb is betting big on its Experiences program, which enables hosts to earn money on the platform by hosting an activity for guests to experience rather than a property for guests to stay in.

What began with limited tests in San Francisco and Paris in 2014, Airbnb Experiences officially launched in November 2016 with about 500 experiences in 12 cities. As of early 2020, Airbnb already offers more than 40,000 Experiences around the world, tripling the Experiences listings from the year prior. However, that still pales in comparison to the more than six million property listings on the platform.

With continued aggressive growth expected, Airbnb Experiences presents the biggest growth opportunity on the platform. In this chapter we explore what the advantages and challenges of being an Experiences host and how you can meet the requirements, submit a strong application, and ultimately design a successful and profitable Airbnb Experience from day one.

Introducing Airbnb Experiences

According to Airbnb, an Experience is "an activity that goes beyond the typical tour or class, designed and led by locals all over the world" that enable hosts to "show off their city, craft, cause, or culture."

An Experience is

>> Led by a knowledgeable and passionate host

>> Hands on or immersive for guests

>> Special or uncommon where guests couldn't easily have discovered it on their own

>> The host's unique perspective on a place and/or activity

>> A great story for guests

However, an Airbnb experience is not

>> Large and impersonal

>> An event without a clear host

>> A service such as airport transportation, babysitting, or resume reviews

>> Something guests could easily find on their own outside of Airbnb

Airbnb Experiences are typically activities that last one to five hours long, ranging in price from as low as $10 to several hundred dollars, with the majority below $100. They can be activities for one guest or several guests at a time and can often be booked by companies looking to host team building events with their employees as well.

In return for providing payment handling, 24-hour customer service, and a $1 million Experience Protection Insurance policy, Airbnb takes a 20 percent fee from Experience hosts on all bookings, much higher than the 3 percent fee charged to property hosts. Although the few top Experience hosts can earn more than $300,000 in a year, according to Airbnb, the average Experience host earned about $2,500 a year.

TOKYO AIRBNB EXPERIENCES

A quick search on Airbnb for Experiences in Tokyo, Japan, review a large selection of both popular and new Experience listings. Here are a few of search results you see:

- **"Eat/Drink like A LOCAL - Taverns & Ramen":** Hosted by Akira, "an international sake sommelier and whiskey expert," this popular three-hour Experience (www.airbnb.com/experiences/183804) takes guests on a private food and drinks tour in the Ueno neighborhood.

- **"Tsukiji (old) vs Toyosu (New) S.S Tour":** This six-hour tour of both the old and new world famous fish markets in Tokyo, hosted by local restaurant owner Toshi, is one of the most popular Airbnb Experiences in Tokyo (www.airbnb.com/experiences/71924) with more than 2,000 guest reviews as of early 2020.

- **"Sushi-making Experience":** A 1.5 hour Experience, sushi chef Kazuki teaches guests five techniques for making sushi in a 100-year-old sushi shop (www.airbnb.com/experiences/53271).

- **"Tokyo waterway night paddling":** Host Takashi takes guests on a three-hour kayak tour of the city's nightscape for epic night photos (www.airbnb.com/experiences/107865).

- **"Local bike ride to see Mt.Fuji":** Host Hayato takes guests on a relaxing 4.5-hour bike ride through nature and rice fields in the backdrop of Mt. Fuji (www.airbnb.com/experiences/13586).

- **"Personal Photographer & Guide in Tokyo":** Taking guests on a two-hour visual tour of Shibuya, host and photographer Kenji takes epic photos for guests (www.airbnb.com/experiences/959073).

WARNING

Although the $1M Experience Protection Insurance policy covers most Experiences, certain activities are excluded from coverage, such as anything involving aircrafts. Check with Airbnb's webpage for more detailed coverage at www.airbnb.com/experience-protection-insurance.

Considering the Advantages and Disadvantages to Hosting an Experience

Hosting an Experience has its share of pros and cons, just like hosting a listing. These sections focus on both.

The advantages of hosting an Experience

In addition to Airbnb pouring millions to further develop and expand this program, hosting an Experience over listing a property has the following advantages:

» **No property needed:** Perhaps your house or apartment isn't a good fit for hosting on Airbnb due to location, lack of proper amenities, or poor condition. Finding a new property or renovating an existing property takes much more time and money. But with an Experience, you don't even need to have a property. You can host it somewhere else or even out in nature.

» **Location choice:** Even if you live outside of the main travel destinations in your city, you can host your Experience in a well-chosen location where it can attract the most bookings. You're no longer limited by the location of your own home. Depending on the activity, Experience hosts can often choose their designated location to their advantage.

» **Great reach for greater earning potential:** With a property, hosts can only attract the guests who want to stay within a close radius of their intended travel destinations. But with Experiences, hosts are often able to draw from a much larger pool of travelers willing to take that long rideshare to experience that unique activity.

» **Greater flexibility:** Unlike a property where hosts may need to respond to guests during any hour of the day (or night!), Experience hosts only interact with the guests during the window of their activity. Experience hosts often choose availabilities only when they're available during nights or weekends. For hosts who want to earn extra income without the commitment of managing a fully available property listing, Experiences are the way to go.

» **Less competition:** Although it has grown tremendously, Airbnb Experience listings still face far less competition in the markets. All property listings are ultimately competing with property listings, but Experiences are far more distinct. Even in large cities, it's difficult to find more than a handful of identical Experience listings — a tiny difference makes an experience unique in the market.

» **Easier to start:** Many Experiences require minimal up-front investment from their hosts, unlike a property that needs expensive furniture and appliances. Some Experiences, such as guided walking tours, require no up-front investment.

» **Higher earning potential:** A property listings earning potential is limited by the number of nights it's available for booking times its nightly rate, which is limited by its occupancy capacity and location. With Experiences, hosts aren't limited by any physical occupancy capacity, though Airbnb explicitly prefer

Experiences that host ten or fewer guests at a time for a more intimate experience. Experiences also have higher profit margins and higher return on time for hosts.

The disadvantages of hosting an Experience

Hosting an Experience isn't without a few important challenges. Those contemplating becoming an Experience host need to consider the following:

» **Still relatively new:** The Airbnb Experiences program is now available in most markets, but most guests are still learning about it and haven't made booking an Experience an automatic addition when booking their trips. Airbnb is also still figuring things out. In many markets, only the few best performing Experiences see enough bookings to make it worthwhile economically. New Experiences outside of major markets often experience a slow start.

» **Very high expectations:** To create and maintain a winning experience listing, hosts will need to aim to achieve near perfect guest ratings (4.95+) to remain competitive. An April 2019 update from Airbnb states that more than 90 percent of all Experiences have 5-star reviews. If your Experience listing isn't essentially getting exclusively 5-star reviews, it'll have a hard time showing up on the first page of search results.

The relative newness and slow start potential will change as Airbnb Experiences continue to grow. However, as more hosts discover the great opportunity in Experiences, the very high expectations will persist, if not become even more so.

Understanding the Keys to Successful Experiences

Getting your new Experience approved and listed is one thing. Getting bookings right way and building it into the must-try activity for guests traveling to your city takes much more. Here we explore the most important strategies to ensure success right from the start.

Knowing your target audience

Just as property hosts should cater their property listing to specific types of travelers, so too should Experience hosts. Trying to be something for everyone means your Experience will be nothing for anyone. You must identify a specific traveler you want your Experience to attract and then specifically design your entire listing to appeal to that traveler. Refer to Chapter 3 for a discussion on key traveler segments and how property hosts can cater to their needs; the same strategies apply for Experience hosts.

The top performing Experience listings in most cities often appeal to specific travelers seeking a specific Experience. For instance, a high-octane trampoline lesson that appeals to thrill seekers won't at the same time appeal to yoga enthusiasts seeking quiet mindfulness medication.

For example, consider a quick search for Experiences in Los Angeles that yields the following top search results:

>> Honey Bee Therapy

>> Legendary Sunset Strip Tour and Bar Crawl

>> Easy Rider: Discover Los Angeles by Sidecar

>> Meditation and Creation by the Beach

>> Hike Runyon Canyon with a Rescue Dog

>> Yacht Cruise with Avocado Toast Buffet

>> Learn to Surf in Venice Beach

>> And various Hollywood sign tours

Notice that from their titles alone, these Los Angeles Experiences paint very different settings and activities for their guests. Some are outdoors, some indoors. Some are very active. Some are very relaxing. All are distinctive.

The Hollywood sign listings are targeting tourists seeking to take photos with the iconic sign. A very high demand activity can give opportunity for multiple hosts to succeed with only slight variations — some in the mornings, some at sunset, and some with a photographer and photos included.

Creating a meaningful story

As Airbnb works hard to grow and promote Experiences, one important way for you as an Experience host to gain new guests is through word of mouth. Happy guests going home and telling family and friends, "Guess what I got to see/do/experience on my trip?" to rave about your Experience beats any recommendation from strangers online.

REMEMBER

Top performing Experiences give stories for their guests to take back with them. Do you have insider knowledge to share about your city, culture, or craft? Are you able to grant guests special access to places, people, or events? Can you deliver an Experience that connects guests to a meaningful story or purpose? Hiking a trail with dogs can be fun, but hiking a hidden trail with a backstory with rescue dogs to help a local animal shelter takes the Experience to another level.

Engaging and immersing the guests

Regardless of the Experience, guests prefer active participation, full immersion, or both. Here we explore various ways successful hosts design active participation and immersion into their Experiences:

» **Classes centered:** No successful class-based Experience has guests watch from the sidelines as the hosts merely show how to do something. Guests want to learn something about the topic they signed up for, so they'll always prefer to try tasks out on their own. For example, cooking lesson Experiences have guests make their own dishes that they later get to eat. Arts and crafts lessons Experiences have guests make their own art piece to take home with them.

» **Places centered:** For all location-based Experiences where hosts take guests to specific locations, successful listings incorporate other elements to immerse the guests. Host tell stories, add food and drinks, use a specific mode of transport, pick an ideal time of day, or incorporate an activity to enhance the immersion for the guests. For example, a host may add a guided meditation session in addition to taking their guests to an epic sunrise view of their city.

» **Activities centered:** With activity-based Experiences, such as surfing, kayaking, hiking, walking, meditating, biking, or climbing, that emphasize the Experience over the teaching of the activity, hosts act more as guides than instructors. Hosts can create a more immersive Experience by pairing the activity with something memorable, sometimes entirely unrelated to the main activity.

For example, a traditional guided yoga session in a yoga studio is far less appealing and memorable than a guided yoga session with miniature goats as in the Experience at www.airbnb.com/experiences/125756. Guests get to experience a popular and highly rated yoga session with friendly miniature goats hosted by certified yoga instructors. The session starts guests with a short introduction into goat etiquette, followed by the yoga class where goats may join in by doing their yoga on top of guests, and finally finishing with a goat therapy playtime session.

In the later section, "Brainstorming Unique Airbnb Experience Concepts," we explore various strategies to come up with your own Airbnb Experience, one that can be immersive and memorable for your guests.

Choosing the ideal location

One of the biggest advantages for Experience hosts is in being able to choose the specific location for their listing. Without being tied to a specific physical location, you can and should choose your location carefully.

An ideal location for an Experience is

>> **Easy to get to:** Even for more remote Experiences, their starting locations are often easy for guests to find and get to. They're a short rideshare away. All things equal, try to locate your Experience in or near the epicenter of your nearest major Airbnb market. Especially for markets where travelers are on short stays, guests will shy away from committing hours just to get to an activity. Experiences targeting travelers on extended multiweek stays could locate in more remote and inconvenient locations. In addition, Airbnb has stated that search rankings for Experiences are in part based on the proximity to the guests' property bookings.

>> **Legal for your activity:** Not all locations are accommodating for many activities. Check whether local laws allow your specific activity on the targeted location. Some places may require a license or permit.

>> **Economical:** All things equal, choose a location that is less costly for you and your guests. Having to pay a higher rental fee may cause you to set a higher minimum guest fee, resulting in fewer sessions and lower profit margins. Think creatively! This is the reason many yoga Experience hosts choose free outdoor locations over indoor locations that require renting.

>> **Unforgettable:** Choosing the right location can help create a more memorable and sharable setting for guests. Successful Experiences choose locations that are as much, if not more, of a draw for guests than the activity itself.

Although finding a location that satisfies each of these criteria isn't easy, putting in the extra effort up front can make all the difference in creating a consistently profitable Airbnb Experience.

Building and sustaining momentum

Just as with property listings, Experience listings may only get one first impression when they go live on the platform. During this ramp-up period, hosts should design their listing to build momentum for bookings and guest ratings as quickly as possible, rather than to maximize profits.

According to an April 2019 article published by Airbnb data scientists who manage and optimize the search algorithms that rank the Experience listings the platform tracks more than 25 metrics in determining the search rankings for Experience listings.

Among the most important (and controllable by hosts) for building early momentum are

>> **Number of reviews:** Experience hosts should aim to get to 50 guest reviews as quickly as possible. The average search ranking for Experiences with fewer than 30 guest reviews are twice as worse as those with more than 30 guest reviews. Airbnb ranks listings with fewer than 10 guest reviews only nominally better than listings with zero reviews. Getting to 50 guest reviews or more as quickly as possible is crucial for search rankings and provides social proof to potential guests.

>> **Overall guest rating:** Listings with an average guest rating of 4.5 or lower perform just as poorly as listings with no ratings. The top performing listings have average guest ratings of 4.7 or higher, often 4.9 or higher in highly competitive markets. Besides getting as much guest reviews as possible, Experience hosts must also get primarily 5-star ratings by consistently over delivering for guests.

>> **Number of bookings in last seven and 30 days:** Listings that are getting more bookings than their competition over the prior week and month, will rank higher. To do so, hosts must create an appealing listing that has

- **High click-through rates:** That is, the listing can get more guests to click through from the search results to view their listing than competition. A higher click-through rate means a better designed listing with great profile photo, great title, and an attractive pricing.

- **High booking rates:** Out of every 1,000 guests who view their listing profiles, the top performing Experiences often achieve 30 or more bookings. In comparison, poorly performing experiences only achieve 10 or fewer bookings from the same 1,000 views of their listing profiles.

- **Approachable pricing (total price and price per hour):** All things equal, guests prefer lower-priced Experiences, which also seem to rank higher on search results compared to their higher priced counterparts. When initially launching a new Experience listing, pricing it as low as possible enables the listing to achieve higher search rankings and more bookings. Hosts can then raise pricing gradually to go from momentum building to profit maximizing.

>> **Occupancy rate of past and future availability:** Listings with more availability have a higher chance of being shown to potential guests because the search algorithm only shows guests Experiences that have availabilities that fall within their check-in and check-out dates. However, having more availabilities isn't enough — the listings also get bookings. Airbnb search ranks Experience listings that book a higher percentage of their availabilities higher.

>> **Percentage rating "unique" and "better than expected":** After the completion of every Experience, Airbnb asks guests to rate their overall satisfaction on multiple dimensions, including whether they felt the Experience was "unique" and "better than expected." The top performing listings have about three in every five guests agreeing to both.

To build and sustain momentum for a new Experience listing, you as a host must make deliberate choices about both the activity and the listing profile to maximize these important metrics.

An April 2019 article published by the Airbnb data sciences team outlined the search rankings of two Experience listings where one went from an overall ranking of #30 to the #1 spot and the other dropping from an overall ranking of #4 down to #94. The improving listing went from 0 to 60 listings and dropped pricing from $29 to $23. The falling listing raised prices from $15 to $35 and fell from booking 200 to 50 bookings per month during that same time.

Making the economics work from day one

Hosting an Experience on Airbnb takes time, money, and effort. Whether you want to earn an extra income for yourself or to help a worthy cause you believe in, you want to make sure you design an Experience that's profitable from day one. Hosts considering a new Experience must ensure that the activity is not only profitable overall but also worthwhile for amount of time it requires from them. Here we dive into the math.

Gathering your start-up costs

What do you to have in place before you could host even one guest? Is there equipment or tools that you must purchase but can utilize for all the sessions? Any one-time expenses that hosts must incur before hosting their first session that they can utilize over multiple sessions are *start-up costs*.

For example, an outdoor drawing Experience host may need to purchase all the drawing easels and chairs. This host may need to buy a small number first and purchase more as she achieves more bookings to meet demand. If the easel and chair combos cost $150 each, then purchasing 10 initially costs $1,500 (10 times 150).

For most Experiences, hosts will have an option to rent before purchase. Cooking classes can rent a kitchen rather than buying all the expensive appliances upfront. A photography experience host can rent her equipment before purchasing expensive camera gear right away. Some Experiences may not have any start-up costs. For example, a walking tour of a public natural reserve requires no significant up-front start-up costs.

Understanding per session economics

From a per session basis, you'll want your revenue to be greater than your expenses to ensure a profitable Experience effort. To do so, it needs to be profitable from a per guest basis and address the following:

- » **Revenue per session:** This is the Price Per Guest times the Average Number of Guests Per Session. For example, an outdoor drawing Experience that charges $30 per guest and averages 8 guests per session will achieve an average session gross revenue of $30 times 8 = $240. Factoring in Airbnb's 20 percent service fee, the net revenue per session becomes $240 – $48 = $192.

- » **Expenses per session:** Session expenses consist of general expenses that the host incurs for hosting each session regardless of the number of guests attending and the average session expense per guest. For example, that same drawing Experience could incur $20 in general session materials and an additional $2.50 for drawing materials and light refreshments for each guest. With 10 guests per session, the average session expenses become $20 plus 8 times $2.50 = $40.

- » **Hourly input per session:** How many total hours of input does it require the host to set up, deliver, and break down an entire session? For example, the drawing host may take an hour to set up for a three-hour long drawing Experience and another hour to break down and pack up. For this host, her total hours of input for their three-hour drawing experience becomes 1 + 3 + 1 = 5 hours.

- » **Profit per session:** This is the Net Revenue Per Session minus Expenses Per Session. For our example, the Profit Per Session becomes $192 – $40 = $152.

- » **Profit per hour:** Just because a session is profitable doesn't mean it's worthwhile for the host. In this example, with the drawing host spending a total of 5 hours for each session, her profit per hour becomes Profit Per Session divided by Hourly Input Per Session, or $152 divided by 5 = $30.40. However, that same $152 in session profits is less appealing if the host had to spend twice as much time per session: $130 divided by 10 = $15.20.

As you can see, an economically viable Experience must both be profitable on a per session basis and achieve a high enough profit per hour for the host.

Understanding long-term economics

Hosts should explore their long-term economics to see what their Experience will generate in profits on a weekly, monthly, and annual basis. The crucial decision to make is deciding how many sessions you'll host in a typical week.

Continuing our example from the previous section with the drawing experience host who makes $240 in gross revenues and $152 in net profits per five-hour session, say they decide to host three sessions per week, which equals to approximately 13 sessions per month and 156 sessions per year on a 52-week year.

Here long-term economics now become as follows:

>> **Weekly economics:** Total weekly revenue becomes 3 times $240 = $720. Total weekly profit becomes 3 times $152 = $456. The host is spending 15 hours a week hosting the three sessions. To be more conservative and account for demand fluctuations, you can assume a lower weekly average number of sessions, such as 2.5.

>> **Monthly economics:** Assuming 4.33 weeks per month in a 52-week year, the total monthly revenue becomes 13 times $240 = $3,120. Total monthly profit becomes 13 times $152 = $1,976. The host is spending 65 hours a month hosting the 13 sessions.

>> **Annual economics:** Assuming 52 weeks per year, the total annual revenue becomes 156 times $240 = $37,440. The total annual profit becomes 156 times $152 = $23,712. The host is spending 780 hours a year hosting the 156 sessions.

>> **Payback period:** How long does it take the host to recoup her start-up cost from the profits earned? In our example, if the host spent $1,500 in start-up costs, it will take less than one month to payback, assuming she achieves guest bookings immediately.

Even with a moderately priced Experience, a host can make a tidy extra income from hosting with a few sessions on a part-time basis. However, most Experiences won't book an average of eight guests per session just starting out. This level of performance is achievable; it just may take many months of ramping up to get there.

To run your own analysis for your Experience concepts, download the companion *Airbnb Experience Profit Calculator* through our online resources page located at www.learnbnb.com/airbnbfordummies. The provided calculator is an Excel-based spreadsheet that enables you to make the key assumptions as outlined in this section and determine the economics for your Experience concepts.

ANATOMY OF A MULTI SIX-FIGURE EARNING EXPERIENCE

One of the most popular and most booked Airbnb Experiences is this 3.5 hour guided food tour experience in Lisbon, Portugal (www.airbnb.com/experiences/64564). At the time of this writing, this Experience listing has achieved more than 5,000 guest ratings at an average rating of 4.95 and having hosted more than balance 10,000 guests already in just a little over four years of operations.

At 6 available sessions per week, if the host averages about eight guests per session, then they are booking nearly 2,500 guests per year. Charging $84 per guest, this host is achieving gross booking revenue of approximately $200,000 per year from taking guests on the guided food tour!

Although the host must pay a good portion of these revenues to the restaurants for the cost of the food and service, this is a win-win-win for guests, host, and the restaurant partners. Even if they gave 40 percent to their restaurant partners after Airbnb's 20 percent fee, they still pocket over $100,000.

Note: All income estimates are our conjectures.

Finding the right balance between price and volume

Just as property hosts must find the right between pricing and occupancy, you must too if you're an Experience host. Pricing your Experience too high will cause fewer (if any) bookings, but pricing too low will also mean a lot of work for little return.

REMEMBER

One important factor to consider is the cost of the Experience versus the cost of the total stay for the target audience. If, for example, your target audience is primarily visiting for short two-night stays that on average cost $75 per night (for a total stay of $150), then a $150 Experience will double the guests' travel cost. However, that same $150 Experience targeting guests who are staying on average for a week at $150 per night (for a total stay of $1,050) will seem more appropriate.

REMEMBER

Both the low price but high volume and the high price but low volume Experiences can perform well. But Airbnb's search algorithm tends to favor the Experiences priced at $40 or lower per person, especially toward first-time Experience bookers who are shy with booking more expensive outings initially.

Hosts price Experiences from as little as $10 to several hundred dollars with most falling in the $25 to $150 range. For example, in Los Angeles, the average price of Experiences is about $77 per person.

Brainstorming Unique Airbnb Experience Concepts

To design an Airbnb Experience that is uniquely yours doesn't mean you have to come up with something no other host is doing anywhere in the world. In these sections we explore various strategies to help you come up with novel ideas for your experience.

Ask yourself these questions to generate ideas:

>> **Do I have specialized knowledge or skills?** Could you host a workshop or teach an engaging class on something you know well? You don't have to be a world-class expert in the topic (although it doesn't hurt). You just need to deliver the learning experience in a fun and engaging way. Popular Experiences in this category are cooking lessons, arts and crafts workshops, and outdoor lessons such as surfing, yoga, or even chainsaw carving. Go to Airbnb's website (www.airbnb.com), pick any major city, and explore how other hosts are structuring and charging for their Experiences that may be like the one you're envisioning.

>> **Do I have unique insider knowledge or perspective?** Many successful Experiences have hosts providing their own unique spin on an otherwise free activity. For instance, do you know enough about the local history of mural art and the artists behind them that you could give a fun and engaging tour? Do you know special hidden gems that outside tourist would find thrilling to learn and experience? Look for "walking tour," "biking tour," or "guided tour" on Airbnb for inspiration.

>> **What do I love doing already and feel confident in teaching others?** Examine your recent travels and look at the Experiences you've enjoyed most taking part in. Could you host your own version of that in your city? Could you reinterpret it by adding a personal or local flair to it?

After you've gathered some initial, albeit rough, ideas for potential Experiences, look at what various strategies hosts around the world have used to create their own unique and personal spins.

Using the mix-and-match strategy

One fun way to come up with creative new Experience concepts is to mix and (mis) match activities and/or places.

Sometimes the pairings are obvious and complementary:

>> **Alcohol plus almost anything:** Wine with cooking class. Wine with art. Wine with cheese tasting. If it's safe and allowed, alcohol is a welcomed pairing with just about any activity.

>> **Tour with almost anything:** Beer tours. Wine tours. Food tours. Art tours. Bar tours. Farm tours. Walking tour. Biking tour. Kayak tour. Include something appealing for guests to consume or immerse in.

>> **Interesting place with any activity:** Practice yoga on the beach at sunrise. Learn night photography in an historic neon district. Learn urban sketching with haunted historical buildings. Combining popular activities in exotic or unusual settings can create appealing and memorable pairings.

Sometimes, purposely mismatching unrelated situations with an activity can produce great Experience concepts. One popular mismatch strategy is to add animals to any activity. Practice outdoor yoga with miniature goats. Make and enjoy gourmet coffee with 30 cats. Taste microbrew beer with puppies. Hike a popular trail with rescue dogs. Hosts of these types of Experiences often partner with an organization to provide the animal friends and donate to a worthy cause.

Capitalizing on a growing trend

Another popular strategy is to create experiences that cater to trends that are rapidly growing in popularity. Here are a few ideas:

>> **Yoga:** Yoga and related categories such as meditations have seen tremendous growth interest in recent years. As a result, many travelers are actively seeking experiences in this category. Visit the Experiences page on Airbnb for any major market and you'll probably see dozens of yoga, meditation, or mindfulness-related listings, all with their own variations. According to statistics gathered by The Good Body, an organization that compiles research findings on yoga, there were 300 million yoga practitioners worldwide in 2018, having grown substantially from a decade earlier.

>> **Vegan:** Because of growing awareness of health and environmental concerns, interest in veganism has grown substantially worldwide, with interest in the United States growing by 600 percent from 2014 to 2017, according to Forbes. *The Economist* even declared the year 2019 as the "Year of Vegan." For any

popular Experiences that utilize animal products, consider offering a vegan alternative equivalent Experience.

>> **Doing good:** More travelers will look to book Experiences that help a good cause and are fun. Many popular ones donate 100 percent of their proceeds to support a nonprofit cause helping animals, the environment, or some other worthy local organization under Airbnb's Social Impact program. For example, guests of the "Plastic Fishing" Airbnb Experience (www.airbnb.com/experiences/44548) spend two hours fishing plastic to help clean a local river in Amsterdam while all proceeds support Plastic Whale, the world's first professional plastic fishing company.

Keep an eye out for other fast-growing trends that resonate with you and then adapt an existing, already popular Experience concept to fit the trend.

Going extreme

Another strategy to create novel Experience concepts is to take a popular concept and add an extremeness to it. For example, Airbnb recently partnered with select Guinness World Record holders to offer the "Record Holders Collection" of Airbnb Experiences. These include hula hooping, balloon making, stone lifting, brick breaking, and cow milking — all with a world record holder.

TIP

Find an existing popular Experience concept and look for ways to make it extreme. Highest. Fastest. Most expensive. Tallest. Find an extreme adjective or an extreme setting to add to an otherwise vanilla Experience. For example, turn camping extreme with "Camp on a Cliff in Colorado" (www.airbnb.com/experiences/234689) where guests literally set up camp and sleep on the side of a sheer cliff, way up in the air. Or "Taste the Most Expensive Milkshake" (www.airbnb.com/experiences/1050185), where guests learn to make and then eat a $100 milkshake made with 24 karat edible gold served in a Swarovski crystal glass.

Going weird and one of a kind

If you want to create a one-of-a-kind Experiences found nowhere else in the world, you have to be extra creative. We could only point to some one-of-kind Airbnb Experiences we found from around the world. Here are some examples:

>> **"Play mermaid for the day in San Diego":** Guests are "glammed up with a mini makeover" to turn them into a mermaid, complete with photographer to help with poses at this Experience (www.airbnb.com/experiences/120266).

>> **"Make Smudge Sticks with a real Witch":** Guests learn to make their very own sage smudge sticks from a "witch and spiritual healer" host (www.airbnb.com/experiences/358388).

>> **"Extract Your Own DNA into a Necklace":** Guests extract and make visible the strands of DNA from their own cells and turn it into a necklace keepsake in this Social Impact Experience (www.airbnb.com/experiences/370392).

The more unique, the more it stands out. However, it also means a smaller pool of potential guests. These one-of-kind Experiences work best at a higher price point with higher margins given their expected lower volumes.

Submitting Your Airbnb Experience for Approval

Because of Airbnb's high-quality expectations for Experiences, it continues to reject applications that don't meet its standards. In these sections we explain the application process and strategies to increase your odds of approval.

Understanding Airbnb's three pillars of quality Experiences

Airbnb is looking for intimate and memorable activities difficult for guests to find easily find elsewhere. For a new Airbnb Experience to gain approval for publication on the platform, the proposed Experience must show the following qualities:

>> **Expertise:** For Experiences that require hosts to teach or coach the guests in an activity, they must be able to show their expertise to Airbnb when applying. Hosts who can provide concrete examples of their expertise, such as prior teaching experience, awards, credentials, or portfolios of quality work, have a much better chance of gaining approval.

>> **Insider access:** For Experiences where the location is as much as, if not more of, a draw than the activity itself, Airbnb wants to know what makes the location special and why only the host can gain access or provide that unique perspective of the location. For activities, hosts must show their unique angle that makes for a compelling take on the activity.

>> **Connection:** Aspiring hosts must be able to describe in detail how they'll create a "meaningful human connection" with their guests. How will the hosts create an engaging and connected Experience for guests in a safe and immersive environment? What potential issues could the hosts foresee and how would they mitigate them?

As you go through the detailed application process, keep these three pillars in mind and always ask yourself, "Which of these pillars am I showing?"

Preparing to apply

Before you dive into creating your application online, you can do the following to help craft your application and make it more polished:

>> **Book some Airbnb Experiences.** The best way to get a feel for what Airbnb Experiences is to *experience* them from the guests' perspective. Browse through the Experiences in your city on Airbnb and book one, two, or three. Find ones that share some commonality with what you're envisioning. Pay attention to your own experience and those of your fellow guests. Listen. What do they love (or hate) about the Experience? What do they whisper to each other when the hosts can't hear?

>> **Soft launch your Airbnb Experience.** Try it out with friends and family or complete strangers even before creating your application. Doing several dry runs can give you the chance to spot opportunities for improvement and to address any points of confusion or frustration for guests.

>> **Take great photos.** Hire a photographer to take professional photos for at least one of your dry runs, perhaps during the second or third one when you've already made some adjustments. Like property listings, Experience listings need to have well-composed and well-lighted photos to succeed. Great photos also show your seriousness to Airbnb in your application. Having nice videos can also help.

>> **Build supporting materials.** The best way to show Airbnb's three pillars of quality Experiences is to show rather than tell it. For example, to show your expertise and ability to teach an activity, compile all relevant photos and videos into an online portfolio where you can then share the URL as part of your application. Show Airbnb you are already demonstrating, teaching, and delighting others in your proposed activity.

Filling out the application

To begin the application process, you must already have an existing Airbnb account. From the Airbnb homepage after logging in, you can then click "Host" in the main navigation bar on the top right-hand corner.

The homepage then opens a secondary menu with the options to "Host a home" or "Host an Experience." Click the latter, which takes you to a welcome screen with a brief introduction. After clicking the "Continue" button, it takes you to the application page for you to fill out.

You have 21 items to submit as part of the application process. The application has five main sections, each with multiple questions inside.

Step 1: Your idea

In the first step in the application process choose your experience type (in person or online), add some basic details such as the location of your Experience and finally, select a theme for your proposed Experience.

SELECTING YOUR THEME

When you click the "+ **Select a main theme**" bold text link, it opens a new dialog window with the primary theme options. You can choose from one of the many available options including: arts and culture, nature and outdoors, entertainment, sports, wellness, food, drink and a few others.

Selecting one and then clicking the "Save" button on the bottom right-hand corner takes you back to the main theme selection page where you can then choose to add a secondary theme, or keep it at just one. For hosts combining two distinct themes, choosing the right options can help attract guests based on both themes.

Step 2: What Airbnb is looking for

After completing the first step, you move on to the second screen where you walk through a series of pages that explain in more detail exactly what it is that Airbnb is looking for when it comes to Experiences. This is a bit different depending on whether the experience you're hosting is online or in-person. Here's what Airbnb is looking for with online Experiences:

>> **Expertise:** Airbnb is looking for Experience hosts who have exceptional skill or a background in the Experience they're hosting.

>> **Participation:** They really want experiences that encourage participation and engage guests.

- **Easy to do:** Experiences will ideally require minimal supplies or advanced preparation.
- **Technical quality:** Airbnb is looking for Experience hosts who are comfortable using technology such as Zoom for hosting their Experiences.

When it comes to in-person Experiences, the list varies slightly:

- **Expertise:** Airbnb is looking for Experience hosts who have exceptional skill or a background in the Experience they're hosting.
- **Access:** Ideally, your Experience is something that guests can't do on their own.
- **Connection:** Airbnb wants their Experience hosts to make meaningful connections with each of their guests.

Step 3: Experience page

In this third portion of the application, you fill in all the information that goes into the actual Experience page itself:

- **What we'll do:** Describe your Experience here in detail from start to finish and in the order that guests do the activities. Be descriptive and show the readers what makes the Experience special and what they can expect. Airbnb provides helpful tips and examples. You can use up to 1,400 characters.
- **About you:** First, you need to write a description that establishes both your expertise and passion for the activity. Airbnb provides several examples and some tips to help you. You can use up to 850 characters.
- **Where we'll be:** Select the location(s) and provide a description. You can choose up to three types of locations from nine categories. In your brief description, tell the readers why they should care about the location(s) or why it's meaningful to you. You can use up to 450 characters.
- **Location:** Add details for everything you provide for the guests by adding one item at a time. The categories include Food, Transportation, Drinks, Equipment, and Tickets. Within each category, you can choose from subcategories. For example, under Tickets, you can select Event Tickets, Show Tickets, and Entrance Fee. After selecting the subcategory, you're asked to provide a brief description. For transportation or equipment provided by third parties, Airbnb requires you to name the business along with any relevant details guests may need.

- **What I'll provide:** Specify items that you provide such as drinks, tickets or special equipment. Anything that you can provide which to make your guests more comfortable is a plus.

- **What guests should bring:** Specify items that guests should bring. Try to keep this to a minimum because most guests appreciate the convenience of having everything provided. Ideally, require nothing from your guests.

- **Guest Requirements:** This section is where you add details on any strict requirements around age, skill level, or certifications.

- **Title:** Give your Experience a catchy and descriptive title. Look at examples of the top performing Experiences. Find a strong action verb if possible that shows guests what they'll be doing or experiencing rather than just describing what the activity is. Perhaps turning something like "Private homecooked dinner" into "Feast on private six-course tasting menu." You can use up to 40 characters.

- **Photos:** Add your photos starting with the profile photo followed by up to nine additional and optional photos for your gallery. **Remember:** All photos must have a minimum resolution of 480 pixels wide by 720 pixels tall. There will be a preview of your listing card, which is how your listing will appear in the search results to a potential guest. Because the appearance will cut off the sides of your profile photo, ensure each photo appears as you want it to appear. Use the extra photo options to your advantage by showing different parts of the activity and/or different locations. Include both wide and closeup shots. Also, ensure all subjects shown in photos are having a great time! Look at top performing Experience listings around the world that are similar for inspiration.

Step 4: Settings

In this fourth portion of the application process, you enter additional information to determine the settings about your Experience:

- **Group size:** Determine your maximum group size, which can range from one up to ten. **Note:** Airbnb has a one guest minimum. Hosts are expected to honor their sessions even if only one guest books with them.

- **General availability:** Set the time when you start your Experience.

- **Guest pricing:** Set your price here. Airbnb provides a preview of your earnings based on the price you set and the number of guests attending after it takes its 20 percent service fee.

>> **Discounts:** Decide if you want to offer group rates to make your Experience more attractive to larger groups and attract more bookings.

>> **Booking settings:** Set how much advance notice you need to prepare for your Experience.

- The first is if your Experience session already has bookings and additional guests want to book.

- The second is when your Experience session has no bookings yet and a first guest makes a booking.

For both, you can set anywhere from one hour up to one week. Think carefully about your Experience and how much time you need to organize and prepare. Some Experience sessions already planned can easily accommodate new guests, even just an hour before start time. But some activities require significant planning.

TIP

For sessions without any bookings yet, we recommend giving yourself at least one day rather than risk scrambling your day to accommodate one last-minute booking. For existing sessions, we recommend always building in excess capacity to allow last-minute bookings to maximize reach. According to Airbnb, going from a one-hour cutoff to a one-day cutoff for existing sessions could reduce guest reach by 32 percent.

>> **Cancellation policy:** Choose whether you'd like to allow guests to cancel and receive a full refund up until 24 hours before the start of the Experience or only if they cancel more than 7 days out. *Note:* Guests will still be able to cancel within 24 hours of booking as long as they booked more than 48 hours before the start time of the Experience.

Step 5: Your submission

In this fifth and final portion of the application process, answer one more question and acknowledge Airbnb's many policies before you can submit for review:

>> **Which of the following applies to you and the experience?** Given that all Experiences must comply with local laws and regulations, Airbnb requires you to say that either you have all the licenses, permits, or permissions needed for your Experience or that none are needed. For some Experiences, Airbnb may request proof of compliance before final approval.

>> **Review policies:** For the last and final step before you can submit your application.

Getting approval

After you're approved, your work is only just beginning. What is approved may not necessarily be what performs best for you. Over the first few months as you get bookings and deliver your Experience, you'll have plenty of opportunities to adjust and improve your experience page and the experience itself.

TIP

Airbnb has a ten-point checklist for the Experience page to help you think through some of these opportunities. You can find these resources at `https://blog.atairbnb.com`.

Re-applying if rejected

If Airbnb rejects your initial application, don't panic. Airbnb wants to add more Experiences on its platform so most initial rejections aren't forever rejections. Instead, according to Joseph Zadeh, chief stakeholder officer of Airbnb, the company will typically provide its rationale for the rejection and give clear specific remedies to improve the proposed Experience.

Airbnb may indicate that the proposed Experience is too mundane or doesn't cater enough to specific traveler passions. Read the company's feedback carefully. Get advice from others you trust on how you could incorporate the feedback into a winning resubmission.

Looking at the Future of Airbnb Experiences

With the listings, bookings, and revenue all growing for Airbnb Experiences, Airbnb's big gamble outside of property rentals seems to be paying off. But as we see already in just the last few years, Airbnb will continue to experiment to explore new channels of growth.

Two growth areas in Airbnb Experiences include the following:

>> **Airbnb Adventures:** Officially launched in June of 2019, Airbnb has expanded its foray into activities by including multiday experiences called Adventures. These are completely planned activities that include meals, accommodations, and a full itinerary. These Adventures can range from same day trips that cost

just under $100 to week-long journeys that cost more than $7,000 per person. To find out more about Airbnb Adventures, go to `www.airbnb.com/d/adventures`.

>> **Co-branded experiences and adventures:** Airbnb has also begun to partner with other well-known entities to create co-branded Experiences and Adventures, including a recent partnership with Atlas Obscura, the popular guide to the world's hidden wonders. Check out `https://news.airbnb.com/atlas-obscuras-hidden-world-wonders-now-available-on-airbnb/`.

Looking forward, we expect to see a similar growth trajectory for Adventures as we have seen for Experiences — more listings, more bookings, and more revenue. Similarly, we expect to see many more brands working with Airbnb to created co-branded Experiences and Adventures.

IN THIS CHAPTER

» Comprehending the essentials of Airbnb taxes

» Getting your earnings report

» Tracking your expenses

» Focusing on a profit and loss statement

» Grasping recent tax law changes

Chapter **17**

Understanding Airbnb Taxes

A s an Airbnb host, you have several tax-related issues to consider. For the income that you earn from hosting, you almost certainly need to pay your federal and state income taxes on it. If you own your property, you must pay property taxes. And increasingly, more hosts will be subjected to local occupancy taxes as cities enact short-term rental regulation to begin capturing this previously missed tax revenue opportunity.

This chapter discusses the most important strategies to not only do your taxes right, but also to pay what you owe and nothing more. In additional, we point out common pitfalls to avoid when it comes to your taxes.

WARNING

Taxes can and often do get complicated, and tax laws are often changing. They differ from jurisdiction to jurisdiction and for everyone's unique financial situation. What we present in this chapter is by no means an accurate or complete coverage of all relevant tax matters for all hosts in all markets. Instead, the chapter presents a limited set of (mostly U.S.-centered) tax-related matters that are useful for most hosts to become aware when thinking about their Airbnb taxes. Don't make major financial decisions, including tax-related matters, without consulting with your financial advisor or accountant who understands the local tax regulations for your unique situation.

Getting Serious about Taxes

There's good reason for the overuse of the trope, "The only things certain in life are death and taxes." It's true! No one can avoid either. Although paying taxes is all but guaranteed, how much you end up paying is not.

According to accountant Miguel A. Centeno of SharedEconomyCPA, an expert tax group specializing in helping shared economy individuals, such as Airbnb hosts and Uber drivers optimize their tax filings, the average Airbnb host can often achieve up to $10,000 or more in taxable deductions. However, having worked with thousands of clients in recent years, we've realized most hosts are only claiming a fraction of their available tax deductions, resulting in them unnecessarily paying higher taxes.

Pay what you owe in taxes but not a penny more. Even though most hosts aren't making major tax mishaps, many are leaving a few hundred dollars or more in potential savings on the table.

These sections discuss the many ways in which Airbnb earnings can be taxed as well as important questions you may have about your tax filings.

THE NEARLY $2,400 TAX MISTAKE

Elaine and her husband, both full-time working professionals, have a combined household income of $184,000. Filing jointly, their marginal tax rate was about 24 percent.

Last year they purchased and renovated a three-bedroom home in the heart of New Orleans, and instead of renting it out to a long-term tenant, they decided to list the property on Airbnb. To their surprise, their property was an immediate hit, and they've been booked solid ever since. During the first year, they booked an additional $40,000 in gross earnings from Airbnb.

Having done their own taxes, they were about to report the entire $40,000 on only $10,000 expense deductions, creating $30,000 in additional taxable income, which would have been taxed at the next marginal tax rate of 24 percent, or nearly $7,200 in additional taxes. However, by working with an accountant who understands Airbnb hosting, they were able to document an additional $10,000 in deductible business expenses, helping them lower the tax burden from their Airbnb earnings by $10,000, cutting their tax bill by $2,400.

Knowing how Airbnb income is taxed

Come tax season, new hosts are often surprised that they owe more than the typical federal and state income taxes on their Airbnb income. In fact, most hosts are subject to federal income taxes, state income taxes, occupancy taxes, the self-employment tax, and the net investment income tax.

Here are the ways your Airbnb income can be taxed:

>> **Federal and state income taxes:** No surprise here. All hosts who made any profit from Airbnb are subject to federal income taxes, and most also owe state income taxes unless they reside in a state with zero income taxes, such as Nevada. The specific income tax rates vary due to your income, filing status, and your state of residence.

>> **Occupancy tax:** Also known as the Transient Occupancy Tax (TOT), this tax is charged to travelers who rent accommodations in hotels, motels, inns, vacation homes, and short-term rentals as in Airbnb.

>> **Self-employment tax:** Unlike owners of passively managed rental properties, hosts who actively managed their Airbnb listings are subject to the self-employment tax, which covers Social Security and Medicare taxes. Active hosts must report their Airbnb rental income and expenses on Schedule C of their tax return. As of 2020, the tax rate is 15.3 percent.

>> **Net investment income tax:** If you derive passive income from your Airbnb property by outsourcing all the management and operation to a property manager or co-host and you have adjusted gross incomes greater than $200,000 as a single tax filer or $250,000 for joint tax filers, then you may also be subject to the net investment income tax of 3.8 percent.

REMEMBER

How you operate your Airbnb and where you live ultimately determines the taxes your Airbnb income is subject to. If you rent out your Airbnb rental property for 14 or fewer days and personally use the property for 14 or more days, or greater than 10 percent of the total number of days the property was made available for rent, then your Airbnb income isn't subject to any federal income taxes. In fact, if you satisfy these conditions, you won't even have to report the income on your taxes, regardless of how much you earned in those 14 days. Except for Alabama, Arkansas, Mississippi, New Jersey, and Pennsylvania, you'd also avoid paying state income taxes.

Asking the important questions

The goal for Airbnb hosts is not to minimize the taxes that they owe but to make sure they don't pay more than they need to. To not overpay, you must account for all your Airbnb earnings and expenses accurately.

To do so, ask yourself these important questions that ultimately determine how much taxes you owe:

>> **Am I subject to U.S. federal income taxes?** Before you calculate how much you owe, first determine whether you owe. With respect to U.S. federal income taxes, here's how they work:

- If you're a U.S. citizen or permanent resident, any rental income derived from both U.S.-located or internationally located listings are subject to income taxes. For example, you're a U.S. citizen host with listings in California and Hong Kong. You're subject to federal income tax on all the rental income, regardless of the location of the listings.

- If you're a non-U.S. citizen or permanent resident, you're only subject to U.S. federal income taxes for rental income derived from U.S.-located listings. For example, a French citizen host with an Airbnb located in Florida is subject to U.S. federal income taxes on the rental income derived from that U.S.-located listing only. Her rental income from her Paris-based listings are exempt.

>> **Is Airbnb collecting and remitting the occupancy tax on my behalf?** Although Airbnb is automatically collecting and remitting occupancy tax on behalf of hosts in more and more cities across the United States and beyond, the hosts are still held responsible for manually collecting and remitting the occupancy tax due in many locales. To find out, you can log into your Airbnb account and go to Account Settings—> Transaction History—> Gross Earnings. See Figure 17-1 for an example of what you can expect to see from your Airbnb gross earnings report online.

- If the numbers in the Occupancy Taxes column are non-zero, then Airbnb is collecting and remitting on your behalf. You no longer need to worry about this.

- However, if the figures in that column are all zeros, then Airbnb isn't collecting and remitting the occupancy taxes on your behalf. In this case, you need to collect this tax manually from each guest. In the past, hosts had to collect from guests in person or utilize the Resolution Center to issue their occupancy tax charges, neither of which was ideal. Today, Airbnb lets hosts add a custom tax collection to their listings by turning on professional hosting tools under Account Settings.

If Airbnb is automatically collecting and remitting the occupancy tax on your behalf, your online Gross Earnings report looks like this example with the numbers under the Occupancy Taxes heading reflecting the occupancy tax rate in your area.

Date	Type	Details	Gross Earnings	Occupancy Taxes
12/31/22	Reservation	Dec 29 - Jan 2, 2020 HZXHIDEA8F	$297.00	$29.70
12/26/22	Reservation	Dec 26 - 30, 2020 HZ79VRQO2G	$440.00	$44.00
12/23/22	Reservation	Dec 22 - 27, 2020 HZ43OJRG4R	$645.00	$64.50
12/18/22	Reservation	Dec 18 - 23, 2020 HZ60GRSA4B	$600.00	$60.00
12/13/22	Reservation	Dec 13 - 19, 2020 HZ72WKIX3W	$630.00	$63.00
12/8/22	Reservation	Dec 11 - 14, 2020 HZ63PMRK1D	$288.00	$28.80
12/5/22	Reservation	Dec 5 - 11, 2020 HZ96XIVP8E	$684.00	$68.40
12/2/22	Reservation	Dec 1 - 6, 2020 HZ54NXJI5Q	$515.00	$51.50
11/28/22	Reservation	Nov 26 - 1, 2020 HZ87KNLQ3F	$545.00	$54.50
11/24/22	Reservation	Nov 21 - 27, 2020 HZ77QTAE8S	$636.00	$63.60
11/20/22	Reservation	Nov 17 - 22, 2020 HZ91LLBE8B	$625.00	$62.50
11/15/22	Reservation	Nov 12 - 17, 2020 HZ88TRCM1Z	$650.00	$65.00
11/11/22	Reservation	Nov 9 - 13, 2020 HZ88OTDZ6X	$380.00	$38.00
11/6/22	Reservation	Nov 5 - 10, 2020 HZ26CMQB2K	$610.00	$61.00
11/3/22	Reservation	Nov 1 - 5, 2020 HZ61YHWA3R	$504.00	$50.40

FIGURE 17-1: Example of Airbnb collecting and remitting occupancy tax.

© John Wiley & Sons, Inc.

>> **How much gross earnings did my Airbnb generate?** *Gross earnings* are the rental revenue generated by your listing before accounting for any adjustments, such as refunds and allowable expenses, such as utilities fees. Gross earnings is also known as the gross rental revenue collected on Airbnb from your listing. For example, a $125 per night reservation for four nights generates 4 times $125 = $500 in gross earnings. Note that this excludes the Airbnb service fee and any additional cleaning fees charged to guests.

>> **How much did I pay in hosting fees?** The *hosting fee* is simply the 3 percent hosting fee paid on each reservation. Because this fee is included in the gross earnings calculation, you need to calculate this figure and subtract it out from gross earnings to match your actual payout figures.

>> **What is my gross revenue figure?** The *gross revenue* is where you tabulate all the additional adjustments that both add to and subtract from your gross earnings figure, which only pertain to rents collected, to arrive at a gross revenue figure that account for all sources of revenue from your Airbnb operation.

Gross revenue items include cleaning fees collected, payments or credits from a resolution, and any additional revenue generated. For example, if you collected an additional $100 cleaning fee and another $40 for providing breakfast to your guests, your gross revenue from this reservation will become $500 (gross earnings) + $100 (cleaning fee revenue) + $40 (additional revenue) = $640 gross Airbnb revenue. If you had to issue a refund, you'd adjust your gross revenue down.

>> **What and how much are my allowable expenses?** Of course, that $40 in payments you collected for providing breakfast to your guests had expenses, you had to buy the materials to make it. And even if you did the cleaning yourself, you had to purchase and use cleaning supplies. Many items are generally considered allowable expenses to help offset your gross Airbnb revenue and ultimately reduce your taxable Airbnb earnings. Given that your expenses, not your gross earnings, ultimately determine the amount of tax you owe, we discuss this topic in greater detail later in this chapter under "Taking Account of Your Airbnb Expenses."

Ultimately, from a tax perspective, you want to go from gross earnings to the final taxable earnings, as Figure 17-2 highlights.

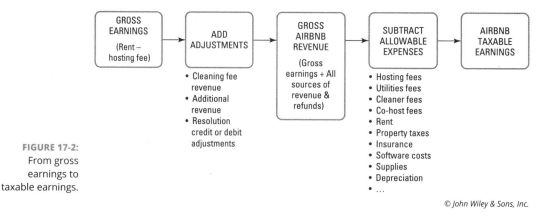

FIGURE 17-2:
From gross earnings to taxable earnings.

© John Wiley & Sons, Inc.

Although your gross earnings won't match what was paid out to you, the IRS requires you to report your gross earnings and then add in all the revenue adjustments and allowable expenses to arrive at your final taxable Airbnb earnings.

If you kept poor records and can only claim a fraction of the expenses you incurred, you'll overpay in taxes. By how much? For every dollar you spent but forget to claim, that's another dollar subject to income taxes. For example, if you're at the 25 percent marginal income tax bracket and you forget to claim $2,500 in allowable expenses, you'll pay an additional $625 in taxes.

Taking Account of Your Airbnb Earnings

Although getting your expenses right is key to minimizing your tax burden, you must start with gross earnings. Luckily, this figure is easy to obtain directly from your Airbnb account.

What Airbnb collects from guests for them to "rent" your property, the *rental revenue*, is also known as *gross earnings*. You're required to report this figure on your tax filings. However, this figure isn't the same as what was paid out to you because this figure is before factoring in Airbnb's hosting fees. The following sections walk you through what the different numbers on the gross earnings report mean and how you can acquire a tax form from Airbnb.

Deciphering the gross earnings report

You need the gross earnings figure to start. To do so, export your gross earnings report by following these steps:

1. **Log into your Airbnb account.**

2. **Click Account Settings.**

3. **Click Transaction History.**

4. **Click Gross Earnings.**

5. **Choose from January to December for the taxable year.**

6. **Click Download CSV.**

The downloaded common-separated values (CSV) file is a spreadsheet that contains the relevant details for all your Airbnb transactions for the taxable year. Your CSV includes the following important information:

>> **Date:** This date is when the transaction was recorded in your transaction history. It's typically the day after the start date of the reservation, but on occasion it can take two to three days.

>> **Type:** This indicates the type of entry in your transaction history, whether it's a reservation, payout, or adjustment due to resolution.

>> **Confirmation Code:** This alphamerical code is associated with each reservation. For any resolution requests, you use this code to reference the specific reservation in question.

>> **Start Date:** The start date of the reservation in question.

>> **Nights:** The number of nights the guest booked that reservation.

- **Guest:** This field is the names of the guests for each corresponding reservation.

- **Listing:** This field shows the name of the listing for the reservations. For hosts with more than one listing, this distinction allows them to filter the results by listing.

- **Details:** Here you can find additional information for the specific record in the transaction history, including the bank account where the payout was made and any resolutions. A resolution includes a resolution number.

- **Reference:** This field shows any reference numbers for refunds or resolution center items associated with the reservations.

- **Currency:** This tells you the currency associated with each record. Hosts operating in one country have the same currency in all the records.

- **Amount:** This entry is for the amount in question affecting the host. For reservations, it's the amount to be paid out. For adjustments, it's the exact amount adjusted from the host's accounts.

- **Paid Out:** If a payout occurred, the amount paid out shows up here and matches the figure amount in the corresponding reservation.

- **Host Fee:** This entry is the 3 percent host fee charged to hosts from each reservation. Adding this figure to the figures in Amount gives you your gross earnings for your Airbnb listing.

- **Cleaning Fee:** These are the fees collected for cleaning from guests. Although they need to be reported as additional sources of revenue for your Airbnb operation, which you then offset with your actual cleaning expenses, they don't count toward the gross earnings calculation as it applies to your "Airbnb rental."

- **Occupancy Tax:** If Airbnb is automatically collecting and remitting the occupancy taxes on your behalf, the amounts collected show here.

After you download and export the CSV file from your Airbnb account, you see a spreadsheet of all relevant transactions for your listing, as in Figure 17-3. Note that for hosts without additional sources of revenue by not collecting cleaning fees, have no issued refunds, or received credits from resolutions, their gross Airbnb revenue equals their gross earnings.

The export doesn't have a Gross Earnings column so you need to calculate that manually. In Figure 17-3, the column is created by adding the figures from Amount and Hosting Fee columns together. For example, in the first column where the amount was $149.17 and the hosting fee was $4.61, the gross earnings from that reservation became $149.17 + $4.61 = $153.80. For the full calendar year calculation, add all the gross earnings calculations for all the reservations. *Note:* We formatted it slightly for clarity.

Date	Type	Confirmation Code	Start Date	Nights	Guest	Listing	Details	Reference	Currency	Amount	Paid Out	Host Fee	Cleaning Fee	Occupancy Tax	Gross Earnings
6/15/22	Reservation	HUZCGHR926	6/14/22	3	James Bond Jr	Luxury 2BR apartment			USD	149.19		4.61	24.2	14.92	153.80
6/15/22	Reservation	HUZCGHR926	6/14/22	3	James Bond Jr	Luxury 2BR apartment			USD	596.74		18.46	96.8	59.67	615.20
6/15/22	Co-hosting Adjustment	HUZCGHR926	6/14/22	3	James Bond Jr	Luxury 2BR apartment			USD	–121					
6/14/22	Resolution Adjustment						Resolution adj		USD	–60					
6/13/22	Reservation	HX3D1338AY	6/12/22	2	Ben and Jerry S	Luxury 2BR apartment			USD	100.49		3.11	24	10.05	103.60
6/13/22	Co-hosting Adjustment	HX3D1338AY	6/12/22	2	Ben and Jerry S	Luxury 2BR apartment			USD	–120					
6/13/22	Resolution Adjustment						Resolution adj		USD	–199					
6/13/22	Reservation	HX3D1338AY	6/12/22	2	Ben and Jerry S	Luxury 2BR apartment			USD	401.97		12.43	96	40.20	414.40
6/6/22	Reservation	HX31CZZ11E	6/5/22	6	Joe Some	Luxury 2BR apartment			USD	211.46		6.54	24	21.15	218.00
6/6/22	Reservation	HX31CZZ11E	6/5/22	6	Joe Some	Luxury 2BR apartment			USD	845.84		26.16	96	84.58	872.00
6/6/22	Co-hosting Adjustment	HX31CZZ11E	6/5/22	6	Joe Some	Luxury 2BR apartment			USD	–120					
6/3/22	Resolution Adjustment						Resolution adj		USD	–225					
6/2/22	Reservation	HJJ8EAXISC	6/1/22	2	Izzy Bizy	Luxury 2BR apartment			USD	110.58		3.42	24	11.06	114.00
6/2/22	Reservation	HJJ8EAXISC	6/1/22	2	Izzy Bizy	Luxury 2BR apartment			USD	442.32		13.68	96	44.23	456.00
6/2/22	Co-hosting Adjustment	HJJ8EAXISC	6/1/22	2	Izzy Bizy	Luxury 2BR apartment			USD	–120					

FIGURE 17-3:
Example of Airbnb earnings report export.

Getting tax forms from Airbnb

Depending on your status and how much in gross earnings your listing achieved in the prior calendar year, Airbnb may be required by law to send you certain tax forms, which can include any of the following:

» **Form 1099-K:** And as of January 1, 2022, if you earned over $600 during the calendar year, Airbnb issues you a Form 1099-K. Previously, only hosts who earned more than $20,000 and have 200 or more reservations in the calendar year had their gross earnings reported to the Internal Revenue Service (IRS). If you meet the current threshold, the form is available online in your Airbnb account under Payout Preferences:

  • Airbnb sends both an email confirmation to you as well as a physical copy, unless you have specifically selected to receive electronic delivery only. The form typically is delivered by the end of January.

  • Hosts with taxpayer information listed on multiple Airbnb accounts may receive multiple 1099-K forms, one for each account.

» **1042-S:** Non-U.S. citizens or residents who submitted a Form W-8 receive a Form 1042-S in the mail. The form typically is delivered in late February.

» **Special cases:** Hosts who also provided services to Airbnb, such as photography or translation services and earned $600 or more from those services, also receive a Form 1099-MISC, typically in late January. Hosts operating in California, District of Columbia, Illinois, Maryland, Massachusetts, Missouri, Vermont, and Virginia have special considerations. For additional information, visit Airbnb's official help center resource on tax forms located at www. airbnb.com/help/article/414/should-i-expect-to-receive-a-tax-form-from-airbnb.

Taking Account of Your Airbnb Expenses

Ultimately, whether you owe taxes and how much you owe for your Airbnb operation depends primarily on your documenting and factoring back of allowable business expenses to offset your Airbnb revenue.

You need to be aware of two classes of expenses that are treated differently for tax purposes: those you can deduct and those that you capitalize. These sections examine these two classes in greater detail and explain what expenses to track and what documents to keep so you're well prepared to file your taxes.

Understanding deductible expenses

Deductible expenses are normal business expenses incurred in renting your property and hosting your guests. For tax purposes, they're considered *ordinary and necessary*, which means they're ordinarily incurred for such a business operation and necessarily helps with the business.

For example, fees paid for cleaning qualify because they're typical and necessary for operating an Airbnb listing. However, paying a professional composer to create theme music for your listing is neither ordinary or necessary. A good way to tell is when you must incur the expense for each reservation, such as a cleaning fee, or on a regular basis to operate your business, as in utility bills and subscriptions to software. Refer to the later section, "Knowing what deductible expenses to track" for a specific list of deductible expenses.

Comprehending capitalized expenses

Capitalized expenses are expenses that either add to the useful life of or long-term value of your Airbnb listing. For example, replacing an old air conditioner or refrigerator, renovating a bathroom or kitchen, repaving the driveway, or buying and installing a hot tub. These purchases can have a useful life from a few years up to 27.5 years.

To determine how much you can depreciate, you can deduct for a capital expense each year. Consider these three factors:

>> **Cost basis:** Typically the total cost to acquire and install the depreciable asset. If you purchased a brand-new refrigerator for $1,500 and paid another $250 for delivery and installation, then your total cost basis will be $1,500 + $250 = $1,750.

>> **Useful life:** The length of time in years that you expect to derive value from your capitalized asset, and thus depreciate the asset. Useful life is also known as the *recovery period*. For example, a refrigerator is often depreciated over five years. When purchasing used assets, the useful life is the number of years for a new unit minus the number of years the asset has been used. Buying a used two-year-old refrigerator means a remaining useful life of three years.

>> **Salvage value:** The third factor needed to determine the depreciation of a capitalized expense is known as the *salvage value* of the asset, or what you can sell the fully depreciated asset for at the end of its useful life. Even if it no longer works, a refrigerator can have its parts sold for scrap value.

Most hosts utilize a straight-line method to calculate the depreciation schedule, where the depreciation is divided evenly over the useful life of the asset. The depreciation amount is then calculated by taking the difference between the cost basis and the salvage value, and then dividing that by the useful life. See Figure 17-4 for an example of a depreciation schedule for an asset that is depreciated over ten years.

Total Cost Basis	$1,200	
Useful Life	10	years
Salvage Value	$200	

Year	Book Value (Beginning of Year)	Depreciation	Book Value (End of Year)
1	$1,200	$100	$1,100
2	$1,100	$100	$1,000
3	$1,000	$100	$900
4	$900	$100	$800
5	$800	$100	$700
6	$700	$100	$600
7	$600	$100	$500
8	$500	$100	$400
9	$400	$100	$300
10	$300	$100	$200

FIGURE 17-4: A ten-year depreciation schedule.

© John Wiley & Sons, Inc.

Here, the capital expense has a cost basis of $1,200, a salvage value of $200, and an estimated life of 10 years. Notice that the depreciation amount per year is $100, which is equal to ($1,200 − $200) divided by 10.

ON THE WEB

You can download a depreciation calculator from our online resources' webpage located at www.learnbnb.com/airbnbfordummies. For this calculator, all you need to input are the cost basis, useful life (choose between 1 and 50), and salvage value to automatically create the full depreciation schedule.

Determining exactly which repairs and maintenance expenses are deductible and which are capitalized can be confusing. The appropriate useful life to use in depreciating furniture, appliances, fixtures, and other capital improvements varies by jurisdiction. Talk to your accountant to verify what is an appropriate depreciation schedule for your situation in your location.

Knowing what deductible expenses to track

To minimize your taxable Airbnb earnings, and thus how much you owe in taxes, you must deduct all the allowable expenses from your gross Airbnb revenue. To do that, however, you must first keep accurate and complete records of each expense item and their amounts that you incur during the taxable calendar year.

Allowable expense items typically include the following:

>> Advertising and marketing

>> Airbnb hosting fee

>> Car expenses

>> Cleaning fees

>> Contract labor

>> Depreciation of all capitalized expenses

>> Education

>> Guest incidentals and amenities

>> HOA fees

>> Insurance

>> Laundry services

>> Legal and professional services

>> Meals and entertainment

>> Mobile phone and data plans

>> Mortgage interest

>> Office supplies

>> Permits and licensing

>> Property management or co-host fees

>> Property taxes

>> Rent (if renting property or equipment)

>> Repairs and maintenance

>> Subscription fees

>> Software

>> Supplies

>> Travel

>> Utilities

Not all these categories apply to every host, so carefully consider each category to ensure you're not leaving money on the table. According to SharedEconomyCPA, hosts often undertrack and underclaim on expenses, often those related to travel. For example, a multi-listing host who makes frequent travel to, from, and between their multiple Airbnb properties, stores, and meetings with vendors or partners can incur travel-related expenses that make up nearly 20 percent of her total expenses.

TIP

One great way to track your expenses is by creating dedicated checking accounts and debit or credit cards for your Airbnb operation. By running all your expenses through only these accounts, you only need to look at the year-end statements from these accounts to tabulate your expenses. Additionally, by connecting these accounts directly to an online accounting software, you can automatically keep accurate books to make for easy reporting come tax season.

ON THE
WEB

For the latest list of allowable expenses, reference the IRS Publication 527 (Residential Rental Property) located at www.irs.gov/forms-pubs/about-publication-527.

Knowing what documents to keep

To avoid being unable to provide the IRS documentation to support all your Airbnb-related earnings and expenses, you need to keep records of all supporting files and documents.

Here are the documents to keep in your records:

>> **All 1099 forms:** If you paid an independent contractor or service provider $600 or more, you're required to issue them a Form 1099-MISC before the end of January. Improper 1099 filings can lead to fines and having the expense barred from use as a deduction, leading to higher taxes. If you hired a cleaner and paid the individual for cleaning services of $600 or more in the calendar year, you need to issue the 1099. However, if you paid a cleaning company for services rendered, you don't need to issue the company a 1099.

- » **Full depreciation schedule:** For all capitalized assets, keep a schedule that includes the purchase date, purchase amount, expected useful life, and depreciation calculations showing how much depreciation has already been taken.

- » **Home office documentation:** If you manage your Airbnb from your home office, you may be able to deduct expenses, such as equipment, office supplies, and a portion of your utilities expenses based on a percentage of the size of the office to the total livable space on the property.

- » **Insurance receipts:** If you purchased additional short-term rental insurance or liability insurance for your Airbnb operation.

- » **Log of travel expenses:** Clean records of travel with dates, mileage, expense items, and amounts make it easy for determining deductible travel expenses, especially if vehicles are also used for personal travel.

- » **Mortgage interest paid:** If you own the property, the interest paid on the mortgage is typically tax deductible.

- » **Prior tax documents:** If you operated your Airbnb at a loss in the prior year, you may be able to carry forward some or all the rental losses to offset earnings in the current year.

- » **Professional service receipts:** For any professional services, whether for plumbing or an accountant, keep your receipts.

- » **Property tax receipts:** For property owners, keep documentation of all property taxes paid because you may be able to deduct a portion of or all the taxes from your income.

- » **Related purchase receipts:** Keep receipts for all deductible purchases of items or services pertaining to your Airbnb operation, including all repairs and maintenance receipts, as well as the purchase of regular supplies, such as soap, toiletries, cleaning supplies, and incidentals.

TIP

Accidents happen. Documents get misplaced or lost. For tax-related documents, you never need them . . . until you do! Although the IRS recommends keeping all records for at least three years, some situations have a period of limitation of seven years or more.

To avoid the pain of keeping years of physical filing cabinets filled with old paper receipts and documents, digitize them with receipt digital scanners to quickly turn physical documents into digital equivalents. And by keeping the digital files organized by year in a secured cloud storage account, you have quick and easy access, and you never have to worry about not being able to produce the relevant supporting document.

Exploring Recent Tax Law Changes

The passage of the Tax Cuts and Jobs Act of 2017 (TCJA), which went into effect in 2018, is considered by many as the biggest tax code change in recent decades. The changes presented new and enticing tax deductions for hosts, which we discuss in the following sections.

Deducting 100 percent bonus depreciation on personal property

If you purchase personal property for use in your Airbnb unit, such as a new sofa or a new television, you can now deduct the entire cost of the purchase in a single year, compared to the typical five- to seven-year useful lives applied to personal property.

Before the TCJA, you could only deduct up to 50 percent of the purchase amount, which could significantly reduce your taxable Airbnb income if you had made sizable purchases of personal property.

ON THE
WEB

However, to qualify for the 100 percent bonus depreciation, special rules must be met. You can find the latest requirements on the IRS website (www.irs.gov) and searching "Tax Cuts and Jobs Act."

Getting the 20 percent pass-through deduction

From 2018 to 2025 under the TCJA, owners of pass-through businesses, such as limited liability companies (LLCs), may deduct up to 20 percent of their business income from income taxes. For short-term rental properties, this change means deducting up to 20 percent of their Airbnb rental income from their overall income taxes.

Prior to this option, small business had to pass their business income directly to their personal income, which was subject to personal income tax rates as high as 39.6 percent. However, ensuring that you qualify for the deduction isn't a straightforward matter.

To qualify, you must meet the following requirements:

>> **You operate your Airbnb like a business.** Unlike owning a passive rental property investment, running an Airbnb requires much more active engagement to run properly and profitably. As such, hosts who actively manage their Airbnb listings are generally considered as operating like a business.

>> **Airbnb rental activity must be pass-through.** Because most Airbnb hosts manage their own listings, they're almost always considered a pass-through business. Some hosts form legal business entities, such as LLCs, to own and operate their Airbnb listings. This situation is more common with professional hosts operating multiple listings or for those hosts whose Airbnb rental is just one of several businesses that they run through their business entity.

>> **Your Airbnb rental must be profitable.** Given that the deduction only allows you to deduct up to 20 percent of your Airbnb rental income, you must operate a profitable Airbnb business to take advantage of this deduction.

>> **You must have taxable income.** If you don't have taxable income, there will be nothing to deduct the 20 percent of Airbnb rental income from.

In addition, the specific rules for the deduction depend on your annual taxable income. As of 2020, if you have a total taxable income of less than $163,300 (or $326,600 for joint filers), then you' likely qualify for the full 20 percent deduction. However, if your taxable income exceeds those income thresholds, then calculating the deduction becomes more complex.

Chapter **18**

Making Big Bucks as an Airbnb Co-Host

As an Airbnb host who's truly optimized your performance and streamlined your operations, you might be asking yourself how you can do more hosting. Buying another property can be quite expensive and requires a much greater risk than a lot of hosts are looking for.

That being said, as a successful Airbnb host you have a valuable skillset. Very few hosts on Airbnb actually put in the time and energy that it takes to optimize their returns and streamline their operations. Many hosts are wildly excited by the prospect of partnering with someone who can help them to boost their returns and save them some time. That's exactly what being a co-host on Airbnb is. In this chapter, we explain in greater detail what it means to be a co-host, help you to determine whether co-hosting is a good fit for you, and show you how to successfully manage other people's properties on Airbnb.

Co-Hosting: What It Actually Takes to Manage Other People's Listings

For hosts who want to increase their income from hosting without purchasing a new property, co-hosting is a great option. They can help others manage their properties on Airbnb.

Having another property to manage opens the opportunity to earn about double the money. You may find that with the right property, you can earn an even better return on your time than from your first property.

The following sections focus on helping you figure out whether co-hosting is a good option for you, what types of properties you may be able to co-host, and how to stay legal.

Understanding the basics of co-hosting

Essentially, *co-hosting* is managing someone's property on that person's behalf. It means taking all aspects of hosting your own property and doing it for someone else. You're telling another property owner that you're going to effectively run his Airbnb listing. You don't physically undertake all the tasks associated to hosting but rather you facilitate everything. Co-hosts typically earn a percentage of the property's overall revenue, which you can negotiate with the property owner. Generally, this percentage ranges from 20 to 50 percent.

REMEMBER

Starting to co-host may be easier after you've already had experience managing your own property on Airbnb; however, having hosting experience isn't completely necessary. I (James) started hosting ten other people's properties on Airbnb before ever being able to host my own. If you host for others before hosting for yourself, then you want to take matters a bit more slowly and ensure you're performing well with one property before growing to two, three, five, or ten.

If you're a current host who's considering co-hosting, make sure that your own hosting is optimized before expanding into managing other people's listings. When it comes to your own property, if you've done a good job of maximizing your returns and minimizing your time, instead of doing the cleaning or guest communication yourself, you're simply facilitating it.

You hired cleaners and now you manage them. You outsourced your guest communication. Now if you decide to start co-hosting, the same principles apply. You hire cleaners and a guest communication team. You can even use the same groups you use for your own property. You now manage and organize them for the new property or properties that you're co-hosting. Anything you do for your own listing you can do for your additional properties as well.

For example, whether you're optimizing pricing or enlisting a great photographer, you extend those services toward any additional properties you co-host. You add a new lockbox and facilitate having your photographer come to the new space.

After managing your own property, you know what it takes to be a great host. Now as a co-host, you continue to optimize that skill set over the course of your hosting journey. You can help a property perform at its optimal level in a way that is effective and efficient and ensure you're producing the maximum dollars per hour for you.

Considering co-hosting: Is it right for you?

When figuring out whether to co-host, think about the following questions before you make your decision:

>> **Are you maxed out with what you can do with your own listings?** A great reason to co-host is when you either don't have your own property to manage or you don't have the amount of properties to maximize the time you're putting into hosting. If you've optimized your own property as much as possible, then managing properties for other people can make a lot of sense. For most people, if you have a valuable skill set, then you want to put more time into it.

>> **Do you enjoy hosting?** Another reason to consider co-hosting is if you've come this far with hosting, then you most likely enjoy hosting in and of itself. If hosting is something that you truly enjoy, consider taking it one step further and earning more income by co-hosting.

REMEMBER

If co-hosting is up your alley, the best way to start is through friends or family members who are a great fit for renting their space on Airbnb or who already do. After you have the hang of managing properties for other people, there are a number of ways to continue growing your business. It's important to note that managing properties for other people is more than just a hobby and truly is running a business. Naturally, if you don't have any business experience, then specific training such as the training that I (James) offer in BNB Mastery Program can be quite helpful to avoid mistakes.

If you aim to grow hosting into a full-time income, where you manage five, ten, or more properties, then you want to keep them all centrally located. You don't necessarily need to host in the same place as where you live, but we recommend that all the properties be in one centralized location so that you're not managing ten sets of cleaners. You're just managing one cleaner who handles all your properties.

However, if you're just managing one or two properties as a hobby or as a part-time gig, then you can feasibly manage two properties in two locations that aren't close to one another. The scalability can become a bottleneck so keep in mind your ambitions with co-hosting and where you want to take it.

Identifying the benefits to co-hosting

Co-hosting a property includes the following benefits for both you and the property owner:

>> **It's a win-win situation for both people.** Consider what it was like for you as a host when you first started hosting and you were doing everything yourself.

Maybe you started off on the right foot and nailed everything from the get-go; however, more than likely you struggled with some aspects. Many hosts don't have training, experience, or education on hosting. Most likely they're doing all the day-to-day work by themselves and they're making a low dollar per hour wage. Furthermore, these day-to-day responsibilities of hosting are probably not what they want to be spending their time doing. They want to focus on other parts of their lives so by having you co-host their property you're offering a valuable service.

>> **You can make a great income without putting in much additional time.** Because many aspects of hosting can be outsourced and automated as we discuss in Chapter 10, you don't need to put a huge amount of additional time into managing properties for other people.

>> **You can help the property owner earn more money.** Many hosts are hosting inefficiently and leaving tons of money on the table. They're not optimizing their property the way they could or should. When someone like you walks into the equation who knows what it takes to make their property succeed, you can improve their overall performance so that it offsets your management fees.

>> **You don't need to invest more money into buying properties.** Co-hosting is a great way to still be able to host more without needing to invest thousands of dollars into buying another property.

Running your co-hosting business through a legal entity

If you decide to start co-hosting, speak with a local attorney before you begin. They can advise you on how to set your co-hosting business to ensure you're legally protected. The specific requirements depend on where you live, your own personal situation, and what kind of entity you need to set up if one is needed at all. For example, your attorney may advise you to set up a limited liability company (LLC) or a corporation for tax or liability reasons.

When co-hosting and providing this service to other hosts, you're operating a business. Before you begin, make sure to check with local laws and regulations to ensure you're completely compliant. In most areas, co-hosting is legal, although you may need to follow certain regulations.

WARNING

It's also a good practice to mandate short-term rental specific insurance for all the properties you manage. Many companies offer this type of insurance, such as Guard Hog and Square One. Having the property owners you work with carry this type of insurance can dramatically reduce your risk as a co-host. The worst-case scenario for you as a co-host is that something bad happens to the property and you get sued because the owner can't go after the guest. Having the property owners you work with carry additional insurance mitigates against this. The property owners bear the cost for this insurance. It's a fraction more per month for the owner and a no-brainer.

Scaling Your Income through Co-Hosting

After you decide that co-hosting is something that you want to pursue, you're ready to find someone's property to manage. The following sections walk you through the practical aspects of how to actually begin managing other people's properties.

Starting to co-host: The how-to

After you decide you want to co-host, you have to find a property, a spare space, or a vacation home. Consider looking here:

>> **Your friends, family members, or professional network:** They may already be hosting or not hosting, or perhaps they may want to host or potentially would be interested in it. Anyone you can think of in your network who would want you to manage his or her property is the easiest initial hosting partner.

   Start with these people if you want to manage a couple of properties. Begin slowly by selecting a couple and then proceed the same way you did with your own property.

>> **Online communities such as Facebook groups:** These communities allow you to connect with fellow hosts. Consider any host where you can help add value to make their life easier.

After you have a property to host, co-hosting is as simple as the property owner giving you access to his Airbnb account and you then going through the same process you did with your property with this property. If the property owner doesn't already have an account on Airbnb, then he needs to take a few minutes to set one up and you can take care of all the rest. You can create the listing and use the strategies we outline in Chapter 6 to do so. Make sure you optimize everything so you don't miss out on earning any money and so that you're delivering a great guest experience. Doing so will benefit both you and the property owner. From there, focus on reducing your time spent managing the property so that your dollars per hour are maximized.

If your ambition is to grow your hosting into a full-time income, then you're going to have to spend a lot more effort and gain more expertise. You can check out a company such as BNB Mastery Program for additional training, which gives a full overview of how to grow a co-hosting business and earn a full-time income managing other people's properties on Airbnb.

Turn hosting for others on autopilot

After you get to your desired number of properties under management, you want to start focusing your energies on outsourcing and automating. In other words, you remove yourself from all the daily operations of managing properties and replace such activity with the automation tools we discuss in Chapter 10. This way, you are earning a great income and have the freedom to spend your time the way you want to.

When managing more than five properties or managing properties remotely from afar, we recommend having a dependable handyman on call for any maintenance issues that come up because you won't personally be able to tend to maintenance issues the way that you can with just one property.

The best way to find a quality, reliable handyman in your area is often through referrals. Ask your friends, family, or fellow Airbnb hosts for recommendations. Otherwise, a quick online search for handymen in your area should help you to find the right person for the job.

Growing your co-hosting business to your desired level of income in record time

When you're co-hosting, you have the following two important points to consider as you put your co-hosting plan in place and grow your business:

>> **Know what your goal is when you begin.** Do you want to manage one or two properties? Or do you want to manage 15 properties?

>> **Determine what it takes to achieve your goal.** Plan out what areas of the business need to shift in order to reach your goal so you can set up systems to be ready before you need them.

For example, if you want to manage an additional two properties along with your own listing, then not much needs to change from what you're currently doing. The systems that work for one property more than likely will work the same if you have two additional properties. Your cleaners likely won't have trouble adding two properties to their plate. The guest communication team you have won't be stretched too far with the additional work. The pricing optimization you're doing won't be too different either.

However, managing 15 properties is a different story. Adding 15 more properties under one cleaning team's belt is going to take up most of the team's bandwidth and much more of its resources. You need to plan ahead so that as you grow, your cleaning team doesn't get maxed out and start missing cleanings or have standards drop.

WARNING

Plan ahead in order to avoid experiencing growing pains such as your cleaning team missing turnovers. In the case of your cleaners being overbooked, you need to let them know well in advance that you're growing so that they can prepare, or you need to hire an additional team to help with the workload.

If you start co-hosting and you're managing a number of properties and facilitating different teams of people, you risk running out of resources and being unable to support all the properties that you manage. As a result, you could run into issues that lead you to default on delivering the necessary services and satisfying your customers. Conditions can slide and you'll wind up taking steps backward rather than forward.

Obviously, this situation is less than ideal and adds a tremendous amount of time and effort for little reward. Overwhelming yourself early on leads to less than gratified clients and poorly performing properties. In order to have the most satisfied clients and grow as quickly as possible without having to take steps backward, you must plan ahead so all systems are intact before you need them. Be proactive and prepared to effectively grow your business and avoid taking any steps backward. Ultimately, your clients worked with you because they didn't want to put their own time into managing their properties themselves.

6

The Parts of Tens

Avoid the ten common pitfalls that many new Airbnb hosts make so that you can get your hosting journey off to the best possible start.

Make the ten best purchases according to hosts to reduce operating expenses and hosting headaches. Less wasted time and effort can be just as rewarding as increased profits.

Find out ten proven ways to increase your long-term earning potential by finding opportunities both on and off the Airbnb platform.

Chapter **19**

Ten Tips to Become a Better Host

E ven though both launching and maintaining a successful Airbnb listing takes planning and effort, as a host, doing some simple tasks can help you earn more, stress less, or both. Here are ten helpful tips for happy hosting.

Become a Guest First

The best hosts know what it's like to be guests first. So, before you jump into hosting with both feet, book your stays on Airbnb for your next trips. Experience the entire process from start to finish as a guest — from searching on the platform and booking to checking in and checking out. Note all the moments you felt confused, irritated, relaxed, or elated. These moments can point to both aspects to replicate or avoid in your practice as a host. Even better, enjoy a few "staycations" by booking reservations at existing local listings in your city. Chapter 5 gives you the lowdown on what to note when staying as a guest at an Airbnb listing.

Research Your Market Before Hosting

Smart hosts research their market before hosting to know exactly what to expect in their market. Some would-be hosts choose not to become Airbnb hosts after finding out that a traditional rental of their unit would perform better in their particular market. Chapter 4 covers the ins and outs of doing market research.

Invite but Never Impose

Guests traveling from different places come stay at your listing for different reasons. Some come to relax. Some want to meet and hangout with strangers. Some want quiet time. Never assume you know the preference of any guests unless they tell you explicitly.

For example, if you're hosting a dinner party with friends and family and want to extend an invitation to your guests, make sure they know it's an open invitation with zero expectations. Come if they want. If not, no biggie. The more you host, the more you develop intuition for how and whether to extend invitations with each specific guest.

Offer More Than Promised

Promise the stars and deliver the moon? Disappointment. Successful hosts who wow their guests consistently know to properly manage expectations with their listing profile and their communications with potential guests.

TIP

This success means having great but honest photos and descriptions and then offering little unexpected extras for the guests. Offering killer home-baked cookies? A bottle of wine from a local vineyard? Fresh roasted coffee beans from a local roastery? Let your guests discover them as surprises when they arrive. Check out Chapter 12 on what it means to deliver great guest experience.

Touch Base with Your Guests

For every guest who reached out to you directly with a question or complaint, there probably were a few more with the same question or complaint who didn't reach out to you. Some people are shy. Some don't want to feel bothersome.

TIP

Send a short and inviting message to your guests, such as "Good morning! Just wanted to see if you had any questions or requests. Call/text me anytime. Here to help," the day after check-in. Check in at least once every two to three days. Doing so lets the guests know it's more than okay to reach out to you if they need something. Chapters 13 and 14 cover guest communication best practices from prior to check-in to post check-out.

Use Tiny Helpful Labels

Checking into a stranger's home after a long day of travel, many guests want to settle in and relax before the next day's adventures. But that can be tough if they don't even know which switch works for which light or if they have to open all the cabinets just to find the extra trash bags.

TIP

One simple way to show your guests you're thinking of them is to place small but conspicuous labels next to switches, cabinets, drawers, or doors in the house. Keep these small and visible only up close so they don't show up on normal photos. Use a color scheme and a font that fits your overall decor, and they will look as intentional as they are useful.

Always Have Extra Essentials

Not having an extra supply of essentials, such as toilet paper, paper towels, soap, and all linens can ruin an otherwise great Airbnb experience for your guests. No one enjoys having to make a trip out to the local store to get toilet paper because the host provided only a starter roll in each bathroom.

WARNING

Being penny-wise and pound foolish may save you a few bucks now but create unhappy guests who could leave you scathing reviews that cost you bookings in the long run. Keep the extra supply out of sight to encourage more frugal use of supplies and note the details in your house manual. Chapter 5 discusses all the items you need to make your property Airbnb ready.

Use Action Shots in Your Photos

Showing guests what they could be doing in your listing is much better than telling. Yes, well-composed photos help, but putting people in some of the photos enjoying the space or showing the action makes a more compelling pitch and results in more bookings.

TIP

Have a hot tub in the backyard overlooking a picturesque sunset? Put a couple of friends in there and silhouette them against that sunset. Have a firepit in the back ideal for making marshmallow s'more sandwiches? Show the marshmallows roasting on the open fire. Have a billiards table for guests to enjoy? Don't show an empty table but take a photo with the blurry moving cue ball just about to collide with another ball. Check out Chapter 7 for additional strategies to creating great Airbnb photos for your listing.

Disclose and Highlight Potential Negatives Up Front

Getting long-term success for your listing is as much about avoiding the wrong kind of guests as it is attracting as many guests as possible. Have an extra friendly cat on the property who enjoys greeting guests? Talk about Waffles and his nosy manners in the descriptions and add a photo. Yes, doing so can turn off many guests who don't want to share their stay with a cat, however friendly. But it also makes your listing more appealing to guests who love cats.

Honest disclosure enables you to both attract the right guests who would appreciate the listing as it is and discourage those who wouldn't enjoy it from booking in the first place.

Measure Return on Time

Could earning more from your listing ever hurt? Yes, if it means having to put in a disproportionate amount of extra effort. Would you rather earn $1,000 a month from two guest stays or $1,200 from 15 guest stays? Many will choose the more relaxed two guest stay with far less turnover work.

As you host, instead of only seeking ways to squeeze every dollar out of your listing, look instead on how you can free up your time by using automation tools to simplify pricing and communications or using smart locks to eliminate time-consuming in-person check-ins. Sometimes, profit per hour of input is more important than total profits. Chapter 10 offers suggestions to use your time wisely.

Chapter **20**

Ten Best Purchases for Hosts

We asked the thousands of hosts through our blog and online courses, "What was the best purchase you've made as an Airbnb host?" Some were obvious, and some were surprising. Here are ten that you should consider when hosting on Airbnb.

Futon Couch or Sofa Bed

If you have enough space for a traditional couch, you likely have enough space for a sofa bed or futon couch instead, which increases your listing's occupancy capacity to sleep an additional guest and permanently increase your earning potential. Be sure to provide a set of quality pillows, linens, and a bed topper to improve the comfort of these notoriously uncomfortable sleeping options.

WARNING

Don't overdo it by adding a sofa bed in every common area or turning every bed into a bunk bed just to add capacity. Local fire codes still apply. Be sure to check with your city to determine the maximum allowable occupancy for your listing.

Floor Mats for Every Entrance

Especially for those hosting near the beach or the outdoors, guests can bring in a lot of sand and dirt, making for a longer and more difficult cleaning during turn-arounds. Having floor mats at every entrance can encourage guests to wipe their shoes before entering. Adding fun messages, such as "Please wipe paws before entering" with paw prints can serve as gentle reminders for the guests. Refer to Chapter 6 about setting house rules where you can ask guests to remove their shoes upon entering.

Shoe Racks

To decrease the amount of dirt and grime from getting inside the house and on the furniture, invest in a shoe rack for guests. A conspicuously placed shoe rack inside the main entrance offers an easy and accessible way for guests to take off and store their dirty shoes. Put another one in the backyard or offer slippers and sandals guests can use outside.

Universal Device Chargers for Every Room

Assume your guests will travel with their smart phones and devices. Most will bring their own chargers, but many will occasionally forget to pack them. To save your guests the hassle and headache of going to a store, keep a set of universal chargers and cable in each bedroom available for guests to use. Even if they do bring their own cables, the extra option comes in handy when charging multiple devices at the same time. An alternative is to include USB power adapters in each room, allowing for easy USB usage in addition to being a regular plugin.

TIP

If you're in a location that attracts a good number of international guests, we also suggest you invest in an international converter plug.

Large Capacity Appliances

If you must buy a new dishwasher or washer and dryer combo anyway, opt for the largest capacity unit you can afford and that can fit in your unit. The one-time extra cost more than pays for the continuous savings in fewer loads and washes, resulting in lower utility bills and faster, less stressful turnaround times between guests.

Storage Lockers with Locks

Flights can get delayed. Rides can get stuck in traffic. Plans can change. As you host more guests, you can receive requests from guests to check in earlier or check out later. Accommodating the requests can lead to rushed turnarounds, but simply refusing when guests are in need can lead to a bad start or ending to their stay. Having storage lockers that are large enough to stow large luggage bags paired with combination locks can fix the problem; it allows guests to put their luggage in a safe place while they move about town before the unit is ready or before they need to head to the airport for their delayed flight. If you are a host who resides on the property or nearby, you can offer to keep the luggage until the guests can pick it up later that day.

High Quality Mattress and Linens

Investing a little extra upfront on a comfortable mattress and the softer, higher thread count bedsheets and pillowcases can lead to better sleep experiences for the guests. Well-rested guests equal happy guests. And happy guests mean happy guest ratings. Scroll through the raving reviews from the most popular listings or the scathing reviews of the struggling listings in any city to read about a "super comfy bed" or "the worst sleep ever."

Smart Locks

Most guests prefer the ease of checking in themselves whenever they show up, whether at the designated check-in time or late in the evening. One of the best ways is by using a smart lock that allows the host to remotely change the access codes, for example, to the last four digits of the guest's phone number. A smart lock is more convenient and less stressful for both host and guest. Refer to Chapter 13 for more on how smart locks can simplify your Airbnb hosting.

Automation Tools

Hosting a profitable listing on Airbnb doesn't work with a "set it and forget it" strategy. It requires continuous monitoring and updating of prices and availability for your listing and timely communications with potential guests. Even though you can technically do all this manually, you get better results with less stress by using automation tools to automate your pricing, most of your guest communications, and scheduling. Explore the many choices available, test some out through free trials, and then choose one. The small nominal fee pays back many folds. Chapter 10 discusses the ins and outs of automation for Airbnb hosting.

Better Coffee Options

Many guests enjoy coffee, and although most hosts now provide some options to make coffee, most aren't taking advantage of an easy way to wow their guests. Instead of just providing a coffee pot and stale store-bought pre-ground coffee beans, provide some alternatives, such as whole roasted beans with a hand grinder for a pour over or a French press to show the coffee-addicted guests you're looking out for them. Be sure to showcase it in your listing descriptions and photos. All things equal, the coffee-drinking travelers will choose your listing over your competition for better coffee.

TIP

Not all guests are coffee aficionados. For the tea lovers, keep a couple of options available in case they want a cup. Another favorite to have on hand are hot chocolate options.

Chapter **21**

Ten Ways to Increase Your Earnings

"No, I don't want to earn more money while putting in the same effort," said no Airbnb host ever. If you're already putting in the time and energy to hosting on Airbnb, why not get the most from your hosting efforts? In this chapter, we provide ten strategies that have helped hosts to earn more while hosting.

Putting Your Best Listing Forward

Most new hosts who complain about not earning enough as hosts also leave low hanging fruits with their property listing, which can include having poor photos taken from the wrong angles with poor lighting at the wrong time of day. Or they have poorly written descriptions and boring listing titles. Unless you have the best listing profile you can have for your property, you won't come close to earning your full potential as a host. Refer to Chapter 6 for specifics on building the perfect listing for your property.

Asking Guests to Leave Reviews

While Airbnb reminds guests to leave a review after their checkouts, hosts who reach out to guests with a friendly reminder get more guest reviews. Having more reviews, especially from happy guests raving about their wonderful stays, lead to more bookings and profits by making your listing more appealing to future guests. However, asking for more reviews when you're not meeting guest expectations consistently is just asking for trouble. Review Chapters 12 thru 14 for the ins and outs great guest service.

Tailoring Amenities to Your Audience

Understanding who your guests are can help you better cater to their specific needs. For instance, business travelers have very different needs than families with young children. Pay attention to the recurring types of guests who stay at your listing and look for ways to add relevant amenities. For example, having family-friendly games can help attract family travelers while having a dedicated work station can appeal to the business travelers. The more you can make your listing an easy decision for your target traveler audiences, the more bookings you get.

Offering Add-On Goods and Services

After your guests book with you, you have a captured audience during their entire length of their stay. Why do hotels offer minibars? Some guests want to drink without having to leave their rooms. You can do the same by offering a menu of extras, such as alcohol or breakfast to earn extra income. Hosts can also provide services, such as pickup and drop-off, guided tours, home-cooked meals, or equipment rental to increase earning potential. Chapter 9 discusses additional strategies for increasing your Airbnb profits.

Using Appropriate Pricing

Charge too much and you risk having too many unoccupied nights. Charge too little and you miss out on profits you could have earned from guests who already chose your listing. Figuring out the right price to charge for your listing for any given night requires that you account for many factors that affect pricing, including your competitors' pricing and availability, seasonality, and special events. Successful hosts understand they can't do that manually and instead use a third-party pricing tool to set the ideal pricing for your listing automatically. Check out Chapter 8 for all the important factors in properly pricing your Airbnb listing.

Hosting More Listings

You can earn only so much from a single listing. After you reach maximum occupancy charging the highest rates your market can support, there is little you can do to increase your earnings from that listing. But add another listing or two, and you can quickly grow your earnings on Airbnb. You can create a win-win by offering your hosting services to a property owner who doesn't want to host themselves. Or, you can even buy or build another property yourself to scale your profits significantly. Chapter 3 discusses specifics regarding buying or building a property for Airbnb.

Listing an Airbnb Experience

Renting a property is not the only way to earn money on Airbnb. A recent but fast-growing opportunity on the platform is for hosts to list an activity rather than a property. Hosting an Experience over a property has many benefits and can help you grow your earnings substantially on the platform. Chapter 16 discusses the ins and outs of hosting an Airbnb Experience.

Thinking Long Term

Would you take $10 more now to lose $100 later? Probably not. Yet many new hosts make a similar trade-off by taking small short-term gains for bigger long-term losses. Yes, providing an extra supply of incidentals means higher costs per stay as guests use more of those items, but this small investment now prevents negative guest reviews that later lead to long-term losses from fewer bookings.

Although Airbnb is by far the most prominent example of the growth of sharing economy, if you find that your listing isn't getting enough bookings on Airbnb, you can look at alternatives, such as VRBO, HomeAway, FlipKey, and Bookings. com to just name a few.

WARNING

However, putting your listing on multiple platforms requires the use of vacation rental management tools to help you manage the multiple listings and calendars to avoid double bookings and scheduling conflicts. These tools can be costly, so the option isn't ideal for single listing hosts in low travel demand markets.

Renting Something Else

If you search online, you quickly find Airbnb-like platforms targeting some other underutilized asset. Have a rarely used car you can rent? There's an Airbnb for cars. A boat, backyard, garage, tools, gear, office, you name it. There's an Airbnb copycat for whatever *that* is. Some platforms can complement your Airbnb hosting operation while others are an entirely separate operation.

Avoiding Catastrophic Losses

Getting a huge fine from the city or having to make a costly replacement due to damage can wipe out an entire year's worth of earnings. To avoid potential big losses, be sure to check and comply with local laws, keep all receipts and documentation if you need to make an insurance claim, and make timely repairs of all safety-related issues to limit liability risk. If you have assets greater than one million dollars, you should purchase additional insurance coverage on top of Airbnb's hosting insurance policy.

Index

About the Authors

Symon He is a co-founder of LearnBNB.com, a leading online educational destination for all things Airbnb hosting. His research and works have been cited in the Wall Street Journal, Reuters, Forbes, CNBC, and SKIFT. Through his training and coaching programs, he has worked directly with thousands of aspiring Airbnb hosts to begin their hosting journeys.

Symon is also a best-selling instructor of real estate and business courses, with over 750,000 students worldwide. You can find his popular courses on the top educational platforms including Udemy, LinkedIn Learning, StackSkills, and LearnFormula.

Previously, he was head of marketing analytics at the Panda Restaurant Group after serving as a senior financial analyst focusing on real estate underwriting efforts. Before that, he was a global M&A manager for Ingram Micro, a Fortune 80 company. Prior to that, he worked on commercial real estate acquisitions at HG Capital, covering a wide range of asset classes across the western USA.

He is a licensed real estate broker and consultant based out of Los Angeles, helping private clients on real estate acquisitions and deal structuring. Symon also writes on his personal blog at symonhe.com.

He graduated Magna Cum Laude in Computer Engineering and Economics from UC Irvine and received his MBA from Stanford University. He lives with his wife and son in Los Angeles, CA.

James Svetec is the co-founder of BNB Inner Circle, where he helps people to build cash flow and long-term wealth by investing in short-term rental properties. He's also the creator and founder of BNB Mastery Program, where he helps people to earn a full-time income managing other people's properties on Airbnb.

Through his coaching and training programs, James has worked with hundreds of investors and entrepreneurs from all around the world helping them to build successful businesses and become masters of Airbnb.

James is also the co-owner of LearnBNB.com, the No. 1 resource for people from all over the world to learn about the world of Airbnb hosting.

Dedications

To my beautiful wife and best friend, Hillary. –Symon

To my mother, father, and sister who epitomize unconditional love and support, and to my many friends and coaches who have made this all possible. –James

Authors' Acknowledgments

First, I'd like to express my gratitude for the great team at Wiley. This book — from idea to printed copy — would not have been possible without the continued support and guidance from each of you. Specifically, I'd like to thank Tracy Brown Hamilton and Elizabeth Stillwell for all your patience and support in making this second edition possible.

I'd also like to thank acquisitions editor, Ashley Coffee; and project, development editor, Tracy Brown Hamilton; copy editor, Jerelind Charles; and technical editor, Chad R. Sievers. Thanks also to associate publisher Katie P. Mohr for ensuring all the pieces came together smoothly.

Thank you to all the Airbnb hosts, students, and readers from LearnBNB.com and the Hosting Accelerator Program, your stories inspire and inform others to explore the exciting, fun, and sometimes complicated world of Airbnb hosting. Special thanks to Clara Reeves and Elio Mondello Anza for sharing your inspiring Airbnb hosting journeys with us.

Thank you to Pierre-Camille Haman of SmartBNB, Neel Parekh of MaidThis!, Miguel Alex Centeno of SharedEconomyCPA, and the many fine folks at AirDNA, WheelHouse, and NoiseAware. Your guidance and support were invaluable to writing this book.

Thank you to my co-author James Svetec. I wouldn't have been able to complete this book without you. What a journey to complete together! I look forward to many more fun and fruitful ventures with you.

To James Breese Jr., thank you for introducing me to the world of short-term rentals and Airbnb and founding LearnBNB with me all these years ago. None of this would have been possible without your continued support and friendship.

To Travis Chow, thank you for your friendship, patience, and support. Your encouragement empowered me to both begin and complete the writing of this book.

Lastly, thank you to Airbnb for making it possible for people to belong anywhere in the world and for giving ordinary folks the opportunity to earn an income through genuine hospitality.

—Symon

I first want to thank the incredible team at Wiley for providing us the opportunity to share our knowledge of hosting with the Airbnb community. Working with the Wiley team from the initial ideation phase through to final edits has been a fantastic journey and an even better learning opportunity.

Thank you to Airbnb and the Airbnb community at large for providing such an incredible environment for people all around the world to come together and live like locals. From hosting to managing to traveling, being a part of the Airbnb community has been and continues to be a truly great experience.

Thank you to all of my students in BNB Mastery Program who allow me to guide and inform them on managing other people's properties on Airbnb. They say that one of the best ways to learn is to teach, and I certainly learn from all of my students as they continue to grow their businesses around the world.

Thank you to all of the readers and students at LearnBNB.com and in the Hosting Accelerator Program. Striving to become the best hosts we can be is fun and exciting, and doing it alongside such a fantastic community makes it all the more enjoyable.

Thank you to my business partner, co-author, and friend, Symon He. I never would have had the opportunity to share in writing this book if not for you, and doing so has been a great journey. I'm very excited for many more projects to come in our future!

Thank you to my family who continues to support me in everything I do. To my eternally supportive mother, who encourages and challenges me to be the best I can be while loving me no matter what. To my loving and hardworking father who taught me what it means to put my all into something that I love, never allow obstacles to get in my way, and who over the years has become a truly great friend.

To my sister and soon-to-be brother who keep me grounded, always make life fun, and have always got my back. Last but not least to my loving and supportive girlfriend Christine whose partnership amplifies my life to no end.

Thank you especially to my first ever mentors, Chris Thomson and Patrick Lalonde. Words of course fall short in being able to express the contributions you've made to my life through both guidance and friendship, but know that I am eternally grateful for all that you've been and continue to be for me.

Thank you to Sam Symons, whose partnership and friendship have gotten me through tough times and who continues to be supportive in everything that I do. Of course, I would never be where I am without you. Your unwillingness to settle or give up is both admirable and inspirational.

Thank you to Paul Carleton and Esbe van Heerden, who have been right by my side throughout this entire journey. You are truly wonderful people and exceptional friends. There are many things I could thank you for, but thank you most of all for just being who you are to me.

Thank you to the many communities of entrepreneurs that I've been able to be a part of over the years and whose guidance and support have allowed me to avoid countless mistakes and overcome many obstacles. Notably, I've built many truly great relationships, met countless incredible people, and gained a seemingly end-less amount of wisdom from the DC, GIA, and Student Works communities, and for that I am exceptionally thankful.

—James

Publisher's Acknowledgments

Acquisitions Editor: Elizabeth Stilwell

Project Manager: Tracy Brown Hamilton

Copy Editor: Jerelind Charles

Technical Editor: Sam Symons

Senior Managing Editor: Kristie Pyles

Production Editor: Mohammed Zafar Ali

Cover Image: © Africa Studio/Shutterstock